Woodstock Census

WOODSTOCK CENSUS

THE NATIONWIDE SURVEY
OF THE SIXTIES GENERATION

Rex Weiner and Deanne Stillman

Research Consultant
Linda Z. Waldman

The Viking Press | New York

ACKNOWLEDGMENTS

Warner Bros. Music Inc: Lyrics on Page 205 are from *My Back Pages,* words and music by Bob Dylan. ©1964 Warner Bros. Inc. All rights reserved. Used by permission.

Photographs on pages 12 and 28, Ken Regan, Camera 5
Photographs on pages 66, 102, 178, 204, Charles Gatewood
Photograph on page 132, Christopher Little
Photograph on page 160, George Gardner

First published in 1979 by The Viking Press
625 Madison Avenue, New York, N.Y. 10022
Published simultaneously in Canada by
Penguin Books Canada Limited

Library of Congress Cataloging in Publication Data
Weiner, Rex.
  Woodstock census.
  Bibliography. Includes index.
  1. Youth—United States—Attitudes.
  2. United States—Social conditions—1960–
  3. Conflict of generations.
  4. Radicalism—United States.
  I. Stillman, Deanne, joint author. II. Title.
  HQ793.W26 301.43'15'0973 79-13665
  ISBN 0-670-78206-8

Printed in the United States of America
Set in CRT Baskerville

"Break on through to the other side"
    —Jim Morrison and the Doors

ACKNOWLEDGMENTS

Thanks to all the people who helped us put this book together: most of all to Linda Z. Waldman, whose advice and expertise were invaluable; to Kurt Shulman, who did the coding; to Ann Sanfedele and M. G. Data, who did the processing; to Nancy Stillman, who did the typing; and to Shay Addams, Hank Alrich and the staff of Armadillo World Headquarters, Larry Alton, Chip Berlet, Ron Brawer and Jill Diamond, Mike Chance and Nancy Borman, John Daily and Ken Segal of KWKI radio, Mike Fellner and the *Takeover* staff, the late Reverend Thomas King Forcade, Gates's Barbecue, Mark "Hey, this was my idea" Jacobson, Susan Leon, Ron Lichty, Lee Mason, Tom Miller, Peter Moore and the Roxy Theater staff, Bertel and Paule Ollman, Debbie Oppenheimer, Cindy Ornsteen, Joe Nick Patoski, Mark Salditch, Cindy Spain, Eleanor Stillman, Susan Toepfer, Ben Weaver, Phil and Edith Weiner, Becky Wilson, and our very groovy editor, Amanda H. Vaill.

Contents

8
Looking Back, Looking Ahead

Like a Rolling Stone . . . Sex and the Single Hippie . . .
"When I Die I'll Go to Heaven, 'Cause I've Served My
Time in Hell" . . . Changing the World . . . Groovin' . . .
Flipping Out . . . Brothers and Sisters . . . Three Days of
Peace and Music . . . "Don't Think Twice, It's All Right"
. . . The Future . . . The "New Narcissism" . . . The
Community . . . The Trouble with Kids Today . . . The Wild
Card . . . When Will the Sixties Be Over? . . . Some Final
Comments

Introduction

Once upon a time there was a decade of wide-eyed idealism and youthful dreams called the Sixties, which suffered an abrupt reversal, becoming a sadder but much wiser decade called the Seventies (which, as some people tell it, was actually a return to a wasteland called the Fifties).

Right?

We have heard this version of recent history so often that it seems almost to be the truth. We read in a popular national magazine, for example, a writer's parenthetical remark about the counter-culture of the Sixties, "whose only two enduring contributions appear to be blue jeans and marijuana." Or a book reviewer makes an offhand comment on "the shocking slide of the Seventies when our values changed faster than a bargain basement markdown sale." And one of those celebrity magazines, under the heading "Where Have All the Radicals Gone?" gives the soothing answer that all the wild idealists of the Sixties are now safely parked in offices, peddling insurance.

Veterans of the Sixties react variously to this picture. To some, mention of the Sixties brings a faraway look to the eyes, a trembling to the lips. Others smile with cynical tolerance, as though hearing a bad joke. And there are those unreconstructed types who can still barely muster a "Far Out!"

But we liked the Sixties and we still do, not as a flowery fantasy or an LSD flashback, but as an exciting and important time in history, which shaped our lives and the lives of an entire generation.

And that's really why we wrote this book. In the post-Sixties period, people have increasingly come to view the events of recent

3

times less as history than as a matter of mood, as if America were alternately greening and browning according to whim. The effect has been to place a dead weight of indecisiveness on the present and to hobble the future with chic cynicism.

Certainly there was a welter of folly and silliness in the Sixties, just as in any decade. But what made those years special was the extraordinary amount of energy and imagination people invested in attempts at making life better. To dismiss that time with glib comments and superficial sociology is to denigrate the best efforts of the past and to discourage them in the future. To a large degree, how we see history is also how we make history.

Are blue jeans and pot all the Sixties add up to? Did our values really take a nosedive in the Seventies? Are all the hippies safely settled in suburbia and are all the radical protesters bank presidents? Has an entire generation *sold out*?

We decided to find out by asking a few of our friends—1005, as it turned out—who, like us, were part of what was called the "Now Generation," the "Love Generation," and other dopey labels the press invented to describe the giant bulge we made in the demographic charts (the postwar baby boom of 50 million). We felt it was about time that ordinary, everyday people told their stories about the Sixties and Seventies; social commentators always speak so knowingly about "the people," but rarely do "the people" get a chance to speak for themselves. Too often, it is the celebrity version of the Sixties that we're given, narrations from people who happened to be famous at the time for one thing or another and are therefore considered experts. Though sometimes entertaining, their viewpoints are far out of the ordinary—if not, on occasion, downright self-serving.

So we put together a lengthy questionnaire that we hoped would allow people to describe some of their activities and feelings during the Sixties and Seventies and to draw comparisons between the two periods. From the fall of 1977 to the spring of 1978, we distributed the questionnaire as widely as possible around the nation, with the aim of collecting at least a thousand responses.

The people we were looking for were not hard to find. In fact, they found us. And this was our very first survey result: Veterans

4

of the Sixties are eager to relate their experiences of that era. We found that we had tapped a huge reservoir of emotion. Other people felt, as we did, that the Sixties had been misrepresented, and they were willing to spend an hour and a half filling out a questionnaire in order to set the record straight. One person wrote: "Everything just gets forgotten or explained away simplistically—please don't, in writing your book, explain away what we did as passing fancy. I think we all cared so much."

HOW WAS THIS SURVEY CONDUCTED?

With as much of a sense of humor as possible. While our goal was to amass a pile of solid data upon which we could build accurate conclusions, we also wanted to capture some of the fun, spontaneity, and craziness of the Sixties. We don't pretend to have been strictly scientific in our methods, nor are we experts in sociology, polling techniques, or statistical analysis. The truth is that even those who are experts—including the biggest and best-known polling outfits, like Harris, Gallup, and Roper—obtain contradictory results, differ over correct methodology, and have to allow for biases.

Our greatest advantage in conducting this survey has been the fact that, having grown up in the Sixties, we know the times and the people well. There are things that only true veterans of the Sixties understand. Would Lou Harris think to explore the political implications of armpit hair on women? Would George Gallup grok* the significance of love beads? They have enough trouble figuring out Republicans and Democrats.

Still, we are writers, not pollsters. In order to follow the basic requirements of a survey, we employed a professional pollster, Linda Waldman, who helped us to put all our questions into a form compatible with computer processing, and to devise a method by which the questionnaire was applied. Some surveys send armies of interviewers to canvass door-to-door in communities around the country. Other surveys are done over the tele-

*grok (grahk) vt. 1. To understand. 2. To grasp the meaning of. From Robert Heinlein's *Stranger in a Strange Land*, 1961.

phone by interviewers who dial numbers at random from directories. These are the most frequently used methods, but for our purposes they were impractical, if not impossible.

Our intent was to survey the kind of people we used to see every Saturday night at the Fillmore rock concerts, the ones who showed up at be-ins, antiwar rallies, and campus hootenannies. We wanted to reach ex-SDSers, former freedom riders, and Haight-Ashbury alumni. We were seeking those who had been Clean for Gene and those who had been Loose for Leary, the kind of people who could recognize the names of the Chicago Eight as well as the names of the Grateful Dead, who could remember reading the Port Huron Statement, the *East Village Other*, and R. Crumb's comics; the commune dwellers, draft-card burners, hippies, yippies, and trippers.

These people don't have doors, they listen to the Doors. And they are reluctant to dispense intimate details about their lives over the telephone to strangers, who could just possibly be minions of the CIA.

Therefore, we hit on the idea of making this survey an event in itself, a kind of be-in, which by its very nature would attract the people we were looking for. We accomplished this in two ways. The first involved publicizing the survey through the national press so that people all over the country could read about it and mail to us requests for questionnaires, which they would fill out and mail back. In this manner, we were able to collect more than a third of our sample.

The rest we obtained by traveling around the country holding what we called "census sessions." We did this in order to have as much personal contact with our respondents as possible and to guarantee that we received a fair national sampling. The places we chose to survey in person were New York City, Boston, Madison, Wisc., Kansas City, San Francisco, Berkeley, Tucson, Austin, and Atlanta. We picked urban areas because this is where we were most certain to find large numbers of the kind of people we wanted to survey—whether they had grown up in Centerville, U.S.A., or Chicago. We didn't visit the Deep South or Des Moines or the backwoods of Vermont or (regrettably) Hawaii. But through the mail we received questionnaires from every one of the

6

states, and one from what was once called the Canal Zone. (For complete demographics, see Chapter One.)

Like most Sixties events, our census sessions attracted mobs of reporters—before, during, and after each session. This was one way we publicized our cross-country canvassing and attracted mail-in as well as on-the-spot questionnaires. We also put up posters in each city to advertise the fact that at a certain time (usually around 7:30 P.M.), at a certain place (most often a rented hall), veterans of the Sixties could take part in a survey that was all about them. Anywhere from fifty (Boston) to one hundred and fifty (Kansas City) would show up. We supplied presharpened pencils, questionnaires, and the admonishment, "No cheating!" While they went to work, we played a specially programmed tape of great hits from the Sixties: music to reminisce by.

Our respondents treated the event like a reunion, saying hello to people they hadn't seen in years, passing joints and wine, giggling whenever "Ballad of the Green Berets" came on the tape, singing along with the Supremes or Country Joe and the Fish. Lou Harris or George Gallup would have been appalled, but for our purposes it couldn't have been better. When handing in their completed questionnaires (some people took hours to finish, painstakingly laboring over their answers), our respondents occasionally complained of the length, or that some of the questions were tricky. More often, they said they were glad for the chance to express their views, and some even reported reaching new self-realizations ("In the Sixties, I went to demonstrations; in the Seventies, I fill out questionnaires about *why* I went to demonstrations"). Just about everybody enjoyed the experience.

"It was nice to come here and remember when. All the people who participated seem to have a happy and powerful common memory."

(For additional notes on survey methodology, see Appendix B.)

WHO TOOK PART IN THE SURVEY?

"Dear Surveyors—I would really like to fill out one of your questionnaires. I don't consider myself a typical product of the U.S.A.

"Born and raised in San Francisco, I began to raise my consciousness with beatniks in North Beach at the age of 11. As a junior in high school I attended Bill Graham's 3rd rock concert (1965) and dozens more as the 60's passed. I first saw Cream when they had second billing. As a graduation treat, my girlfriends and I went to Monterey for the Pop Festival (and we lost Janis Joplin to the rest of the world). I attended S.F. State College. My black English teacher didn't receive tenure, subsequently the student body, followed by faculty, went on strike. And we rioted.

"The longest I have been out of S.F. is the four months I spent in Europe.

"I am now 29 years old. I still associate with radical artist types. I work as a telephone installer. I have never married. I own my own home. I do not dwell on the past but recall the times with much affection and sometimes think my experiences are unique.

"I installed the phone for Patty Hearst's kidnappers—the FBI talked to me about it.

"So it goes . . ."

Diane P., who wrote the above letter, may not be a "typical product of the U.S.A.," but she is in many ways typical of the people we surveyed. Anybody who heard about the questionnaire could send away for one or fill one out at one of our census sessions. Age was the only qualification.

We were looking for that "Sixties Generation" that everybody loves to generalize about, the people who received *Time*'s Man of the Year designation in 1966 when they were twenty-five and under. Certainly anybody who was alive and conscious during the Sixties was affected by that era. But we wanted to focus only on those whose values and goals were shaped by the era. We wanted our survey to include people who were old enough to have participated in the civil rights struggles of the early Sixties, and those young enough to have been on campus during the climactic antiwar activities of the late Sixties and early Seventies.

So we limited the survey to people between 25 and 37 years old at the time the survey was being taken—in other words, anybody born between 1940 and 1952.

Of course a vast number of people older and younger than those included in this survey played significant roles in making the Sixties what they were. Our age limitation excluded people like

Allen Ginsberg, Abbie Hoffman, Gloria Steinem, Ken Kesey, Chubby Checker, Betty Friedan, Eldridge Cleaver, Andy Warhol, Richard Nixon, Tiny Tim, and perhaps you, the reader. Sorry, but we *had* to stop somewhere.

BUT ISN'T THIS SURVEY BIASED?

Biased in favor of what, or whom? The question implies a misunderstanding of the survey's purpose.

We did not set out to poll *all* Americans on their feelings about the Sixties. Or the feelings of Young Republicans. Or the Ku Klux Klan's view of the Sixties. We were interested in that special group that Abbie Hoffman once referred to as "Woodstock Nation."

Our sample was self-selected; just as people *chose* to attend rock festivals, they *chose* to be surveyed. The response to the survey was intended to be a finding in itself, to help answer the question of who and where are the people who identify strongly with the Sixties era.

HOW DO YOU TURN 1005 QUESTIONNAIRES
INTO A BOOK?

First, get a computer; then find somebody who knows how to operate it. We took our questionnaires to a data processing company (where the keypunchers regarded this survey as a welcome change from the usual surveys on attitudes toward mayonnaise and fabric softener).

The computer transformed the questionnaires into a thick sheaf of tables that cross-referenced people's feelings about armpit hair, marijuana, and acid rock, for example, with their degree of political activism in the Sixties and their present yearly income. We had a staggering amount of data to decipher.

In this book, you'll find we've used certain terms to help bring the data into focus. Our respondents are divided into age groups: older (born 1940–45); middle (1946–49); and younger (1950–52). When we refer to activists, we mean people who have defined themselves as "totally involved" or "very active" in politics during the Sixties. By heavy drug users we mean those who have defined their involvement in the Sixties drug scene as "total." And when speaking of the entire group of respondents (and, by extension, those they represent), we frequently use the term "Woodstock Nation," although this group reveals itself to be less monolithic than that term implies.

Before actually writing the book, we spent weeks looking over the data, figuring out what they meant, at times arguing over interpretations. Besides the computer results, we had the answers to the essay questions to sort through. We read every one of the questionnaires that formed a six-foot stack in our living room. People had described intimate aspects of their lives over the past twenty years with such sincerity that distinct, almost three-dimensional personalities emerged. The accounts were funny, sad, sobering, and thoughtful (but the whole class flunks on spelling and grammar). In a way, our respondents are the ones who have written this book.

The information they gave us fell into a structure that was formed by our inquiry into the subject. First we find out who our respondents are, where they live, what they do for a living; this is Woodstock Nation today. Then we go back to the Sixties and explore what the so-called counter-culture was or wasn't, and how involved our respondents were in its making. This is followed by a line-up of the great heroes of the Sixties (as compared with the heroes of the Seventies), in order to discover some of the influences that shaped our respondents' ideals and goals.

Discussions of drug use, political activism, and the sexual revolution come next, because we feel these areas mark the most distinctive activities and attitudes of the Sixties Generation. In these sections we look into the changes that have occurred—and the similarities that remain—from the Sixties to the Seventies.

Finally, our respondents describe what has happened to the counter-culture in the Seventies, and their own experiences of the changing eras. This leads us to draw some overall conclusions about the Sixties and the Seventies, and to make some predictions about the future.

The results of the Woodstock Census unfold in a manner not unlike the plot of a mystery story. A disappearance has been claimed. We are looking for a decade, an era, a crowd of people that we once knew well—or thought we did. Where did it all go? Our investigation brings together 1005 people who tell, in their own words, what happened to the Sixties Generation.

1
Woodstock Nation

"We are people of this generation,
bred in at least modest comfort,
housed now in universities, looking
uncomfortably to the world we inherit."

—PORT HURON STATEMENT, 1962

A man in Tucson read about the Woodstock Census in the local newspaper and sent us this note: "I'm 28, have two advanced degrees, fought as a marine officer in the Vietnam War, got sick of everything under the sun and finally decided to go into business for myself. I have long hair, love rock music, fight for my freedom every day and came in 4th in the Boston Marathon. Do I qualify?"

Because he was between the ages of 25 and 37, because he felt strongly enough about his experiences in the Sixties to request a questionnaire, he "qualified" to be included in the Woodstock Census. This was not a Representative National Sampling of Average Americans, nor a scientifically controlled cross section of an age group. Instead this survey sought out people who have a sense of having been profoundly affected in one way or another by an extraordinary time in history, people who react strongly to the idea of a Sixties Generation. In the language of statisticians, they were highly motivated respondents—sometimes for quirky reasons:

"I'm 25, a former campus protestor and now—believe it or not—a law enforcement officer, juggling free time to obtain a master's degree in drama. I figure I can really befuddle your survey results, so please send me a copy!"

A New Jersey attorney wrote, "Would like a questionnaire. . . . I feel I am highly qualified since I am 35 years old and still don't know what I want to be when I grow up."

A housewife in Minnesota said, "I told my family I was doing this because the 'squares' needed representation in the survey."

Others seemed, with a good deal of humor, to be trying to recapture something of the "good old days."

"I figured any graying 32-year-old with a persistent rock-and-roll mentality would qualify. Or perhaps it's just that I am fed up with the silly Seventies."

More often, respondents to the survey simply wanted to testify, like a woman in Texas:

"Spring, 1969? I'd love to share with you what I was doing, thinking and even dreaming. . . . I was in San Francisco, married to a musician and dreaming of India. Where I am now is with a different dreamer, gone and come back from India more than once, with three children and one more on the way. Blessed with a Guru, and growing daily in many ways. Still think about revolution and massive change, still believe we can/will/are doing it."

And another man wrote from San Francisco, "Please send me the questionnaire. Some of us acid-crawlbacks want to stand and be counted, too. If only I could find my feet."

The people who responded to this survey came through the Sixties with a wide variety of experiences. Not all were flower children. An inmate at Leavenworth Federal Penitentiary in Kansas wrote, "Although I was a captive in some of this country's most infamous concentration camps for the poor during most of the 60's, that period affected my life and thinking more profoundly than any other since my birth. . . . the changes wrought in my thinking and behavior during that dynamic period in our history will continue to influence and guide me until my death."

And a Connecticut man informed us, "I just might like to take part in your survey. I was a medic in the 82nd Airborne Division and I certainly have some rather definite opinions."

Some people could not resist the chance to tell their life stories. Inevitably, these tales were wrapped up in the surge of nostalgia:

"During the summer of Woodstock I experienced the most tumultuous, traumatic and bittersweet few months of my life down in Chapel Hill, N.C. During the week of Woodstock I tripped on mescaline and LSD for the very first times, made love for the second time, had my heart broken and met a magic (Aquarian) man who let me find the child I was looking for in me at 19. The summer irretrievably changed me. And to this day, in a way, I'm looking, looking for that creature and the feeling of that Time."

And many took part in the survey in the same spirit that had moved them to show up at be-ins, rock concerts, and protest marches. But the most commonly expressed reason why people took part in the Woodstock Census was simple curiosity.

"When you said on a radio interview that Woodstock is ten years old, it put a whole lot into perspective. Since that weekend a whole bunch has happened!! I've gone from carpenter, to farmer, to vagrant, finally to the army, to hold together a family that I also happened to gather along the way. I've got to see how all of us turned out."

"My husband and I'd like to participate in your survey. I'm 28 and went to Syracuse University, involving myself in all those demonstrations. My husband's almost 32, went to a Baptist seminary, and became involved in Chicago in 1968 by picking up a hitchhiker with a gun! I wonder what happened to us all, too!"

The important word is "us." It appears frequently in people's comments on the questionnaire. In their anecdotes and attitudes, the idea of "us," a generation with shared ideals, tastes, values and experiences, is a recurring theme. The things that "we" did and the styles of living that originated with "us" were what made the Sixties so remarkable.

BACKGROUND

Woodstock Nation is populated overwhelmingly by the sons and daughters of America's middle class. Our respondents defined their socioeconomic backgrounds this way:

Class	% of Total*
Upper class	3
Upper middle	30
Middle	43
Lower middle	18
Lower class	5

*In tabulating the results of our questionnaire, we rounded all percentages off to the nearest whole percent. In some tables the percentages add up to more or less than 100. This is because some respondents gave more than one answer where appropriate, and some did not answer every question.

Respondents were not asked to specify their parents' incomes or professions. For our purposes, the way in which our respondents perceive their social status is more important than a strictly economic or sociological classification, because it is a clue to how they perceive their goals and interests.

The fact that Woodstock Nation draws—or thinks of itself as drawing—73% of its members from the middle and upper middle class is something to keep in mind throughout this survey. The term "middle class"—often a dirty word during the Sixties—is used here to reflect a self-image, rather than to define a social condition. The people we surveyed, for the most part, went to college, had the time to participate in protest movements, and could afford to drop out for temporary experiments with poverty, walking barefoot down Haight Street panhandling for spare change. Interestingly, 79% of our respondents say they tried, during the Sixties, "to shed middle-class values," and as we go along, we will see how they tried to do this, and how far they succeeded.

Where Respondents Grew Up	% of Total
Big cities	28
Suburbs	32
Small cities	12
Small towns	12
Rural	5
Moved around a lot	8

The fact that most of our respondents grew up in urban and suburban areas reflects the fact that our survey was conducted and publicized in locations where the counter-culture had flourished. Outside of the heavily populated areas, it was more difficult to get involved with it: "I didn't participate in any protest demonstrations during the Sixties," one respondent wrote, "because there weren't any nearby."

In and around the urban areas, the message of changing styles and attitudes circulated faster than in the outlying areas. The demonstrations, be-ins, and rock concerts that were the counter-culture's public rituals were more accessible. Also, in cities such as Chicago, San Francisco, and New York, there were established avant-garde communities like North Beach, Old Town, and

Greenwich Village that helped spawn the hip ghettos of the Sixties.

The most important fact here, though, is that the largest percentage of our respondents grew up in the suburbs. What could be more middle class than that?

AGE

We assume that those who identify most strongly with the Sixties were most likely to respond to this survey. The heaviest response comes from the youngest age group.

Year Born	% of Total
1952	17
1951	13
1950	13
1949	13
1948	9
1947	10
1946	8
1945	5
1944	3
1943	3
1942	3
1941	3
1940	1

People born from 1950 through 1952 add up to 43% of our respondents—the largest of our three age groups—even though these people caught only the tail end of the Sixties.

Those born from 1946 through 1949, who came of age right in the midst of the decade, make up 40% of the total.

The oldest group, born mostly during World War II, experienced the Sixties in their late teens and twenties. They form only 17% of the respondents.

It may be that people in the oldest age bracket identify more with the Fifties than with the Sixties and were therefore less motivated to respond to this survey. It may be that Woodstock Nation drew most of its members from those who were between the ages of 16 and 20 in the late Sixties. Or maybe people over 32 are simply too tired to fill out a 22-page questionnaire.

SEX

Sex	% of Total
Male	55
Female	45

Without directly seeking an equal number of men and women, we achieved a reasonably balanced sample. The fact that more men than women responded to this survey may say more about the Seventies than about the Sixties. Although slightly more women than men responded through the mail, men outnumbered women in every place we held our census sessions, except Atlanta. Does this mean that women are still reluctant to venture out at night without a date?

RACE

Race	% of Total
White	95
Black	1
Hispanic	1
Other	1
No answer	1

Several respondents were offended by being asked to indicate their race. "This is bullshit!" commented one. Others wrote in "human." This attitude is a remnant of the liberal "color-blind" ethic, the idea that race doesn't matter.

But race must have had something to do with who was in or out of Sixties counter-culture, because in most photographs of folk and rock concerts, hippie be-ins, and antiwar marches there are very few black faces to be seen among the crowds—although the people on stage, making the speeches, singing the inspirational songs, making the rock 'n' roll, were very often blacks: Odetta, Dick Gregory, Buddy Miles, Muddy Waters, Bobby Seale, Richie Havens, Jimi Hendrix. In the hip ghettos, it was common to refer to the problem of "relating to the Third World Community," which should tell us something about the way the flower children perceived the blacks or hispanics with whom they shared the ghettos.

MARRIED, SINGLE, AND OTHERWISE

Kathy D. from Atlanta told us in a letter: "My husband Butch and I met at Woodstock on Thursday, August 15 (1969), and we've been together ever since. We were married in November of '69. I would be very interested in knowing if you have met any other couples that met at Woodstock and are still married."

Now that's a question we never got around to asking, but Butch and Kathy, of course, are not unusual in a more general sense; all during the Sixties, members of the Love Generation were meeting, falling in love, and getting married.

Remember "hippie weddings"? They were a Sixties phenomenon—like Yippie activist Abbie Hoffman's marriage to Anita Kushner in Central Park in 1967. Bride and groom, dressed in flowing white robes and bedecked with flowers, stood in the sunshine amidst a gathering of pot-smoking, bead-wearing friends while a "hippie rabbi" performed a rather loose interpretation of the traditional ceremony. It was like a be-in, or, depending on your point of view, Mom's worst nightmare, with the East Village community turning out in force. Folk songs were sung, people danced and ate picnic lunches, while a horde of reporters recorded the images for the folks back home. Soon, hippie weddings were being reported by the press all across the country.

Despite the counter-culture trappings, the hippie marriage was still a marriage, perhaps even more old-fashioned and traditional than the usual American ceremony. What could be more folksy and small-town-like than having the community turn out to celebrate the union of two of its own? The restructuring of the ceremony to include poems written especially for the event, passages from favorite authors like Kahlil Gibran and J. R. R. Tolkien, and popular rock songs was an attempt to personalize the event and make it more meaningful to the community—a way of strengthening, not undermining, an institution.

One fifth of all our respondents married during the Sixties—

21

whether in a hippie wedding or not, we couldn't bear to ask. In the Seventies, one-third of all respondents got married, and 16% had children.

At the time the survey was taken, the marital status of the respondents was reported in these percentages:

Marital Status	% of Total
Single	43
Married	30
Cohabiting	14
Divorced	13

The unmarried majority is being gradually eroded in the youngest and middle groups: Of those between 25 and 27 years old, 24% are married; of people 28 to 31 years old, 36% are married. This seems to indicate a trend toward marriage that overshadows the 14% of Woodstock Nation that "lives together." Contrary to some opinions, marriage lives.

However, there is also a corresponding trend toward divorce. Although 45% of the oldest group married during the Sixties, and an additional 23% married in the Seventies, only 31% were still married at the time of the survey. In this group, 19% listed their current status as divorced.

The falling-apart of many Sixties marriages may simply be part of the national pattern, for the divorce rate has risen every year since 1960, and in 1970 it was 3.5; in Woodstock Nation it is 3.7.

One woman reports that her worst experience of the Sixties was "my divorce." Her *best* experience was "my divorce. It made me free."

BIG GENERATION ON CAMPUS

At the University of California at Berkeley, there were 43,000 students in 1956. Ten years later the number had doubled. Across the nation, the student population at all colleges and universities, which stood at 2.3 million in 1960, ballooned to 5 million in 1964.* College was an almost universal experience in Woodstock

* Theodore Roszak, *The Making of a Counter-Culture*, 1969.

22

Nation. Of all our respondents, 93% have been to college, two-thirds are graduates, and a third have completed some postgraduate work.

Presumably, parents send their children to centers of higher learning so they can better themselves. It is a cliché that better jobs go to those with college degrees. But our respondents do not seem to feel this happened. More than half (53%) agree, more or less, with the statement, "My education did not prepare me for a job." Only 36% feel their schooling prepared them sufficiently for the work force.

If preparation for a career is not what our respondents feel they got out of college, then what was really happening on campus? What *did* the college experience mean?

"In 1967 I was a sophomore at a small, Eastern women's progressive college where the community spirit that already existed was completely channeled into the antiwar movement, drug awareness, etc. I didn't get involved in the Sixties until I was surrounded."

This is a perfect description of the experience of at least 26% of the respondents, who testified that, for them, the Sixties really began when they went to college.

The fact that most of the people we surveyed had at least some college experience suggests that, to a considerable degree, the campus was the birthplace of Woodstock Nation.

Educational Experience	% of Total
Some high school	1
Graduated from high school	5
Some college	31
Graduated from college	27
Postgraduate work	35

JOBS AND INCOME

The people we surveyed are not the affluent types who are drinking white rum and soda and "making it" in ads for *Playboy* magazine.

23

Respondents' Yearly Income	% of Total
Under $8000	34
$8000 to 9999	14
$10,000 to 14,999	27
$15,000 to 19,999	12
$20,000 to 24,999	6
$25,000 and up	5

A third report yearly incomes of under $8000. About half of our respondents make under $10,000. Those reporting yearly incomes of $20,000 or more number only 11%. Income levels, however, do tend to rise with age.

Our respondents are in a wide variety of occupations. Some are distinctly connected with the style of the Sixties: childbirth teacher, rock concert manager, head shop owner, dope dealer, environmental specialist, "wanderer." A number of people define themselves by a scattershot approach—"actress, dancer, hippy"; "teacher, writer, social activist." Many of the occupations return very little income. One Florida man describes his means of making a living this way: "I scavenge garbage dumpsters for newspapers, aluminum, whatever I can sell."

But there are people engaged in mainstream jobs, too: office workers, house painters, firemen, nurses, electronics contractors, a lab technician, a keypunch operator, a corporate consultant with his own firm, an economist, a minister, and a probation officer, plus two law enforcement officers and two pilots. We encounter a handful of doctors, a score of lawyers, and many social workers.

The most common occupation, however, is in education. More of our respondents are teachers than anything else. Have Sixties graduates been unable to divorce themselves completely from the school environment? As in every generation, being on campus was for many people in the Sixties their best experience of that time. A

24

30-year-old Atlanta woman recalls "being part of a young collegiate community where academic and personal life blended together." Today she is still part of that world (with some misgivings): "I chose the career of college teaching in order to perpetuate the 60's lifestyle. But it's harder than I thought these days."

More respondents fall into the category of professional workers than into any other category. With their high degree of education, this is perhaps predictable. But while the generation as a whole certainly has its share of upwardly mobile corporate strivers and ambitious White House aides, the group we surveyed tends to have more modest goals. Two distinctive occupational patterns emerge: (1) Respondents, in the main, are engaged in relatively noncompetitive fields; and (2) they tend to work in areas where the products are human rather than material.

Job Categories	% of Total

Professional workers
    teachers, doctors, lawyers, entertainers,
    clergy, C.P.A.'s, engineers, writers, artists
	42

Clerical and sales
    bookkeepers, insurance agents,
    secretaries, salespeople, dope dealers
	13

Craftspeople, skilled workers
    jewelers, electricians, plumbers, printers,
    carpenters, mechanics
	6

Officials, managers and proprietors
    buyers, public officials, contractors,
    inspectors
	6

Students	5
Unemployed	5

Service workers
    waiters, hair cutters, cooks, firemen,
    police, military, postal workers
	3

Operative workers
    bus drivers, machinists, mine workers,
    taxi drivers
	2

Housewives	2
Laborers	2
No answer	14

GEOGRAPHY

Responses to the Woodstock Census came from every state in the Union. A few questionnaires were mailed in by servicemen and servicewomen stationed overseas and one came in from somebody cruising on the U.S.S. *Saipan.*

"Both my brother and I were vets of Woodstock. He's in Nepal, but I'm sure I could get a questionnaire to him. . . . Send two and I'll complete one and send the other along to Katmandu."

A woman from Sewanee, Tenn., wrote, "Please send two questionnaires. Lots of us 60's children live in the country now!"

It's a fact that some of the Sixties people are still living in communes. From upstate New York, a woman wrote, "I sure would like to participate, could you please send me a copy of the questionnaire. Uh, better send six. I live in a rural commune. In fact, better make that eight. I make my living as writer/editor of the local hippie paper and it would be nice for the rest of the staff to get in on it, too."

A man at the Twin Oaks commune in Louisa, Va., wrote, "I'm 31 years old, live on a commune with 80 other people, never gave up my Sixties lifestyle, live with 40 women who still have armpit hair, etc. Perhaps you'd like to send 20 or 30 copies?"

And so our responses came in from all over, breaking down in the following percentages:

Area	% of Total
Northeast	30
South	21
Central/Midwest	24
West/Southwest	25

Of a total of 1005 respondents, 37% requested questionnaires through the mail, 56% filled out questionnaires at census sessions around the country, and 6% were given questionnaires by friends who obtained extras from us.

Questionnaires we received in the mail tended to contain longer written answers to essay questions than those collected at census sessions. People filling out the questionnaire at home could do so

26

at their leisure, as described by one respondent who scribbled on her last page: "Time: 2 hours and 30 minutes later, after many bongs, 2 bowls of ice cream, much reminiscing, dreams and renewed hopes!"

Also, people with incomes over $20,000 show up more often as mail-in respondents than those with lesser incomes; attendance at census sessions was greater for those making less money. Could it be that the more affluent members of Woodstock Nation were too busy—or too snobbish—to participate in a "people's event" reminiscent of their hippie past? Perhaps, but more likely it was simply a matter of a free event attracting those most able to afford it.

These are the only differences we could detect between results gained from the two survey methods.

Very little evidence could be found in the survey results to indicate regional differences in attitudes, values, and experiences. Although the smallest response came from the usually conservative South, for instance, the people surveyed there were not significantly different from the rest in their politics, culture, drug use, and feelings about the Sixties. While regional differences all over the nation are slowly eroding, partly as a result of increased access to national communications media, this group seems to have formed its own intercommunal links that, in the course of one decade, transcended the old American boundaries. No matter where you were, Alaska or Mississippi, if you joined Woodstock Nation, you became part of something that was bigger (and, you hoped, better) than your home town. Wearing love beads, listening to rock music, growing long hair, taking part in protest demonstrations, and smoking pot allied you instantly with comrades across the land.

2
Culture

"Wow!"

—COMMON SIXTIES
EXPRESSION

A Pennsylvania steelworker, 26 years old, laid off and "about to hit the road," recalls when it all started: "The 60's really began in about 1959 when *My Weekly Reader* did an article about a highway that would stretch across the nation with no traffic lights, and they'd be working on it through the 60's."

The same vision, a dream, really, of limitless exploration, no stop lights, no rules, of something brand new that could speed Americans across a new frontier, occurred in different ways at different times to many people. It was a state of mind, not a particular year, which defined the Sixties, a collection of ideas that were revealed in flashes of insight, in raw experiences, in the pages of newspapers and magazines, and in bright bursts of music.

Nearly one quarter of our respondents say their Sixties began with music. Some of the older members of the group heard the first notes of change in the Fifties. When did their Sixties begin?

"In 1956 with Pat Boone, Elvis Presley, etc. Sock hops in elementary school. My parents gave me a transistor radio for Christmas and never saw me again—it was when I first realized that things could be different from the way my parents said they could be."

"1955, with Chuck Berry, Little Richard, Frankie Lymon and the Teenagers."

"1954–55 with Johnny Ray, Elvis, and 'Rebel Without A Cause.' "

"When I heard 'Jailhouse Rock' and wanted to dance—even though it was taboo in my own religious training."

The Sixties were a long time coming, a process of awakening to new rhythms, like rock and roll, which emerged in the Forties and Fifties as "race music," an underground phenomenon suppressed by parents and authorities, despised by intellectuals. That rock and roll has become socially acceptable (to the point where it is now the background music for television commercials) is an intrinsic part of the Sixties story. It started almost as mystic ritual:

"When the song 'If I Had A Hammer' by Peter, Paul and Mary became popular, there was born a new philosophy among young people—the trend toward peace and love began for me then."

"It began when I found myself singing stanzas of Bob Dylan's 'Mr. Tambourine Man' to myself at Camp Lai Khai, Vietnam, in 1966."

"In 1966 when I bought my first rock album, read *Saturday Evening Post* (about Haight-Ashbury) and fought with my mother about my hair."

"One night in late 1960's I woke up and the radio was on and I heard the long version of 'Light My Fire.' It was strange and exciting—symbolically a new dawn!"

"The 60's began, for me, in 1967 when WABX-FM started broadcasting in Detroit. I became super into acid and progressive rock which led to dope and the whole counter-culture."

"Seeing the Grateful Dead and Janis at the Fillmore East, the East Village clubs and friendly young women with free bouncing breasts."

"When I saw *Monterey Pop*; then really when I went to Woodstock."

Some of those surveyed mark the beginning of the Sixties with their first experiences with drugs. A 30-year-old physician in New York says her Sixties began this way: "In Christmas, 1966, my boyfriend returned from grad school on the West Coast bearing a batch of Magic Cookies."

Drugs and music are often linked together.

"I first turned on in the Navy, started to like the music, got myself discharged on a drug bust, joined a motorcycle club, about 1967."

"The 60's began for me when my friends and I started doing

drugs. Also when I went to the 2nd Atlanta Pop Festival in Byron, Georgia, and realized how many people were freaks."

Getting "turned on" happened in some unusual places.

"In 1967 I got turned on to dope by a group of progressive ministers in Detroit and helped stage a love feast. Called a hippie by local press. Parents were mortified."

An Arizona electronics engineer, 32, says that during the Sixties, her life "was pretty much dominated by external, mostly political events." This feeling was common in Woodstock Nation—a large number of people remember political events inaugurating the Sixties.

"With the demonstrations in Selma . . ."

"Kennedy assassinated during my birthday party . . ."

"In 1966 when I joined the War Resisters League (but not SDS 'cause I was chicken and the daughter of a career Air Force officer)."

"The Sixties began for me in 1967 when some of us who were in the Peace Corps in Kenya were threatened with being kicked out because we sent an antiwar petition to Johnson."

The older group—not unnaturally—remembers the Sixties beginning earlier. A 34-year-old North Carolina man marks the beginning when "William Faulkner and Marilyn died the summer of 1962. The Ole Miss riots—first modern collegiate violence."

Over 50% of those born between 1940 and 1945 date the beginning of the Sixties prior to 1965. But only 28% of the people born in 1950 to 1952 feel the Sixties go back that far. We are examining not a bracket of calendar dates but a distinct state of mind, which many people first encountered when they left home and arrived at college.

"September 1, 1965, on my first night at college, I discovered the only song known by heart by myself and 12 other freshmen guitar players was 'Mr. Tambourine Man.' "

"Though I graduated from high school in 1965 at Fort Bragg, North Carolina (my father was a Green Beret), the war was status quo and dissent was not even something I ever thought of. In '68, a fraternity brother turned me onto pot and away we go!"

The press helped spread the message, and the Sixties reached many people through the pages of "establishment" newspapers and magazines.

"The first tiny inklings that something special was happening were from fellow art students at high school and *Time* and *Life* in my junior year."

"In December, 1967, I was a freshman in college and unhappy with myself, restless, needing a change, a drastic change in my life. I picked up a newspaper and read my first article ever on 'hippies' and the East Village. I knew then I wanted to be in with them, that they were the answer I was looking for."

Mobility was an important aspect of the Sixties. It speeded up the process of social change.

"In 1964 I moved from dull Midwest to 'aware' East. Soon discovered Beatles, long hair, sex, liquor, Levis, Gant shirts (remember Gant shirts?!)—a typical 60's teenage metamorphosis. Also, discovered gay tendencies, a crushing realization."

Looking back on that time, people often cite as turning points experiences in which they openly broke with family and authority.

"In 1967 I got divorced, became free to think and act on my opinions. I found my own friends, I was 3000 miles away from home and no one to answer to except me!"

"It all started with being removed from school for long hair in 1965."

"My 60's began in 1965 when I started wearing my hair in braids. When I realized that I was not alone in my so-called weird ideas and thoughts."

More people say that the Sixties began in 1967 than in any other year. This was the year that the Black Panthers emerged as an organization, the first be-in occurred in San Francisco's Golden Gate Park, the Summer of Love lured flower children to the West Coast, rock concerts flourished at Bill Graham's Fillmores, East and West, "free-form" FM radio took over the air waves, the first psychedelic albums were released ("Are You Experienced?" by Jimi Hendrix, "Surrealistic Pillow" by the Jefferson Airplane, "The Doors" by Jim Morrison and the Doors, and Cream's "Disraeli Gears"). The Beatles released their "Sergeant Pepper's Lonely Hearts Club Band," and *Rolling Stone* magazine published its first issue. It was also the year that Dustin Hoffman starred in the hit movie *The Graduate.* A 25-year-old law student from New York confesses: "In 1967 I saw *The Graduate* about ten times. The effect of the change it caused in me still lingers. I refused to listen to anything other

WHEN DID THE SIXTIES BEGIN?

Year	% of Total*
prior to 1961	8
1961	3
1962	4
1963	8
1964	12
1965	10
1966	10
1967	15
1968	11
1969	5
1970 or later	1

*87% of the total number of respondents mentioned dates.

EXPERIENCES THAT MARKED THE BEGINNING OF THE SIXTIES

Experience	% of Total*
Educational (Went to college, etc.)	26
Political events (Kennedy assassination, Vietnam, etc.)	25
Music	23
Personal events (Fought with parents, moved out of the house, etc.)	17
Drugs (First smoked pot, etc.)	13
Cultural events	7
Sexual experiences	3

*74% of the total mentioned experiences, sometimes combining two of the above categories.

35

than Simon and Garfunkel for months (with the exception of the Beatles, the Airplane and the Doors).''

However or whenever or wherever they happened, the Sixties were a distinct phenomenon. Those who truly experienced them can look back to a moment in time that divided their lives into "before" and "after"—and one of our respondents, a 29-year-old Michigan woman, can even point to the precise *hour* it dawned on her: "May 28, 7:30 P.M.—really! It was exactly one week after my engagement had been broken and the first time I had gotten stoned. I'll never forget it!''

Many traditional ties were broken when the Sixties came along. By smoking dope, people became law breakers. Favoring the new rock (Blue Cheer) meant leaving the old music (the Lettermen) behind. Adopting a radical political stance pitted the individual against the government. Joining with other young people in a nationwide community of ideas, tastes, and values was a rejection of the American status quo. And just sensing that new freedom to "do your own thing" caused people to shuck a lot of old habits, as the experience of an Oklahoma City bartender illustrates: "In 1968, I ran away from home, stopped wearing underwear, started smoking dope and dropping acid.''

As everyone knows, once you stop wearing underwear, the sky's the limit.

THE COUNTER-CULTURE STYLE

When people talk about the Sixties happening to them, the elements mentioned most often are music, drugs, politics, a sense of unity with other young people, and the feeling of "cutting loose." These are the essential ingredients of what became known as the counter-culture.

Some people plunged into every aspect of the counter-culture, from LSD to SDS, and experienced the Sixties to the utmost. But there were many who touched only one or two of the elemental aspects of the counter-culture, and still entered into the spirit of the time, such as the Iowa teacher who states: "The Sixties for me are an attitude, not a time period. The best part of the 60's was the possibility of adopting a part of the counter-culture without having to adopt all of it (drugs, etc.)."

The easiest part of the counter-culture to adopt was the style. Blue jeans were favored by 90% of our respondents, and 72% wore work shirts. This originated as the proletarian look, which first became popular on college campuses during the early days of the civil rights movement.

But not all of Woodstock Nation was dressed by Levi Strauss and army surplus. There was a clutter of clothing fads in the Sixties that filled closets with "fab" items: 26% of the male respondents confess to having worn Nehru jackets, not to mention skinny ties, Beatle boots, and newsboy caps popularized by Liverpool's Fab Four. The odd plumage of Carnaby Street in "Swinging London" was imported by invading armies of British musicians, so that men costumed themselves in brightly polka-dotted shirts, and cuffless trousers that tightened at the crotch and flared at the ankle into bell-bottoms.

The sleek, high-fashion look exemplified by Jackie Kennedy and Audrey Hepburn appealed to some—"I had no style of my own," remembers a 35-year-old nurse from Atlanta. "I thought Audrey Hepburn was the epitome of all that is pleasing and attractive, so I tried to copy her style." However, just 17% of our female respondents (mostly in the older age bracket) agreed; the majority seems to have preferred the more unconventional style that was labeled "folkie." How many women tried to emulate Joan Baez, Mary Travers, Judy Henske, and all the other folksingers with long, perfectly straight tresses by ironing their own hair? The answer, at least for this group, is 32%, with younger women in the majority.

Whether you copied Hepburn or Baez, you did it with your knees showing: 90% of the women we surveyed wore miniskirts. When they were introduced in 1964 by British designer Mary Quant, they sparked a public debate over fashion, forcing even politicians to take a stand. "It's a functional thing," stated New York's Mayor Lindsay. "It enables young ladies to run faster—and because of it they may have to."*

*Paul Sann, *Fads, Follies and Delusions of the American People*, 1967.

37

For the people we talked to, clothes became as much a personal statement as they ever were for aristocrats at the court of Louis XIV. In Haight-Ashbury, the East Village, and hip ghettos all over the country, people wore clothes that were often as bizarre as they were beautiful—outrageous clothes made of paisley and velvet, silk scarves and embroidered robes, purple bell-bottoms and long, flowing skirts, cast-off military jackets emblazoned with peace symbols and hats blooming with flowers and feathers. "Outrageous" clothes, we called them—and they were worn in the Sixties by 62% of the people we surveyed (a few were still wearing them when they showed up to fill out their questionnaires).

Under the outrageous clothes another revolution was going on: The "natural look" came into vogue during the Sixties. Both men and women appreciated the idea of discarding brassieres, although men, not surprisingly, were more in favor of bra-lessness than women (81% to 63%). Most of the women—80%—rejected the practice of altering their figures with girdles.

Although the pages of *Seventeen* and *Glamour* and *Mademoiselle* reflected little change in the cosmetological status quo, makeup got a no vote from 53% of the men, as well as from 40% of the women who were supposed to be buying it. And 59% of the women we surveyed say that during those years they stopped using makeup altogether. This was more than a fashion fad. Three quarters of the women who abandoned makeup during the Sixties described themselves as political activists. An "honest" physical appearance was linked to a general antiestablishment outlook in the belief that (as the popular Movement slogan dictated) "the personal is political."

That this slogan was taken seriously is proven by examining the seemingly silly phenomenon of armpit hair on women. Just 15% of the entire group was inclined toward letting it grow (with men and women equal in their attitudes on the matter). But among political activists, the percentage of those who liked females with fuzz is higher (24%). The same attitude was held regarding the practice of women shaving their legs—significantly more of the female activists (58%) stopped shaving their legs during the Sixties than women in general (40%). What a dilemma: A woman had to choose between hairy legs or the appearance of bourgeois decadence. In fact, in certain radical circles, smooth legs were considered the sure mark of an FBI hireling.

Trivial as they seem today, these statistics testify to the super-charged political atmosphere of an era in which hair parted people to the left or to the right.

A few hairy episodes from the files of the Associated Press:

March 13, 1965, Santa Monica, Calif.—Beatle haircut lands 18-year-old student in jail. He was arrested on charges of suspicion of violating Board of Education rules and disrupting the classroom.

July 13, 1965, Louisville, Ky.—A man made his son get a dog license because he "didn't get those bangs cut." Son's breed was described as "American Beetle."

January 24, 1966, Salt Lake City, Utah—Twenty-one-year-old Don Pasternak's shoulder-length hair sparked a fight between two groups of youths. He and two teenage boys were arrested and charged with assault after two other youths were stabbed during the fight. The fight was caused by catcalls aimed at Pasternak's hairdo.

May 3, 1967, Providence, R.I.—Gregory Arthur Smith, 20, president of the sophomore class at Providence College, refused to cut his hair and staged a hunger strike because school officials wouldn't let him eat in the cafeteria.

September 10, 1968, Houston, Tex.—124 boys were sent home from Westbury High because of long hair. 100 returned with haircuts and were allowed to reenter the school. The rest planned to picket.

August 28, 1969, St. Petersburg, Fla.—Three teachers at Lakewood High were ordered to get haircuts or be dismissed from the faculty.

January 30, 1969, Norwalk, Conn.—Fifty-three students at McMahon High were suspended for long hair. They staged a protest march carrying signs that read, "DOES SOCIETY HANG BY A HAIR?" "BEETHOVEN WITH A CREWCUT?" and "IT'S 1968, NOT 1984." Nearby, the barbers' union had erected a billboard featuring a long-haired youth and the advice, "BEAUTIFY AMERICA—GET A HAIRCUT."

September 24, 1969, Marlboro, Mass.—Senior Robert Richards, 17, was reinstated at Marlboro High by Judge Charles E. Wyzonski in a seven-page opinion from the U.S. District Court in Boston which upheld the right of students to wear long hair to class. The opinion cited historical, aesthetic, and legal precedents and issued a permanent injunction against Principal Robert Thruston who had suspended Richards since September 11.

In the Sixties, *Hair* was the title of one of the most successful Broadway musical productions of all time. Billed as a "tribal love-rock musical," *Hair* was loosely based on the predicament of a reluctant draftee whose long hair is clipped by the army. After four years and 1742 performances, it was one of the longest-running shows in Broadway history, evidence that middle-class Americans were intrigued by the "do your own thing" ethic of the counter-culture—symbolized on the simplest level by long hair.

The symbol had a very real significance. One woman reports: "I was cold to anyone who had short hair, wore a suit, or had a pig job." The majority (83%) of the women surveyed preferred long hair on males, so it was tough during the Sixties for men with crew-cuts to get even to first base. And as 75% of the men we talked to had been "long-hairs," short-hairs tended to stick out in a youthful crowd like J. Edgar Hoover at a be-in. The situation created many cases of split personality. Men who enlisted in the military reserves or campus ROTC programs to avoid going to Vietnam had to wear short-hair wigs if they wanted to please their proudly crew-cut officers while at the same time preserving a full head of hair. The only short-haired men accorded respect among long-hairs were deserters from the army and recently released convicts.

Nearly three quarters of the men we surveyed grew mustaches and/or beards at a time when police frequently assumed that the more hair a man had on his head and face, the more likely he was to be a drug user, a political radical, or both. The assumption happens to have been correct: among our respondents, 87% of the male political activists and 94% of the heavy drug users had long hair in the Sixties—significantly higher percentages than for the group as a whole. Here again is evidence attesting to the political nature of fashion during the Sixties.

40

THE PEACE SIGN AND OTHER MYSTERIES

What do we make of the fact that 81% of the people we surveyed say that during the Sixties they flashed the "peace sign" to perfect strangers? And what about all those other rituals of the counter-culture—what did they mean?

For instance, there was the hippie smile, a kind of wide-eyed, open-faced grin that was chock full of innocence and wonderment, with just a hint of brain damage. "We used to smile a lot more and give people flowers," remembers one former hippie. Used on another hippie, the smile usually elicited the same in return, along with the response, "Peace," or its Indian equivalent, "*Om shanti.*" Used on certain kinds of cops, it drove them crazy.

There was the "power handshake," appropriated from black culture, which was accomplished by grasping the other person's thumb and upper wrist, with thumbs entwined.

There was the peculiar aversion to using last names. One fourth of all our respondents once believed that "last names are bullshit." Strangers in Woodstock Nation were often introduced as "Dave from Vancouver," or "Cheryl from San Diego," or else real names were completely obliterated. There was "Panama Red," and "Sunshine," "Che," "Free," "Rainbow," "Mountain Girl," and "Tripper." Grace Slick of the Jefferson Airplane named her newborn daughter "China," while Abbie and Anita Hoffman call their son "america" (with the lower-case *a*). One of our respondents remembers the name she went by was "Rainy Day Blues."

Why did people wear love beads? Why did some paint bizarre designs on their cars and VW buses? Why was everybody hitchhiking all over the country, living in crashpads? What were all those middle-class kids accomplishing by standing around Haight Street or St. Mark's Place begging for spare change? What about all the other odd little customs and practices of the counter-culture?

"Don't forget patchouli oil," a respondent hastens to remind us. Alas, the authors of this book cannot possibly forget patchouli oil, the musky perfume that in proper hippie crashpads mingled with the fragrance of incense (burned to mask the incriminating odor of marijuana). Also very hip was natural body odor. At the height of his Yippie activism, Jerry Rubin declared: "A generation that rejects the middle-class notion of cleanliness is a revolutionary generation."

We find that over a third of our respondents quit using deodorant during the Sixties and one fifth say that in those days they liked natural body odor. By Rubin's standard, this generation was fairly unrevolutionary, or at least the majority of them didn't offend. But those who did reject the middle-class notion of cleanliness and those who were most engaged in the rites and rituals of the counter-culture were those most involved with politics and drug use.

STRANGE RITES OF THE COUNTER-CULTURE

In the Sixties	% of Total Group	% of Political Activists	% of Heavy Drug Users
Liked natural body odor	21	27	31
Stopped using deodorant	37	48	52
Panhandled for spare change	23	28	48
Gave the peace sign to complete strangers	81	89	85
Thought last names were bullshit	25	31	39
Went hitchhiking	73	82	88
Wore love beads	59	65	76
Stayed at crashpads	59	74	85
Painted their cars with bizarre designs	12	15	21

WE'VE GOT A GROOVY THING GOIN'

Another feature of the counter-culture was that its members adopted their own vernacular.

The press picked up the colorful terms used in hip circles and delighted in publishing glossaries, supposedly so parents could find out what their kids were saying. Often, however, the lexicographers cited words that no hip person—or other human being, for that matter—had ever uttered, and some similarly far-out definitions. The following definitions were published in a 1968 paperback with a lurid cover, *Hippie Sex*, by "Dale Gordon, Ph.D.":

BACKWARDS	Tranquilizers, or any chemical depressant.
BUM TRIP	A disturbing experience.
FORWARDS	Any of the so-called pep pills.
FREAK	Somebody's bag, which he grossly over-emphasizes. "To freak out" is to lose all contact with reality.
GROOVY	That which swings or is with it.
WHERE IT'S AT	The psychological or physical locus of real significant activity as opposed to sham and ritual.

"What makes Hip a special language," Norman Mailer once wrote, "is that it cannot be taught—if one shares none of the experiences of elation and exhaustion which it is equipped to describe, then it seems merely arch or vulgar or irritating."* While nearly everybody we surveyed uses hip expressions to characterize the Sixties, the words that the highest percentage of our group (36%) remember as typifying those years are words expressing elation. In other words, the people who shared the experiences of the era regard it as a positive experience in their lives. They think of words like:

far out
peace and love
groovy
right on
wow
hip or *I'm hip*
out of sight
dynamite
good trip
good vibes

*"The White Negro," *Advertisements for Myself,* 1959.

Only 4% sum up the era with negative expressions:

> *freaked out*
> *fucked up*
> *bummer*

The widespread influence of politics on this group is shown by the fact that 20% characterize the Sixties in terms of slogans:

> *Power to the people*
> *Hell no, we won't go*
> *Black power*
> *If you're not part of the solution,*
>   *you're part of the problem*

For 11%, expressions that evoke the drug experience are what best typify the era:

> *turn on*
> *turn on, tune in, drop out*
> *freaky*
> *feed your head*

About 9% mention commonly used exhortations to join the counter-culture:

> *Do your own thing*
> *Get it all together*
> *Let it all hang out*
> *Get with it*

And another 7% quote from the other secret language of Woodstock Nation, the songs and music of the Sixties.

FLOWER POWER

One of the great songs of the Sixties urged people who were going to San Francisco to be sure they wore some flowers in their hair. As a matter of fact, 16% of the people we interviewed did make the pilgrimage to Haight-Ashbury in 1967, the "Summer of Love," and 64% say that back in the Sixties they believed in "flower power," the pacifist philosophy that combined elements of turn-the-other-cheek Christianity and Sgt. Pepper's Lonely Hearts Club Band with Timothy Leary's advice to "turn on, tune in, drop out"—yielding something that sounded like Gandhi on acid.

Flower power was the ideology of the true hippie. Were the young of America hippies during the Sixties? Or is that just a myth? A clear 62% of our respondents say that it isn't a myth— that they did consider themselves hippies in the Sixties. Hippies were not unconcerned about problems like the Vietnam War, civil rights, and poverty, but they believed that the solution lay not in direct confrontation with the establishment, but in transforming it with love and "good vibes."

Serious political activists, however, regarded flower power uneasily. Among our respondents we can see that the number of flower power believers in the activist group is close to the number of flower power-ites in Woodstock Nation as a whole. However, it was the drug users, a less political group, who really went for the flower business.

WHO WERE THE HIPPIES?

In the 60's	% of Total Group	% of Political Activists	% of Heavy Drug Users
Believed in flower power	64	69	80
Considered themselves hippies	62	75	90

For most of the decade, there was a split within the counterculture between the political activists and the cultural activists, a split neatly exemplified in a debate between the two groups that occurred after thirty-eight people were arrested during a 1967 pot "smoke-in" held at Tompkins Square Park in New York's East Village. Hippies and politicos stood on the courthouse steps shouting at each other, as reported in the *Village Voice*:*

*Marlene Nadle, "The Power of Flower vs. The Power of Politicos," *Village Voice*, June 15, 1967.

"Flower power can't stop fascist power."

"The hippies are making it easy for the fascists. Sniffing daffodils is playing it safe. Chanting isn't going to change anything."

"You only want to get rid of the police state to set up your own. You only want to get rid of this establishment to set up another one."

"How can you sing at a time like this? You want to make this into India. You want to chant *'Hare Krishna'* while millions starve."

"We'll never stop singing. What else is there to do except sing?"

Although some revolutionaries agreed with H. Rap Brown, that "you have to fight back and you can't fight with flowers,"* hippies did succeed, in Theodore Roszak's phrase, "in embodying radical disaffiliation—what Herbert Marcuse called the Great Refusal—in a form that captures the need of the young for unrestricted joy."†

This is what made be-ins such powerfully important events that 58% of our respondents attended one or more. Our political-activist and drug-user groups attended be-ins the most, and in nearly equal numbers (78% and 75% respectively). The very first be-in at Golden Gate Park, on January 14, 1967, was conceived as a sort of powwow between the political activists in Berkeley and the hippies of the Haight-Ashbury district. It was billed as a "Gathering of the Tribes," meaning the Hell's Angels and the Hare Krishnas as well as the hippies and the politicos. It marked a milestone in the history of the counter-culture. An alliance was forged that showed its strength the following October, when thousands of people converged in Washington, D.C., to "levitate the Pentagon." The same forces showed up in Chicago in August 1968 under the banner of "Yippie!" What was a Yippie? "A hippie who has been hit over the head by a cop," was Abbie Hoffman's answer. Only 16% of our respondents considered themselves Yippies, proving that this particular initiation was too painful for most. Nevertheless, be-ins were manifestations of the basic alliance between the cultural and political activists.

*Art Spiegelman and Bob Schneider, *Whole Grains*, 1973.

†Theodore Roszak, *The Making of a Counter-Culture*, 1969.

46

FREAKING-OUT THE STRAIGHTS

A 25-year-old factory worker in San Francisco recalls his favorite experience of the decade: "July 4th, 1968, driving in Maine with a car full of acid pranksters handing out flowers to startled tourists as we caroused from one beach resort to another—fireworks in our eyes and foolish grins on our faces."

"Tootling the multitudes," was what Ken Kesey and his Merry Pranksters called this in Tom Wolfe's epic of cultural warfare in the Sixties, *The Electric Kool-Aid Acid Test* (1969). Sometimes it seemed like a game, sewing the American flag to the seat of your pants, wearing buttons that shouted "LSD DID THIS TO ME" and "IF IT MOVES, FONDLE IT." It was somehow exhilarating to deride the squares and sing along with Frank Zappa's composition, "Brown Shoes Don't Make It."

But when it wasn't a game, the division between the counter-culture and the rest of America frequently turned into the kind of open, bloody conflict Peter Fonda and Dennis Hopper experienced in *Easy Rider*. A young Texas woman recounts her worst experience of the Sixties: "Being witness to a beating, with a club, of two males with long hair whose automobile had run out of gasoline, by the owners of the service station (sign on service station read 'no service to hippies') on the drag in Austin, Texas."

"I made a very paranoid journey from New Orleans through South Texas en route to California. I was not married to my traveling companion—we were both in our 20's."

"I was harassed by four crazed Mobile, Alabama, cops while freaking out on mescaline."

These skirmishes in the cultural warfare took place in the South, but New York City had its counterpart of the redneck—the hardhat—and gangs of them went on a rampage in 1970, beating up anyone on the street who had long hair. In fact, the battles over style took place across the country, and in no place was the fighting fiercer than in America's most familiar war zone, the living room.

THE GENERATION GAP

The press labeled the phenomenon the "generation gap." Besides describing the cultural differences between parents and offspring, the term was used as a kind of neo-Freudian theory to explain the entire counter-culture, from pot to protest marches. Spoiled, middle-class kids, according to this proposition, were striking out at their parents in a desperate search for the kind of love that old-fashioned parents used to hand out—namely, a good hard spanking. There was a lot of talk about "permissiveness," and how the child-raising theories of Dr. Benjamin Spock had allowed offspring of the World War II generation to demand instant gratification of their desires. Certainly, the kids may have "gone too far," but according to some of our respondents, the parents went to extremes, too.

"My worst 60's experience was getting kicked out of school for smoking hash and coming home to my parents' McCarthyite hysteria."

"My parents dragged me down to the police station after I came home tripping at 6 A.M. I dummied up, wouldn't tell them anything except what the acid looked like. Bummer!"

"My best friend died in a car crash and my family ridiculed me for grieving. Then when I came home from the funeral I was beaten by my father (who is a professional who earns a good salary and is thoroughly middle class)."

"I was in a hospital giving birth, and was tricked into signing what I thought was permission for X-rays. They were actually adoption papers—my parents lied and tricked me. My life changed that day."

"A constant lack of family communication" is a San Francisco man's chief complaint about the decade. It was difficult for young people to talk to parents, and when Jerry Rubin urged, "Kill your parents," it occasionally may have seemed like a good idea—although only one of our respondents actually did shoot his parents ("We all survived, are best of friends," he adds, having spent time in a "maximum security nuthouse").

The anger and sense of dislocation expressed by youth in the

48

Sixties have been dismissed as nothing more than an adolescent fit, summed up by the absurd phrase, "You can't trust anyone over thirty." This silly motto, coined in 1963 during the Berkeley Free Speech Movement, provided endless opportunities for essayists and commentators; typical of the genre is the classic dissertation, "In Defense of Old Folks Over 25," penned by *Life* Science Editor Albert Rosenfeld:

> The discontented youngsters of this new generation, all the way from the hippies of Psychedelia to the revolutionary activists of the New Left, have every right to carp and criticize. But so far I have seen or heard very little in the way of constructive suggestions from them, other than the most crude and simplistic non-solutions to our very complicated problems. I can't help wondering if they ever wonder what their children will have to thank *them* for. For fouling their chromosomes with LSD? For dropping out at a time when society was never in greater need of their participation? What are their credentials for billing themselves as the take-over generation?*

Mr. Rosenfeld and his cranky comrades can relax in their rocking chairs: Very few of the people we surveyed ever took the "over thirty" idea seriously. In fact, according to our respondents, the generation gap was not a prevalent condition.

THE "GENERATION GAP"

In the Sixties	% Who Agreed Completely*	% Who Disagreed Completely*
You can't trust anyone over 30.	14	26
My parents didn't understand me.	47	6
I was completely different from my parents.	49	5
I felt alienated from the rest of society.	27	10
I liked my parents.	41	30

*Figures do not include those who agreed or disagreed "somewhat" or were "neutral."

Life magazine, August 25, 1967.

It is true that our respondents felt they were different from their parents, and these differences, from the parents' point of view, may have seemed like an almost unbridgeable gap. The hostility this engendered, however, must have existed mostly on the parents' side, since more members of Woodstock Nation *liked* their parents than disliked them. And "alienation" afflicted only a minority of our group.

So, as far as Woodstock Nation is concerned, the generation gap was a counterfeit issue. Some of us knew it back then, too; a 1969 study of college students showed 72% believing that although a gap existed, it was highly exaggerated.* The inflamed rhetoric of the time, however, insisted that the big problem was a difference in age—when the real problem was a difference in politics.

THE POLITICS OF STYLE

In *On the Road*, written in 1951, Jack Kerouac sounded the first note of what was to come.

> At lilac evening I walked with every muscle aching among the lights of 27th and Walton in the Denver colored section, wishing I were a Negro, feeling that the best the white world had offered was not enough ecstasy for me, not enough life, joy, kicks, darkness, music, not enough night. I wished I were a Denver Mexican, or even a poor overworked Jap, anything but what I so drearily was, a "white man" disillusioned. All my life I'd had white ambitions . . .

Disaffection with the middle-class life in postwar America began with the Beats. At first a literary and artistic movement that, unlike previous avant-garde movements in this country, did not look abroad for inspiration, the Beats took their style from indigenous American sources, primarily black culture. When the Beats made jazz their music and adopted black argot and made it into the language of white hipsters, they took on the world-view of disenfranchised blacks, and divided people into "hip" and "square." This division was often explained in terms of alienation

*Daniel Yankelovich, Inc., *Generations Apart*, 1969.

50

or existentialism. But for black people—and oppressed minorities everywhere—it has always had a political definition.

The emulation of black culture by white middle-class kids continued through the Fifties and the Sixties. In the latter decade, more young people than ever were enacting the rituals, and going beyond jazz to the blacker rhythms of folk, blues, and rock and roll. And lacking the distinction of skin color, young whites used long hair and outrageous fashions to mark themselves off from mainstream society. They even took the measure of becoming outlaws through their use of drugs. This induced a tighter unity within the counter-culture, based on fear or, as it was commonly referred to, "paranoia." A 31-year-old Texas woman remembers the effect it had on her: "Paranoia made me feel a kinship with anyone else who followed my lifestyle. It made names and addresses privileged information (and it also made me flush grass down the toilet more than once)."

During the Sixties, 59% of the people we surveyed believed the world was divided into two types of people—hip and straight. Hip people *liked* to think of themselves as an oppressed group. *The Student As Nigger* was a widely read tract that defined the rights of undergrads. Hippies stood with upraised clenched fists whenever the Jefferson Airplane sang about being outlaws in the eyes of America. Belonging to the counter-culture afforded young people at least a taste of the "joy, kicks, darkness" that Kerouac hungered for. And they were proud to gain the approbation of black spokesmen like Eldridge Cleaver, who wrote, "There is in America today a generation of white youth that is truly worthy of a black man's respect."*

By making themselves outlaws, the young, white middle-class members of the counter-culture were able to effect a kind of alliance with blacks. "Police persecution," says one respondent, "made me feel a part of a brotherhood that cut across racial and ethnic boundaries."

In many ways, young people in the Sixties *were* a disenfranchised group. The universities, with their *in loco parentis* rules, treated students like children; the draft board treated them like cannon

---

*Soul on Ice, 1968.

fodder. And although they were ordered to fight and die in Vietnam to defend government policy, they were prohibited from voting on that policy until they were twenty-one.

Without direct access to the system that made the rules, young people in the Sixties expressed their political protest just the way blacks always had, by creating an alternative culture. And so style had power: Clothes were worn like flags; sometimes flags were worn as clothes. When fashion changed in the Seventies, many saw this development as the defeat of the counter-culture. In one respondent's view, "When the paisleys faded into worn jeans (even pre-faded, for God's sake) the dream was gone."

But isn't this mistaking style for substance? For just underneath the surface of a counter-culture that appeared bizarre—even revolutionary—lurked some surprisingly traditional middle-class values.

HIPPIES, GOD, AND HISTORY

In the Sixties, *Time* magazine and something called the "New Theology" declared that God was dead, more than fifty years after Nietzsche had proclaimed: "What are these churches now, if they are not the tombs and monuments of God?"

Some of the people we interviewed, however, report that during the Sixties they often encountered something that looked a lot like Him.

"I took an acid trip where my entire vision disintegrated into a massive, energetic WHITE LIGHT, and I knew then I was in direct contact with the big IT."

"I dropped some Owsley acid and, for the first time in my adult life, I saw the true meaning of ONENESS, or GOD. I was for a short time everything in the universe."

In the Sixties, the religious experiences of our respondents were distinctly not of the Sunday school variety; rather, they tended to be nondenominational and personally spiritual. A substantial number of people select the books of German mystic Hermann Hesse (*Demian*, *Siddhartha*) as the most influential reading they had done in the Sixties. Steppenwolf, a popular rock band of the decade, took its name from the Hesse *oeuvre*.

"His book *Siddhartha* has steered me clear of involvement in large spiritual trips. I'm searching but I'm looking to myself for the answers."

"My lifestyle has progressed to a less and less material scenario after getting farther into his work and my own life."

Nearly 10% cite other spiritual or occult works such as *Autobiography of a Yogi*, the poems of Kahlil Gibran, and the philosophy of Gurdjieff as the major literary influences of the decade.

Nearly half of our sample say they liked Eastern philosophy, and some talked about their gurus.

"Maharishi Mahesh Yogi. Transcendental Meditation is the greatest thing that ever happened to me."

"Paramahansa Yogananda. I read his book, *Autobiography of a Yogi*, and it helped jell all my cosmic thoughts. It gave reason to ideas I had, but had no foundation for."

"Suleman Dede. He is a Sufi Murshid from Turkey. A week of chanting with him was the greatest turning point of my life."

"Guru Maharaj Ji. In the ways a guru does, he revealed to me an experience of internal self-sustaining truth and love."

And there were homegrown gurus, too.

"Grandpa Lone Wolf, an Apache shaman, taught me to look inside myself and to read the eyes and hearts of others. He helped me discover beliefs that have carried me through very difficult times and basically gave me the key to being the person that I am."

The Sixties was a time of intense spirituality, expressed in such diverse practices as the joined hands and raised voices of civil rights marchers singing "We Shall Overcome," or the crossed sticks wound with brightly colored wool that crashpad denizens called "God's Eyes." It was also manifested in the rather naive enthusiasm for astrology, which 35% of our respondents were "into" during the "Age of Aquarius" (women favored it more than men, 48% to 24%).* One person recalls, "There was a free

*In case anyone is interested, we counted among our respondents a high proportion of Libras, Leos, and Sagittarians, and a low number of Pisces and Scorpios. "Can't you tell?" several respondents noted after listing their signs. There were also a fair number of unusual signs, such as "Yield" (four), "Feces" (three), "Slippery When Wet" (three), "Asparagus" (two), and "Fuck You" (one).

53

clinic in Los Angeles that always asked your sign even before your problem."

Religious leaders like Rev. William Sloane Coffin, the Berrigan brothers, and Dr. Martin Luther King were in the forefront of the protest movements. But it was not the time for organized religion. Mia Farrow and the Beatles notwithstanding, more of the people we surveyed were actually negative toward gurus (31%) than positive (23%). And regarding a meditative discipline, namely Transcendental Meditation, those who cared at all were almost equally divided—negative (22%) and positive (21%)—but most were neutral on the subject.

The counter-culture's search for a meaningful form of spirituality had its beginnings in the Fifties Beat scene, with the novels of Jack Kerouac (most of them dealing with a lone protagonist's quest for spiritual fulfillment), the poems of Gary Snyder and Allen Ginsberg, and the Zen popularizations of Alan Watts. But what was the connection between this kind of spirituality and the social experimentation of the Sixties?

A recent survey of religious beliefs among Sixties veterans in the San Francisco Bay area suggests that, in seeking to rearrange their relationship to the social structure, many people in Woodstock Nation also found it necessary to rearrange their spiritual outlook.* There is evidence that far from being revolutionary or antisocial, the new spirituality is highly compatible with today's technological world. Baba Ram Dass, formerly a Harvard professor named Richard Alpert, has many admirers among our respondents, and one states: "His books, like *Be Here Now*, written as they are by one who experienced fully the Western way of life before being enlightened or whatever, have helped me to put different aspects of my life in perspective and have aided my continuing spiritual journey."

This is not the testimony of a saffron-robed disciple with a shaved head, but of a 29-year-old student of finance in Illinois.

---

*Robert Wuthnow, *The Consciousness Reformation*, 1976.

MONEY AND WORK

"You're never the same once you know you can change the world," declares a nattily dressed young man in a recent advertisement for *Playboy* magazine. "I'm part of the generation that forced Lyndon Johnson into retirement and helped end a war. I had my college basketball scholarship taken away for my participation in the protests. I'm also part of a generation that set out to wreck our economic system. However, at some point short of catastrophe, most of my generation got the idea that maybe we'd be better off turning our energies toward building things up instead of tearing them down. Speaking personally, I also got the idea it would be nice to eat regularly. So we went to work within the system to try to make the system work.... By the time I'm 45, I'll have six figures put away. I guess that's what happens when you get more mature. Am I a *Playboy* reader? For sure."

So terrified of the Sixties Generation were those in the American business establishment that today they seem to be rubbing their eyes in disbelief at the fact that young people are working, making money, taking part in the consumer economy. Ads like *Playboy*'s ("his lust is for life . . .") increasingly serve to convince people that there has been a revolution in the "revolution," a reversal in the counter-culture, a return to traditional American values of work, money, and consumerism.

However, few of the people we questioned say they ever had a negative attitude toward money in the Sixties, while half say they always thought cash was a positive thing. Less than one third were against the idea of being ambitious, while a slightly larger number were for it.

MAKING IT

In the Sixties	% of Total Group*
Liked money	51
Disliked money	15
Liked being ambitious	35
Disliked being ambitious	30

*Figures do not include those who were "neutral."

Contrary to the notion that hippies were lazy, the counter-culture actually placed a high value on work. Building the counter-culture involved a tremendous amount of hard labor at the lowest possible wages. A teacher from New York remembers "hitchhiking to Powder Ridge and being put down by people. 'Get a job, cut your hair,' etc. I did work—at three jobs—to put myself through school. Ignorant people."

Tuition bills were not the only motivation for hard work. The civil rights workers who trekked south in the early part of the decade (including 3% of our respondents, mostly the older ones) organized massive voter-registration drives in rural areas under conditions that were threatening and sometimes fatal. About 19% of our group had engaged in community organizing and 32% had helped in fund raising. When in the mid-Sixties, the student power movement became important, similar efforts were made to marshal and maintain the support of thousands of people.

Many people committed time and energy to carry forward the antiwar movement. Every Movement office had a staff. Every demonstration had to be publicized, and 20% of our group put in time at the mimeograph machine, turning out leaflets, posters, and press releases (but not before everybody had wrangled over ideology for hours and hours). Organizing each one of the numerous Moratorium marches on Washington was a monumental task. Then there was the marching itself—often a prodigious effort—which involved three fourths of our respondents. People literally *worked* to end the war.

It took work to import and distribute the counter-culture's favorite recreational drug, pot—and 42% of our respondents dealt dope in the Sixties. Marijuana smugglers worked as hard as Roaring Twenties rumrunners. Like the bootleggers who later became respectable purveyors of fine spirits, dope smugglers have built an industry that today, while not yet legal, is sophisticated, competitive, profitable, and growing. Labor also went into the manufacture of LSD. Underground chemists such as the legendary Owsley spent long hours, days, weeks in makeshift labs, perfecting the little orange or purple tabs, blotters, barrels, and sugar cubes.

There were food co-ops, drug hotlines, crisis centers, free stores, free schools, free clinics and underground newspapers, which, although run somewhat differently from the *New York Times*, still involved selling advertising space, writing articles, setting type, laying out pages, and, yes, meeting actual deadlines. The kinds of work involved in these marginal enterprises may have been of the transitory, volunteer sort, and far from the wage-earning, up-scale careers parents usually envision for their off-spring. But the fact is that when it came to work that seemed fulfilling, young people of the Sixties were not shirkers.

Even the music of the Sixties was created with a lot of work, and 16% of our respondents were members of rock bands. In the Sixties, rock musician Jon Pierson of Ars Nova told *Life* magazine, "Rock groups are really in the magic business. You've got to work hard to make magic." From the guys who constructed the enormous stages and sound systems at outdoor festivals to the gorillas employed as bouncers at the Fillmore, the music involved as much labor as most sophisticated theatrical productions.

The word used to describe work during the Sixties was "gig"— musicians' jargon for a paying engagement, usually a brief one. "Job" was avoided because it sounded too permanent. Some people—Peter Max, Tom Hayden, the Grateful Dead, the Hell's Angels, and your pot connection—made the gigs into permanent careers. Generally, though, people moved on to other things. When they did, it was not necessarily a move for the sake of making money. The majority of our respondents (71%) say that in the Sixties they disagreed with the idea, "It's okay to work at a job you hate if the money's good." In the Seventies, the percentage is exactly the same. This is a consistent vote against "selling out."

BANANAS, COMICS, AND NEWS

Another huge endeavor of the counter-culture was the underground press. The majority of our respondents (87%) got a lot of their news from underground papers during the Sixties. Compared to some of those psychedelic tabloids, the pages of establishment newspapers look and read like tombstones. Within the yellowing pages of the old underground newspapers, amidst the water-bed ads, the Fillmore concert schedules, and the vegetarian classifieds, the entire counter-culture seems to live and breathe with excitement, humor, and startling originality.

The San Francisco *Oracle* was selling for twenty-five cents on Haight Street in August 1967. That month's issue displayed on the front page a bright red rectangle that looked as if it had been tie-dyed, enclosing a geometric arrangement of ten blue spheres.

Opening the front page, one finds a brilliant splash of orange and violet that, upon closer examination, is actually an article entitled, "Programming the Psychedelic Experience," a detailed instruction manual for taking LSD.

On the next page there is an essay, "In Memoriam for Superspade and John Carter," two local personalities murdered during a drug deal. "Some say live by the gun, die by the gun—others say let's get high." Facing this is a collage of black-and-white Haight-Ashbury snapshots, with a story that declares, "The street scene has become an entrance into a phenomenon to which we all have been invited. The word has been passed throughout the country, compliments of the straight media, that there is a scene going down on Haight Street."

On page two of the Los Angeles *Free Press* of February 24, 1967, is Lawrence Lipton's popular column called "Radio Free America," in which he complains about a recent article in *Life* magazine about the underground scene: "Even what's true in it stinks of the underlying motive: to create a stereotype of the Underground that will fasten the stigma of insanity and sadism on it. . . . ONLY THE UNDERGROUND PRESS TELLS THE TRUTH ABOUT THE UNDERGROUND. THE FACT THAT THE UNDERGROUND PRESS IS GROWING SO EXPLOSIVELY SHOULD PROVE THAT LIFE MAGAZINE AND THE REST OF THE SQUARE COMMERCIAL PRESS ISN'T GETTING AWAY WITH ITS STEREOTYPES ALTOGETHER."

The front page of *Other Scenes*, dated June 22, 1969, carries the following declaration:

"NOTICE:

"This special issue costs 25 cents. Most of it consists of blank pages. Do not waste your money buying it unless (a) you want a collector's item, or (b) you are planning to enter our do-it-yourself newspaper contest. First prize is $250. Details in centerfold."

Except for the centerfold and a back-page ad for a new book by Timothy Leary, the pages are really blank.

The cover of *Gothic Blimp Works*, published in 1969, shows "Mr. Natural," disguised as a vacuum cleaner salesman, talking to the "Housewives of America." "Okay lady," says the bearded little guru created by cartoonist Robert Crumb, "let's just say this dirt is your conscious mind." Inside the issue are comic strips by the late Vaughn Bode in his science fiction style, a Trashman epic by Spain Rodriguez (which culminates in a centerfold masterpiece of black-and-white drama titled "Rape of the Toe Queen"), three pages of "Funky Funnies" featuring "Uncle Ed, the rubber wonderman" by Kim Deitch and a two-page comics "jam" called "Come the Revolution" to which all the artists in the issue contribute, including guest spots by former *Mad* magazine artist Harvey Kurtzman. The issue concludes with Crumb's "Sleezy Snot Comics," "Booger Buddies," and "The End Funnies."

In the "Wheel and Deal" classified section of the *East Village Other* of October 1967, there is a crowd of people trying to make contact with somebody, or anybody, or just a body.

"Young man, thirties, interested in erotic pleasures, seeks to exchange visits with distinctive females, call . . ."

"Groovy, virile man of 29, seeks girl, age 19–35, to enjoy sex, love and cunnilingus. Must be attractive, call . . ."

"Genius wants intelligent, sweet-natured girl to bear him a bastard, will provide financial and emotional support, call . . ."

"Kathy M. No need to hide. Mother says you can't be sent to reformatory as you committed no crime. Please call . . . and return to school . . ."

"Annabelle E. Police want you for questioning only. We love you, call collect. Mom & Dad."

"Linda D. Please call your father. Your mother is very sick. Just talk!"

One of our respondents says that his best *and* worst experience of the Sixties occurred when "I wrote, illustrated and published an underground paper in high school in 1969, and caused some havoc in the small town where I grew up."

By 1969, the Underground Press Syndicate, which had begun

three years earlier with six members, had over three hundred newspapers in its membership roster. They had names like *Yellow Dog, Rat, Old Mole, Avatar, Great Speckled Bird, Rising Up Angry, Helix,* and *Kaleidoscope.* There was a high school press, a military press, and papers from Europe and Asia that exchanged issues with each other under the aegis of UPS. Liberation News Service mailed regular twice-weekly packets of news, feature articles, and graphics to its five hundred subscribers. Estimates of the total combined readership of underground papers in the United States for 1969 varied from two million to thirty million. But the numbers alone, whatever they actually were, could never express the true influence of the underground press in the Sixties. A more accurate gauge was the Great Banana Hoax of 1967, perpetrated by the editors of the *East Village Other,* who managed to convince everybody, including the police, that smoking dried banana peels produced a psychedelic buzz. "We took thirty pounds of bananas into the lab," says John Finlator, then chief of the Bureau of Narcotics and Dangerous Drugs, "cooked, scraped, and did everything else to them that the underground papers told us to do. But it was a put-on."*

Bananas notwithstanding, 51% of the veterans we talked to say that back in the Sixties they were more likely to believe a story in the Berkeley *Barb* than in *Time* magazine. "The establishment media inflated the impact of external styles," explains one respondent, "but generally never understood the spiritual context."

Consistent with its movement toward more personalized forms of religion and work, the counter-culture also sought to make the press more responsive to the individual. This is why underground newspapers flourished at a time when local newspapers all over the country were being supplanted by television, which, by its centralized nature, can rarely apprehend the subtleties of local community life. Underground newspapers were nothing more than a return to the tradition of the local community newspaper, filling a need among middle-class young people for communication on an intimate level in the special language of Woodstock Nation.

*Joe Kane, "Banana Appeal," *High Times* magazine, September 1978.

THE SECRET LANGUAGE OF ROCK

Was there a special code by which we understood each other in those years? One respondent reveals that her initiation into the Sixties occurred "when someone explained what 'Rainy Day Women' was all about." For those who were never initiated, "Rainy Day Women" was merely a song on Bob Dylan's 1966 "Blonde on Blonde" album. But there were those who *knew* what Dylan really meant when he repeatedly asserted that "everybody must get stoned."

For a time each new Dylan album was greeted as prophecy, like tablets brought down from the mountain. Was there a "secret language of rock"? One believer, A. J. Weberman, fed all of Dylan's lyrics into a computer. The patterns that emerged were then assembled in a concordance similar to one used by scholars to study Shakespeare's figures of speech. According to Weberman, "rain," for example, means "violence"—as in "A Hard Rain's A-Gonna Fall."

But the real meaning was that there was *meaning* in the music. Music conveyed the message of the counter-culture so powerfully that 62% of our political activists were inclined to believe during the Sixties that rock and roll was a revolutionary political force. Music had a tremendous impact on the people we surveyed, one of whom recalls "going to the second appearance of the Byrds in Ciro's on the Sunset Strip in '64 and knowing we were seeing history being made—the dawn of a new age!"

It all began with folk music. Folk music was the easiest, most accessible form of self-expression. After all, poor illiterates had been making beautiful folk music for centuries. All you needed was a guitar and your own voice. One out of every three people we surveyed played guitar in the Sixties, making this a very tuneful bunch. There is no indication of how well they played, but that really didn't matter. The key thing was to *express yourself.*

Jazz had been the hip sound of the Beats in the Fifties, but it was never widely popular in the counter-culture. Jazz was enjoyed by 36% of our respondents (mostly the older ones) in the Sixties. The trouble with jazz was that it had become a complicated, highbrow musical form. Audiences couldn't participate in it. There was no such thing as a jazz sing-along. The Beat poets, such as Robert Creely, Kenneth Rexroth, Kerouac, and Ginsberg, tried putting words to jazz, but the graft never took. Jazz was too cool.

Folk music was different. Fifty-three percent of our respondents attended "hootenannies," the sing-alongs that were popular on college campuses and in off-campus coffeehouses in the early part of the decade. Some of the performers who advanced the folk music cause were Pete Seeger, Odetta, Leon Bibb, the New Left City Ramblers, Buffy Sainte-Marie, Peter, Paul and Mary, Judy Collins, the Greenbriar Boys, Oscar Brand, Tom Paxton, Jack Elliott, Eric Von Schmidt, Eric Anderson, Tom Rush, Jim Kweskin (and the Jug Band, featuring Maria Muldaur), Dave Van Ronk, Fred Neil, and of course, Joan Baez, and Bob Dylan.

Folk music could be clean-cut and friendly in the style of the Kingston Trio, who first put folk music into the Top Forty with the ballad of "Tom Dooley" in 1959. Twenty-two percent of our respondents, mostly people who had been least involved in drugs or politics, were fans of the Kingston Trio. Activists and drug users, however, tended to favor Dylan and Baez, who used the folk idiom to express anger and rebelliousness. But whatever the style, the words and melodies of folk music evoked the history of oppressed blacks and poor people, and of American radical movements from the Abolitionists to the Communists of the Thirties. The atmosphere that formed around the folk scene was bound not only to attract young people but to reinforce and inspire social consciousness as well. Not surprisingly, among the people we surveyed, those with the highest attendance at hootenannies (64%) were political activists (compared to 40% of those who were not activists).

But the most popular music of the time was rock and roll, which was favored by 87%. In 1962, a watershed year when Dylan released his first album, some of the hit songs were: "Duke of Earl" by Gene Chandler, "Big Girls Don't Cry" by the Four Seasons, "Loco-motion" by Little Eva, "Monster Mash" by Bobby (Boris) Pickett and the Crypt Kickers, "Breaking Up Is Hard To Do" by Neil Sedaka, "Soldier Boy" by the Shirelles, and Chubby Checker's "The Twist," which was followed by Joey Dee and the

Starlighters' "Peppermint Twist," which kicked off a dance craze that had almost everyone (including 84% of our respondents) shaking it up, baby.

As a youth fad, the Twist was no different from past fads like goldfish-swallowing, telephone-booth-stuffing, flagpole-sitting, and the dance mania of the Twenties and Thirties. (Even the marathons were revived, with people doing the Twist instead of the foxtrot or the Lindy.) But as the first nationwide youth craze of the Sixties, it had special significance: It demonstrated the power of youth to attract the attention of the news media. And it forced the older generation to pay attention. On May 2, 1962, as Dwight D. Eisenhower was dedicating the Eisenhower Library in Abilene, Texas, the behavior of contemporary youth weighed heavily on his mind.

"We venerate the pioneers," the former president began, "who fought droughts and floods, isolation and Indians, to come to Kansas and westward to settle into their homes, to till the soil and raise their families. We think of their sturdiness, their self-reliance, their faith in God. We think of their glorious pride in America. Now, I wonder if some of these people could come back today and see us doing the Twist instead of the Minuet—whether they would be particularly struck by the beauty of that dance?"*

In 1964, the Beatles overran America and captured an audience of just about everybody not past the twelfth grade. The number of teenyboppers and Beatlemaniacs who listened to Top Forty AM radio far outnumbered the older, more sophisticated folkies, many of whom were less impressed with Beatle music. While 79% of those who were between 12 and 14 years old in 1964 say they admired and were influenced in the Sixties by the Beatles, a less substantial 65% of those who were 19 to 24 say the same.

And then in 1965 something really remarkable occurred. To the horror of a small number of folk music purists, Bob Dylan took a cue from the Beatles and "went electric," giving folk the power of rock. The Beatles then took a cue from Dylan and began working social comment into their songs, giving rock the expressiveness of

---

*Paul Sann, *Fads, Follies and Delusions of the American People*, 1967.

folk. The vast pop audience and the politically committed folkies were thus merged, and for a period, music ceased being merely entertainment; it was a giant party line with everyone talking at once.

"The Beatles awakened the Sixties for me. I could escape into music and feel there were millions of others lost in the music with me. I was peaceful and accepted."

"Bob Dylan altered my consciousness. He was my spokesperson."

Rock concerts were important convocations of the counterculture. Three fourths of our sample liked the indoor concerts, which many remember very clearly.

"My best Sixties experience was having the Fillmore East around," says a 31-year-old New York man. "There was always a great show there." The light shows that shimmered and pulsated in time to the music were enjoyed by 68% of our respondents, mostly young; and 55% (again, mostly young) liked the black-light posters that glowed in the dark and advised onlookers, among other things, to "Feed Your Head."

Slightly more people enjoyed outdoor rock festivals (79% to 75%), perhaps because of the spontaneity and freedom allowed at the open-air events. A Boston woman remembers: "I went to an outdoor Grateful Dead concert in New Haven when the weather and music were perfect and the crowd loved everything including each other. There was the sensation of no worldly concerns, pure love."

Whether it was at the Fillmore, or Monterey, or Newport, or Woodstock, or even in giant football stadiums, the musical events of those years were concentrated doses of all the things—drugs, sex, politics, fellowship—that characterized the Sixties state of mind. The impact was such that our respondents cite music most often as their best experience of the Sixties.

"My best 60's experience was going to a rock concert in Philadelphia. In a stadium with several thousand young people the feeling of involvement and communication was something I've never been able to recapture in any other experience." (Slide curator, 28, female, Delaware)

"Seeing the Kinks and Yardbirds on Shindig, Rolling Stones

1964 live." (Vice-president record chain, 28, female, Washington, D.C.)

"Seeing Crosby, Stills, Nash and Young at the Fillmore." (Accountant, 30, male, New York)

"Fillmore East at midnight with the Allman Brothers backstage." (Research scientist, 27, male, New York)

"Hitching to Powder Ridge Festival—being with all those people—wine—dope—a real experience—spent one night on a living room floor of some family who quizzed me like I was an alien." (Teacher, 29, male, New York)

"A Grateful Dead concert at the Anderson Theatre in Greenwich Village, New York." (Unemployed, 25, male, San Francisco)

"The last Cream concert in Anaheim in 1968. A very high night throughout the auditorium." (Teacher, 32, female, San Francisco)

"Seeing Cream in Winterland recording 'Wheels of Fire' and being fortunate enough to see Jimi Hendrix on four different occasions—Fillmore, Oakland, Phoenix and Winterland." (Disc jockey, 29, male, Tucson)

"The process of creating a dream into a reality was my best experience—and that was having my own band and being successful at it." (Assistant manager, 29, male, Arizona)

If the music of the Sixties was powerful, so were the people who made the music. An Arizona woman remembers one of her best moments of the Sixties was "meeting Jimi Hendrix." A New York copy writer sighs that her best moment was when "Peter Yarrow kissed me." And a California fashion designer boasts that her best Sixties experience was "having a love affair with a rock star and everyone knowing it! (He really went for me and everyone knew that too!)"

Of the people we interviewed, 61% say that during the Sixties they were inclined to regard rock stars as important people, just as previous generations venerated athletes and movie stars. Obviously, stars like the Beatles and Bob Dylan had a tremendous influence on this group. But what was the nature of their influence? And outside the realm of rock, who were the heroes? A look at the counter-culture pantheon, both in the past and in the present, should give us an idea of the goals and ideals that Woodstock Nation holds highest.

3
Heroes

"The trouble with superheroes
is what to do between phone booths."

—KEN KESEY

"Don't follow leaders," said the singer who, ironically, was one of the most influential leaders of his time. Bob Dylan's words so infused the consciousness of Woodstock Nation that 69% of the people we surveyed say they used to quote Dylan's songs, as the pious might quote the Bible.

"He said poetically and with great force what I was feeling then. He was a public support to all of us. He carried the banner."

"We had the same thoughts many times. He had a way of describing things that was useful to me."

What was it about Dylan's songs that made people listen so intently?

"The more I listened to Dylan, the clearer things became that really mattered to me."

"Dylan made me want to search for personal truth and expression."

"Through his poetry he gave light and voice to the evils happening around the world."

Those who say they admired and were influenced by Dylan are quick to mention either the political aspects of his songs or his open expression of personal sensitivity. It may be that his great power was in transforming the process of self-discovery and growing up into a political adventure; Dylan's songs equated the normal confusion of adolescence with the problems of society as a whole. A San Francisco man remarks, "Dylan seemed to be going through changes and growth like my own in some ways."

Dylan's message was most readily accepted by the most adventurous elements of Woodstock Nation, the ones most heavily involved with political activism and the drug scene.

ADMIRED AND WERE INFLUENCED BY BOB DYLAN

Political activists	82%
Nonactivists	61%
Heavy drug users	84%
Non–drug users	43%

But Dylan's was only one of many voices commanding attention during the Sixties. The decade was rife with "leaders." Cults of the personality flourished; spokesmen and gurus were born overnight, complete with mass followings, fanatical disciples, hungry groupies, and doting hordes of reporters.

In its fall 1965 "college issue," *Esquire* magazine published an article entitled "28 Who Count," about the "heroes of the California rebels (and as Cal goes, so goes the rest)." The twenty-eight included Bob Dylan, Joan Baez, Che Guevara, Malcolm X, Fidel Castro, John F. Kennedy, and the fictional spy, James Bond.* On the walls of college dorms across the nation, the faces of these famous figures were displayed in huge photographic blowups called "personality posters."

For the press, the personalities in the spotlight functioned as bellwethers. By tracking "youth leaders," the press was confident it could predict "where youth is heading." The leaders also served as convenient targets for barbs intended to apply more generally, so that when an editor of the New York *Post* described Bob Dylan as "a walking slum,"† it was understood that this description applied to the singer's long-haired fans as well.

While the press focused on the parade of "youth culture heroes," they ignored the fact that members of the counter-culture were not always marching to the same drummer. The Diggers, a San Francisco group that gave away free food and clothing, pushed the idea of "nonleaders." The Yippies printed up thousands of buttons that identified each wearer as a "Yippie Leader." In their rock opera *Tommy*, the Who spun a morality tale about the folly of leadership and vowed, "We won't get fooled again!" Even Dylan, after a motorcycle accident in 1965, removed himself from

---

Esquire also listed writers Terry Southern, Norman Mailer, and Paul Goodman, along with Chuck Berry, B. F. Skinner and, oddly, the Rand Corporation.

†Paul Sann, *Fads, Follies and Delusions of the American People*, 1967.

the public eye and shrank from his leadership role. In the counter-culture, there was definitely an ambivalent attitude toward leaders, a fact the press preferred to ignore. The result has been the kind of skewed reporting that recently cropped up in one of the weekly news magazines:

> The never-trust-anyone-over-30 generation turned 30 in the Movement, or 35, or 40. They married and had babies and settled down, and turned from making a revolution to writing memoirs about it. The leaders, those who survived, found new faiths. H. Rap Brown disappeared into prison and then Islam. Tom Hayden of SDS and the Chicago Seven cropped his hair and went into reform Democratic politics. His fellow tribesman Rennie Davis is selling insurance and practicing Transcendental Meditation. Stokely Carmichael moved to Africa, Jerry Rubin to Manhattan's monied East Side, anti-war activist Sam Brown and civil rights leader John Lewis to Washington as head men of their own bureaucracy, ACTION. Not many are left at the barricades.*

This is a typical view of the Sixties, less history than polemic. In the effort to declare the end of the decade's progressive movements, the magazine writer uses generally false assumptions that were prevalent in the press in the Sixties: that personalities like Abbie Hoffman, Rennie Davis, and Jerry Rubin actually commanded a large and obedient following; that once the press dubbed them leaders, they remained leaders; that the lives of the "leaders" accurately reflected the lives of the generation they supposedly led; that young political spokesmen were unanimously bent on blowing up the government rather than trying to change it through a variety of means.

The heroes of a generation are invested with the hopes, dreams, and ideals of its youth. If we identify the real heroes of young people in the Sixties, wouldn't that provide a key to what Woodstock Nation was all about then, and where it stands today?

WHO'S IN CHARGE HERE?

From old articles on counter-cultural heroes and from discussions with numerous friends, we developed a list of eighty-five names that were prominent during the Sixties. Our respondents were asked to rate the personalities according to recollections of how

*"Where Have All the Flowers Gone?" *Newsweek*, September 5, 1977.

they felt about them during the Sixties. The six categories—a sort of cross between the Nielsen ratings and a high school slam-book—were as follows:

> Admired and was influenced by
> Admired but was not influenced by
> No feeling one way or another
> Did not admire but was influenced by
> Did not admire and was not influenced by
> Who?

We wanted people to weigh their feelings and to discriminate between admiration and real influence. We wanted to know which personalities actually moved people to find new directions in their lives, to perceive and pursue goals, to dress, talk, or act in a manner that was new to them.

It involved some pretty difficult decisions, looking back over the heroes and villains, clowns and tragedians, visionaries and fools of a whole era. "What the hell does Twiggy or Sammy Davis, Jr., have to do with my life?" demands one respondent in the margin of his questionnaire. Indeed, how do you go about ranking Joe Namath next to Charlie Manson, Rod McKuen against Ho Chi Minh? Who was the more daring, James Bond or George Jackson? Who affected your life more, Dr. Benjamin Spock or Nelson Rockefeller? How many people even remember Mark Rudd?

The category "admired and was influenced by" interested us most. Some of the personalities rated in this category are:*

"Dr. Spock. I was raised by his book and my childhood experiences influenced me and I voted for him for President in the 60's." (Car dealer, 30, female)

"Jean-Paul Sartre. His writing style was uplifting and full of life." (Word processor, 27, female)

"Hermann Hesse and Cesar Chavez. I made tentative steps to a personal theory of mystical non-violence." (Woodworker, 28, male)

---

*The complete list is on pages 242–244.

"Helen Gurley Brown. Her approval of sexual freedom for both men and women." (Administrator, 27, female)

"Mao Tse-tung and Frodo. One was a cultural myth, the other was a mythical culture." (Unemployed, 25, female)

"Jimi Hendrix and Frodo. They both were magical, mystical. I don't especially like reality and they both could take me away from it." (Gardener, 25, male)

"Frodo. I think more than anything, I wanted there to be a Middle Earth and I still do." (Musician and carpenter, 25, male)

"Andy Warhol. He showed the way real life can be when attempting to live in a society like ours." (Unemployed, 28, male)

"Paul Krassner. I subscribed to the *Realist* and picked up Krassner's sense of humor and outrage against hypocrisy. I'm still waiting for the next issue to come out." (Unemployed, 34, male)

"Sonny Barger, president of the Hell's Angels. In the mid-60's, I was getting into cycles. I liked Barger's thinking and the bikers' way of life; not being rebels against the U.S. policy so much, but being free-spirited and doing whatever you felt like doing, no matter how society looked upon you. Maybe not agreeing with the Vietnam War, but not protesting either." (Photographer/bartender, 32, male)

Certain figures appealed mainly to drug users during the Sixties. Of the total group of respondents, 31% admired and were influenced by singer Jim Morrison of the Doors. The percentage of political activists was a little higher (35%). But drug users, at 52%, were the "highest" in favor of the "Lizard King." "Jim Morrison and the Doors, to me, represented sexuality and breakthroughs of awareness." (Law clerk, 30, female)

The pattern was similar for Jimi Hendrix, who captivated 66% of the drug users: "His music was my head trip and re-inforcement for things I was imagining and shaping in my mind." (Teacher, 25, male)

And for Timothy Leary: "His encouragement to explore the realm of inner space transformed my entire life." (Artist, 29, male)

Dr. Leary performed similar transformations on the lives of 77% of those who used a lot of drugs in the Sixties. And of this particular group of drug users, 81% confess to having followed

Dr. Leary's motto, "Turn on, tune in, drop out" (compared with only 48% of the total number of respondents).

Other musical groups of the Sixties are mentioned.

"The Kingston Trio. They were part of the whole folky thing which eventually seemed to lead to progressive musical-political radicalization and change in lifestyle." (Unemployed, 31, male)

"The Grateful Dead. It seemed that while everyone else was out screaming and shouting, they were just partying and having a good time." (Commodity order clerk, 25, male)

"Jefferson Airplane (particularly Grace Slick) influenced me more than the celebrities you listed. They confirmed how I felt about drugs and revolution and life in general. And they made acid seem groovy *before* I tried it. Because they came on like people rather than celebrities, they were very credible. 'Surrealistic Pillow' is still my all-time favorite album." (Hotel night auditor, 35, male)

Satirist Lenny Bruce, who died in 1966, was popular chiefly among the older respondents, and was preferred by political activists.

"Bruce spoke the truth when no one else did." (Publishing vice-president, 33, female)

The most popular literary figures of the decade were Kahlil Gibran and Kurt Vonnegut, both of whom score highest among drug users, although poet Gibran is preferred by nearly twice as many women (44%) as men (25%). Vonnegut, however, inspired the most written comments.

"I love all of Vonnegut's books. He makes you become aware of the humor in everyday situations and sometimes the hopelessness, so the lesson is to take things light." (Gardener, 30, female)

"His books were the first ones to point out to me the duality in life, the first pinprick to see the surreal and the real in life." (Security director, 36, male)

Poet Allen Ginsberg was popular almost exclusively with political activists and drug users. Although Ginsberg's cultural and political activism was evidently the biggest factor in his popularity, he had special meaning to gay respondents.

"He was openly gay and had all the politics I had and I was

74

totally attracted to him sexually, politically, intellectually." (Court reporter, 31, male)

"He was an example of someone who stood up for what he believed and said it. And he was the first openly gay person I saw." (Teacher, 28, male)

Of course there were other influential people, not at all famous or glamorous, who made the Sixties memorable. Some were teachers in school.

"Mrs. —, my high school English teacher. She tolerated bizarre behavior." (Freelance writer, 25, female, Atlanta)

"My 11th grade English teacher, who deserves a special mention as the 'hippie teacher' who even the 'straights' and hawks liked because he was interested in you and made you *think!*" (Unemployed, 25, male, San Francisco)

Some were teachers of a different sort.

"A dealer in Georgia ... taught me how to make money through pot." (Paraphernalia-manufacturing foreman, 27, male, Austin)

"The deserters and draft dodgers who came to Canada. I learned a lot about the States' problems—what was going on. I had no idea why all the demonstrations going on were so important." (Seamstress, 29, Ohio)

And for some people, the best example was set at home.

"My parents. They were Communists in the 40's and 50's and were very supportive of me and involved themselves." (Student, 25, female, New York)

"My husband brought me into the movement—thus a powerful influence–changed my life." (Technical writer, 31, female, Florida)

"My grandmother. She wrote me weekly in Vietnam and included a dollar 'to go have a milkshake with the boys.' " (Ph.D. student, 31, male)

Exactly one person, a 26-year-old paramedic in Alabama, credits the Boy Scouts of America with influencing his life the most in the Sixties: "They gave me a sense of belonging. I probably owe my life to the fact that I belonged. Of all the people I grew up with, two of us are alive. The rest of them became junkies and died in various ways."

MOVEMENT HEAVIES

"Fuck leaders. We were influenced by each other—we all did it, not the media-made leaders!" The woman from Madison who makes this comment has a point. There was something about the leaders—particularly the ones who were always pictured in the press during the Sixties above the caption "Movement leader"—that didn't ring true. A decade later, in articles like the one in *Newsweek* already mentioned, Jerry Rubin, Abbie Hoffman, Eldridge Cleaver, Tom Hayden, Rennie Davis are still in the spotlight, though most of them lack followers and are far removed from leadership roles. The press finds poetic irony in this and often extends the symbolism to prove the failure of the political movements and the generation of the Sixties in general. Columnist Patrick Buchanan, writing about the surrender of fugitive SDSer Mark Rudd in 1977, enjoys rendering this particular event as an allegory of generational defeat. A one-time speech writer for Richard Nixon, Buchanan sneers that the "meek surrender" of an *"enfant terrible"* of the Sixties is cause "to reflect upon the transitory nature of the radical movement." He concludes that "Mark decided to call off the revolution when he read that the big news on his old Columbia campus is the freshman class is wearing beanies."*

The assumption, of course, is that Rudd and the others were all leading the revolution, or whatever the columnists wish to call it. But, for the most part, our respondents never considered themselves followers of these particular personalities.

Movement Heavies	% of Total Who Admired and Were Influenced by Them
Abbie Hoffman	35
Jerry Rubin	35
Eldridge Cleaver	27
Tom Hayden	26
Mark Rudd	19
Rennie Davis	18

*"Mark Rudd and the Left That Got Left Behind," New York *Daily News*, September 20, 1977.

Not only were these alleged leaders not followed by a majority of our respondents, but some of them were to a surprising degree (considering the amount of press they attracted) unknown in Woodstock Nation. For example, Rennie Davis, a defendant in the Chicago Eight conspiracy trial in 1969 and organizer of the May Day demonstrations in Washington in 1970, was unknown to 23% of those surveyed. Mark Rudd, the celebrated SDS organizer and leading figure of the 1968 Columbia University uprising, was unidentifiable to a quarter of Woodstock Nation.

One would think that Rudd and other radical figures would command recognition, and possibly admiration, from those who describe themselves as political activists during the Sixties. And they do—at least more than they do from the entire group.

Movement Heavies	% of Activists Who Admired and Were Influenced by Them
Abbie Hoffman	55
Jerry Rubin	54
Tom Hayden	47
Eldridge Cleaver	44
Mark Rudd	33
Rennie Davis	32

But the fact that these figures attracted no more than about half of the political activists reveals that activism in the Sixties was motivated by many different ideas about the best means of achieving social change.

Abbie Hoffman and Jerry Rubin advocated working from outside the system. They were as popular as they were among activists because they combined the hedonistic elements of the counter-culture with political purpose, and turned protest into a kind of nationwide party (the Youth International Party, to be precise). People liked them for showing that confrontation could be fun.

"Abbie Hoffman was a cheerleader for acid-crazed pranksters."

"Jerry Rubin was an out-front, highly visible symbol of revolution and change. Thanks to the media, I got his message. If he could do it, so could I."

"A teacher of mine got canned because he put Rubin's *Do It* on a book list, so I learned about 'free speech' and 'community standards.' "

In their attitudes toward some of the militant crusaders of the Sixties, our respondents reveal a very definite split between those who were political activists and those who were not.

Revolutionaries of the Sixties	% of Activists Who Admired and Were Influenced by Them	% of Nonactivists
Che Guevara	43	6
Malcolm X	41	10
Ho Chi Minh	35	4
Fidel Castro	31	4

Malcolm X evoked the most response from respondents who were inspired by the black leader's militancy.

"He and his autobiography clued me in to what being Black was all about. The realization shook me and radicalized me significantly." (Radio producer, 30, female)

"I was living in Chicago's South Side and he opened the roots of the Black Movement and experience to me more than prior integrated church and civil rights experience." (Teacher, 31, male)

"Our backgrounds were similar and his philosophy and actions made me reevaluate myself, roots and future." (Entrepreneur, 30, male)

"Malcolm's call to arms and revolution was unmistakable and understandable and the same is true for all the unnamed freedom fighters because they lived and died for a good and just cause in this country's ghetto streets." (Miner, 31, male)

The idolization of Cuban revolutionary Che Guevara typifies the romantic allure of the Sixties political movements. A thirty-one-year-old waitress states: "Che's writings instilled in me the belief that a revolutionary is motivated by the strongest feelings of love for humanity."

The romance of violent revolution, however, was sought by only a few. Even among the activists, the most committed of our respondents, the radical political figures commanded a following of no more than half. So any attempt to portray Woodstock

Nation, either in the Sixties or the Seventies, through these individuals is bound to be misleading. Jerry Rubin, Abbie Hoffman, Rennie Davis, Mark Rudd, and other Movement heavies may have contributed greatly to furthering the causes of the Sixties, but their fates in the post-Sixties period, however ironic, are simply their own.

THE WOODSTOCK CENSUS TOP TEN

If the Movement heavies weren't the real heroes, who were? Astronauts? Athletes? Novelists? Presidents? Out of the long list of potential heroes and villains, there are ten people who were most frequently cited in the "admired and influenced by" category. Although all the others certainly played a part in shaping the times, we may consider these ten the real heavies, the ones who were truly leaders. And now, *the envelope please.*

Top Ten	% of Total Who Admired and Were Influenced by Them
The Beatles	76
Bob Dylan	72
John F. Kennedy	62
Martin Luther King	62
John Lennon	59
Ralph Nader	49
Robert F. Kennedy	47
Joan Baez	44
Eugene McCarthy	43
Janis Joplin	42

Why these people? What values did they represent, what goals did they point to? And what does this list reveal about the people who reacted so strongly to the names and the memories they evoke?

Beatlemania

Date: Monday, August 30, 1965
Time: 7:45 P.M.
Place: Los Angeles, California

79

For more than 12 hours the crowd has been gathering with quiet anticipation. Now, 15 minutes before concert time, the Hollywood Bowl is surrounded. People crowding the security guards to get in, while the guards look less than amused and a little apprehensive. . . . Tiny teen-age girls, dressed in their finest, wave half-heartedly at each other, not anxious to break the privacy of the mood created by the months of waiting for this day. No matter who they are, each of them feels that SHE is the one who will be seen by the Beatles—SHE is the one who will get backstage and see them, talk to them. Of course they dress up! No—those aren't early-American night gowns (what kind of nut are you?)—that's the "London look." Don't you even read *Seventeen?**

"I was 14 in 1964," says a Delaware woman. " For the next two years practically everything I did was in some way related to the Beatles." The coming of John, Paul, George, and Ringo was for many people synonymous with the beginning of the Sixties.

"When I heard the Beatles for the first time, I *knew* something was happening. Something new. Something different. It was the first signal."

In Woodstock Naton, 62% recall having had a "favorite Beatle," whether it was "the cute one" (Paul) or "the smart one" (John) or "the shy one" (George) or "the funny one" (Ringo). Women were especially enamored of the Fab Four; 78% of them had a personal favorite (as compared with 49% of the men). Says one woman, "The Beatles filled a void in pop music . . . after they won our hearts, they broke the rules. They were more popular than Jesus and we idolized them. They took off their suits, dropped acid, grew hair, and along with a few other groups, shattered our conceptions about music."

It was more than just a simple matter of enjoyable music. For example, the Beatles are often remembered in conjunction with the first stirrings of personal rebellion.

"The Beatles made me aware of differences between me and my parents."

"When the Beatles made it big in early 1964, the alienation between my parents and myself grew stronger. Long hair versus crew cuts."

*Los Angeles *Free Press*, September 3, 1965.

80

A Pennsylvania woman, now 30 and a psychotherapist, declares, "The Beatles demonstrated alternatives to the world through their music and their lives. And they put energy into the air."

A San Francisco elementary school teacher says she feels that the Beatles were catalysts. "They seemed to pave the way for most of the changes in the 60's—psychedelics, meditation, protest."

The nature of the Beatles' influence seems to have been that they voiced ideas and feelings that were common to many people. As one person puts it, "They weren't the vanguard, but because of their popularity they became the weather vane of a generation." A West Coast cartoonist describes the Beatles' impact on him: "Their music philosophically and emotionally expressed my values in the 60's."

How did the Beatles do it? One woman mentions "finding hidden meanings in their songs." Was *this* the *secret language of rock?* Did "Lucy in the Sky with Diamonds" really stand for LSD? Who was "the walrus"? And if you played the Sgt. Pepper album backwards, was John Lennon saying "Paul is dead"? (Twenty-nine percent say they believed that rumor!) Was the Beatle magic all subliminal suggestion? Or was it simply the shaggy hair, that cute Liverpudlian optimism, the sound of the first two chords of "I Wanna Hold Your Hand"?

Only a Blue Meanie would subject Beatle music to further analysis. It is enough to understand that, as mystical mass murderer Charles Manson once stated, "The Beatles know in the sense that the subconscious knows."*

All the Way with JFK

None of our respondents was old enough to vote in the 1960 elections when the choice was between Richard Nixon and John F. Kennedy. Some can barely remember Kennedy as president. Yet, he was *their* candidate, a leader of special significance to this generation. A 28-year-old Michigan therapist says, "Kennedy opened doors of awareness to a world outside my elementary

*David Felton and David Dalton, "The Most Dangerous Man In The World," *Rolling Stone*, June 25, 1970.

81

school. I began reading avidly through books on politics and the international spectrum. I became immersed in studying history. He affected my entire intellectual and educational focus until the 70's."

There was the ebullient spirit that Kennedy brought to American politics in the Sixties, a feeling that in the "New Frontier," old problems could be solved with fresh ideas and youthful energy. "I loved his enthusiasm and intelligence. He moved me emotionally and influenced my political feelings."

To the emotional excitement was added a serious commitment to idealism. A 27-year-old Florida physician reflects: "Kennedy helped me define my political philosophy. I admired his honesty and desire to improve the world."

Kennedy's predecessors in the White House had all been old men. The fact that he was president seemed to say that youth could be trusted—even suggested that youth knew best.

"He made me question my parents' political beliefs and think for myself."

On November 22, 1963, Kennedy was assassinated. It has been said that everyone remembers where they were and what they were doing when they heard the news. Certainly, for many people, Kennedy's death marked the end of one era and the beginning of another.

"He was from New England and so was I. He died violently, and violent death has become, unfortunately, something which has become more and more common. I think of him a lot."

"JFK gave me great hope for the future and the system in the early 60's. After his assassination, I felt there was no way I could trust the system."

The Dreamer

"There were several people who influenced me in the 60's, but to say there is only one is hard for me to do," says a 28-year-old Missouri man, now working as a counselor in the Career Education Training Administration. "King sticks out in my memory the most because of his work and how he went about doing it."

Dr. King's idealism inspired many of our respondents to become actively involved in seeking social change. A California woman describes what she learned from King's example: "Courage, inspiration to suffer social contempt for the sake of abstract good."

In fact, 75% of the political activists say they admired and were influenced by King, compared to 45% of those who were not politically active.

A writer in Illinois says that due to King's example, "I became a campus activist and read what he wrote and applied it to my activities, seeking more control over the university by students. Modeled my philosophy for many years on his."

The people who remember Martin Luther King most vividly generally seem to have jobs in fields where they are actively helping people and trying to improve social conditions. A 30-year-old woman in Arizona, working in a rape crisis center, says that King's influence moved her toward social work. "The civil rights movement greatly interested me. In the latter part of the 60's, I was a VISTA volunteer in the rural South. And my best experience of the Sixties was the feeling of making small, but definite changes in the lives of the people I worked with."

A 27-year-old black counselor for juvenile delinquents in Tucson says, "King was somebody I grew up with. His assassination in 1968 triggered in me the belief that there can be no Black Messiah, but a collective movement of many facets on every front. He made me personally aware of racial prejudice and what white America was really like. We're still niggers!"

Dr. King's political tactics and viewpoint were what most impressed a 28-year-old social worker in the Southwest. "His dedication to achieving equal rights for minorities through use of peaceful disobedience, plus his taking a stand against the Vietnam War."

Despite the rift that was to develop in the civil rights and antiwar movements over the use of nonviolence, political activists, whichever way they went, made their decisions in the light of Martin Luther King's life and work.

83

Antiwar Moptop

As one of the Beatles, John Lennon naturally rates high on the list of influential personalities of the Sixties. But Lennon always stood out from the group because of his controversial statements and political activities, and he acquired his own distinct band of followers. It was Lennon who caused an international scandal when he remarked that the Beatles were "more popular than Jesus."

"He seemed such a revolutionary and such an affront to white middle-class values," says a 25-year-old landscaper. "And the music was so good."

As a young art student in Liverpool, John Lennon became familiar with leftist politics and radical attitudes. He seemed to be the most eloquent Beatle, with his off-the-cuff reply to the reporter who asked him what he called his bushy haircut ("Arthur") and his published collections of poetry and whimsical sketches (*In His Own Write* and *A Spaniard in the Works*).

Lennon scores higher among political activists (62%) than among nonactivists (55%). But his real audience was among the heavy drug users, 75% of whom admired and were influenced by Lennon, compared to 37% of those who didn't use drugs. It may be that his political statements put Lennon out front, but it was his example of creative self-expression that our respondents followed most. A 27-year-old nurse explains: "I identified completely with Lennon's music, writing, attitude, and feelings. I learned a lot about life and myself from him."

The Consumer's Pal

Ralph Nader created an image in the Sixties: the citizen's David who regularly sallies forth to slay the corporate Goliaths. Quixotic though it was, the image was not a radical one. For one thing, Nader always wore a suit (the same one, some say), and his hair was short. Not even General Motors, the first target of Nader's muckraking, could find anything controversial about his lifestyle, although they looked pretty hard. No wonder, then, that heavy drug users did not overwhelmingly identify with him (only 44% of his admirers were involved in the drug scene).

Then too, his political method was well within the American mainstream, so that the people who were attracted to what Nader was doing in the Sixties were not necessarily radical or politically active. His admirers included people on both sides of the fence.

"I knew the consumers were getting ripped off," says a 28-year-old New York woman. "Because of Ralph Nader I learned to read labels, stopped being influenced by ads and what I consider fads. I dress simply, don't bother with hair styles or packaged foods."

"I'm glad that consumerism is on the rise," a 26-year-old medical student in Illinois writes, "especially in medicine so people will stop worshipping their doctors and start to be responsible for their own health!"

The consumer movement accepts the capitalist system and seeks only to improve the quality of its products and services. While more of our activists (52%) were behind Nader than nonactivists (45%), these numbers are a measure of how much activism in the Sixties was based on the idea of working within the system to change it.

Bobby

There is a feeling among our respondents that had he not detoured through a certain kitchen pantry during a Los Angeles campaign appearance on June 6, 1968, Robert Kennedy might have changed a great deal of subsequent history. Without a doubt his assassination struck hard in Woodstock Nation; for some it was the worst experience of the decade:

"Waking up and hearing Bobby Kennedy was shot in California. Felt left without hope. Stood seven hours to file past his coffin."

"Bobby Kennedy's death sounded a knell for me, exploding hope for social reform on a big scale."

"I bottomed out and went nuts when he died. It lasted for years."

"To me, he was the symbol of youth with power. Although he was rich, and undoubtedly made establishment compromises, he seemed to radiate ambition and a goal of positive change. His death helped me to become more radical."

"When he was killed, I made my mind up finally to go into federal law enforcement as a career to try to help stop the violence in this country."

Despite the polarization revealed in some reactions to his death, Robert Kennedy—like Ralph Nader—appealed not only to the extremes of our group, but to everyone. Drug users and non–drug users show similar attitudes, with 46% of each group rating him in the "admired and influenced by" category. Almost the same percentage of the political activists (47%) rated him that highly, and in this they were similar to the group that registered as nonactivists.

It may be that many of Robert Kennedy's followers were persuaded by his death to abandon political activism altogether, as a 29-year-old Connecticut teacher says: "I helped run Bobby's presidential campaign on campus in 1968. When they killed him, a little of my zeal and sense of hope died with him."

"Girls Say Yes to Boys Who Say No"

Thirty-two percent of the women we surveyed ironed their hair during the Sixties. Is that evidence of a Joan Baez cult? Perhaps, for as a 31-year-old art director in Austin confesses, "Baez in the Sixties became my alter ago." A Berkeley social worker of the same age says, "I wanted to *be* Joan Baez. Her continuing involvement in social issues is still inspiring."

Those involved in drugs and activism made up significantly more of Baez's audience than those who weren't.

"Reading about Joan's beliefs in non-violence impressed me greatly. I admired her stand against the war. She helped influence me toward non-violent means of protest."

But it is possible that Baez had an impact on the Sixties Generation that was not apparent until late in the decade. In the Sixties, more women than men (52% to 39%) admired and were influenced by Joan Baez—a hint of the women's liberation movement to come.

86

"Get Clean for Gene"

It was a decade for dreamers and poets, and Eugene McCarthy was both. Many people who were part of the campaign to elect the senator from Minnesota president in 1968 recall the experience fondly. A 30-year-old hydraulics engineer in Atlanta remembers: "I felt he was a sane and intelligent voice during a period of great polarization, and that by working for his election I had, for the first time, a direct and meaningful input into the governmental process. My best experience of the 60's was attending the National Democratic Party of Alabama Convention in 1968 as a McCarthy supporter and operating under the illusion that we would be able to sweep away the segregated Dixiecrats in the National Convention in Chicago."

It was the first political experience many had ever had. A 29-year-old Tucson lawyer says, "My first political campaign and the most significant one of that period. I really had a sense of witnessing history being made."

"He got me into grass roots politics," remembers a food co-op worker, "relating me to something outside my world for the first time."

And another respondent reports: "McCarthy got me off my butt and made me realize the power people together have to change lots of reality. Working for Gene made me believe in something again."

McCarthy astonished political experts on March 12, 1968, when he came very close to winning the New Hampshire primary. All of a sudden, his candidacy, and the young people who were working so diligently for him, were taken seriously. Antiwar politics had entered the mainstream. A 26-year-old teacher from New York recalls the feeling of that time: "McCarthy made it seem possible to stand up to the system, that changes could be made."

People who were not active participants in the political movements of the Sixties were more likely to identify with Robert Kennedy (46% of the nonactivists) than McCarthy (23% of the nonactivists). It seems that McCarthy, rather than Kennedy, appealed to those who sought a more direct involvement with the political process; 58% of the activists identified with McCarthy, compared with 47% who identified with Kennedy.

Although both candidates stood for basically the same issues, the McCarthy campaign (often described as a "children's crusade") and the chance it offered to become a part of the political process were what our activists responded to most. A 25-year-old film agent, working today in Los Angeles, asserts that because of McCarthy, "I came to have a real involvement in politics, and that involvement inspired my thoughts and my sense of community with my generation."

But it should be remembered that political activists were influenced by radical Abbie Hoffman (55%) nearly as much as they were by the more moderate McCarthy.

Piece of My Heart

Janis Joplin appears on the list of most admired and influential personalities of the Sixties as one of only two women. Like Joan Baez, she seems to have made an impact through her style of living as much as through her music.

"She was a spirit who gave and gave but never got in return what she needed. Where Janis was, a good time could not be far away."

"People talked about Janis Joplin fucking for days straight. It was the first time I'd ever heard of women's sexuality described the same as men's—I liked that."

Joplin was equally popular with males and females. Says one of the male respondents, "She was a great artist who had a free, independent lifestyle and way of thinking that I greatly admired, as I was 18 at the time."

A female admirer says, "Janis showed women how to party and have a good time, to scream and dance and wear wild, comfortable, sexy clothes."

Those who were the firmest believers in the "do your own thing" ethic of the counter-culture—the heavy drug users—were Joplin's greatest audience among the people we surveyed. The drug users favored her much more (62%) than the non–drug users (15%), or even the activists (49%), and the group as a whole (42%).

Joplin embodied the hedonistic element of the counter-culture, burning her candle at both ends with a blow torch. When she sang *Down on Me* or *Ball and Chain*, a lot of her young fans shared the feelings she sang about. Everybody knew somebody who, like Janis Joplin, destroyed herself before our very eyes. A fan writes, "She knew and understood the temporality of life, and consequently, the value of each moment. She put existentialism into action. I still celebrate her birthday and mourn her death-day."

These, then, are the ten most admired and emulated personalities of the Sixties, the heroes of Woodstock Nation. They are visionaries and idealists, poets and crusaders; they represented the hopes and dreams of the counter-culture. As a group, these ten leaders reveal three aspects of Woodstock Nation.

Half of this list of heroes is made up of musicians—a testament to the bond rock and roll made between the members of Woodstock Nation. Three of the heroes are politicians and symbols of a system in which the children of the Sixties placed more faith than anyone realized. And four of them are dead—victims of tragic accident. If we recall the decade of the Sixties with deep emotion, our memories of John Kennedy, Robert Kennedy, Martin Luther King, and Janis Joplin may explain why.

IN THE SEVENTIES

There are always new heroes, new villains. In the Seventies, our list will change. Before confronting a new list of names, our respondents rated the old list of Sixties personalities according to how they felt about them in the Seventies. Nearly every one of the old heroes dropped in popularity. The only outstanding exceptions were feminists such as Betty Friedan, Simone de Beauvoir, and Jane Fonda. Their slight rise in the "admired and influenced by" category reflects the influence of the women's movement in the Seventies.

But the three Kennedy brothers each slipped about thirty points in our poll, most likely for several reasons: rumors linking Bobby to the FBI's wiretapping of Martin Luther King; the revelation of CIA attempts to murder Castro during John F. Kennedy's administration; and Teddy's misfortune at Chappaquiddick.

Joan Baez, Eugene McCarthy, and John Lennon have all but faded away as influences on our respondents, probably because these three were so closely identified with the antiwar movement, a cause that is past.

The Beatles lost popularity in the Seventies for the simple reason that in 1969 they stopped being the Beatles, and embarked on separate careers. Will those adorable moptops ever get back together again? And if they do, will they play Las Vegas? This, alas, may be something only Charles Manson knows.

Bob Dylan's influence waned, perhaps because of "Renaldo and Clara" (the epic celluloid valentine which he publicly mailed to himself), or maybe because of gossip surrounding a 1978 divorce action brought against him by his wife. Yet, the real reason may have nothing to do with the singer himself, but with the song; after the Sixties, music (as we'll see) lost the power it once had.

The only two figures from the Sixties who continue to be widely admired and still hold a large measure of influence on our group are Martin Luther King and Ralph Nader (their Seventies ratings are 53% and 47% respectively). The fact is that they are the only two heroes to have emerged from the Sixties with their images and reputations intact, despite official attempts, at one time or another, to discredit them. Most important, while most of the other heroes of the Sixties relied heavily on style, which made them into symbols of issues, Nader and King worked with a minimum of style; they *were* the issues.

"I believed, and still do, that Martin Luther King did more to help *all* people than any other person that had lived during those times." (Electronics subcontractor, 30, female)

"Ralph Nader fights the *system*. He is not interested in power or fame, but he is devoted to fighting the corporations when no one else has the ambition to do so." (Archives processor, 25, male)

THE NEW HEROES

Who were the most admired and most influential personalities of the Seventies? And what do they tell us about Woodstock Nation ten years later?

To find out, we assembled a list of newsworthy personalities who captured the spotlight in the Seventies (see pages 245–247). It was a somewhat more difficult task than doing the same for the previous decade, for the choices were not as obvious. One of our respondents points out: "Oh, the most telling indictment of the difference between the 60's and the 70's might well be a comparison of the names on the 60's people list with the names on the 70's list: Mao vs. Ronald McDonald."

But there were similarities, too. Just as in the previous decade, people in the Seventies were influenced by a profusion of minor personalities representing a diversity of styles and ideas.

The 1973 Watergate scandal offered a wide selection of heroes and villains. It was a morality play on a grand scale, and while the headlines and televised committee hearings revealed each new episode, the public drew its own conclusions. A 26-year-old Connecticut store manager picks the tight-lipped White House aide and convicted burglar G. Gordon Liddy as a symbolic figure of the times: "I see G. Gordon Liddy as the extreme example of what the 70's are all about. You are responsible for only yourself and what you say and what you don't say. I admire a strong person. Unfortunately, he worked for Nixon and in the end turned into an asshole."

The first official Earth Day, in May 1970, marked the increasing interest in the environment that had been developing all through the Sixties. The concern with ecology has led some people to admire the back-to-the-land style of singer John Denver: "I'm into conservation and nature—that's what 'Rocky Mountain High' was about. He made me remember that this country is pretty large and I only see a small part of it." (Medical student, 26, female)

In 1974 a San Francisco group calling itself the Symbionese Liberation Army raided a Berkeley house and carried off young heiress Patty Hearst. The ensuing drama of communiques, nonne-

91

gotiable demands, gunfights, and bank thefts often seemed anachronistic, like a page ripped out of an old copy of the Berkeley *Barb*. Most radical political groups, like the Weatherunderground and the Black Panthers, had by that time renounced violence and the idea of a revolutionary vanguard. For a few people, however, the SLA symbolized an ongoing spirit of rebellion that had not died with the turn of the decade.

"There was a true revolutionary force that was crushed by the establishment." (Unemployed, 28, female)

"For a brief moment, the Sixties were alive again." (Researcher, 25, male)

Television and movie stars, as in the Sixties, generally were not influential among our group, although certain female entertainers rate highly with female respondents.

"Mary Tyler Moore. She made it okay to be an independent woman and stay home alone on Saturday nights." (Executive secretary, 32)

"Bette Midler. She's a good example of a strong, sassy, outrageous woman." (Sociologist, 32)

"Jane Fonda. She's always been an ideal woman to me—beautiful, sexy, and intelligent. I admire her political consciousness." (Unemployed, 30)

A computerized entertainer named R2D2, the robot star of the hugely popular science-fiction movie *Star Wars*, seems to have taken over a role previously held by J. R. R. Tolkien's Frodo. In the Sixties, according to our results, Frodo was popular mainly with political activists; in the Seventies, the same was true of R2D2.

"R2D2 is the future made lovable and hopeful. He personifies *Star Wars*, which symbolizes the new positive feelings and the new simplicity." (Clerk, 29, male)

In 1977 the television serial *Roots* captured a nationwide audience of 130 million for one week. *Roots* was based on the best-selling novel by Alex Haley, who had traced his ancestry back to Africa.

"During a period when progress of the 60's was being eroded, Alex Haley focused on commonality of heritage of races, and

dispelled the myth that blacks were rootless, beyond the U.S.A."
(Taxi driver, 31, male)

A 28-year-old slide curator from Delaware makes a point about the Seventies with which many women agree: "Although I wasn't influenced greatly by any one woman on the list, I was influenced by the women's movement—not only by feminists but by female politicians, writers and rock stars."

A 26-year-old Arizona woman says, "Women's liberation seems to concern me so much now. I admire people like Billie Jean King and Barbara Jordan because they aren't simply feminist windbags, but actually show through their lives how women are certainly as admirable as men."

And an Atlanta secretary, 28, explains: "Although I'm not sure I knew it then, all the talk of equal rights, women's lib, etc. was changing the way I would feel about being a woman for the rest of my life."

In particular, women (41%) cite feminist and journalist Gloria Steinem as an influential personality. "She helped women realize that they were equal in every way with men. That women are and should be treated as human beings and they are capable of doing whatever they wanted to, regardless of sex." (Administrative assistant, 31, female)

THE SEVENTIES TOP TEN

Somehow, the personalities of the Seventies don't generate as much excitement as those of the previous decade. Is it possible they just don't measure up to their predecessors? To find out, we assembled a roster of the top ten winners of the post-Sixties period. Without further ado, they are:

Top Ten	% of Total Who Admired and Were Influenced by Them
Woodward & Bernstein	45
Lily Tomlin	34
Carlos Castaneda	34
Mel Brooks	28

Top Ten	% of Total Who Admired and Were Influenced by Them
Alexander Solzhenitsyn	26
Jerry Brown	23
Bella Abzug	22
Chevy Chase	22
Jimmy Carter	21
Barbara Jordan	20

The ten most admired and influential personalities of the Seventies add up to a list that may seem puzzling at first. Comedians and politicians share the same bill (well, maybe *that's* not so puzzling), along with a couple of reporters and a best-selling mystic. But is there a link between all of them?

"Nixon Was a Creep"

A 28-year-old Missouri woman says she admires investigative reporters Bob Woodward and Carl Bernstein because "they showed to me that the media still had guts and this time they were on our side! Of course, they could be classified in the 60's generation."

Richard Nixon was one of Woodstock Nation's biggest villains during the Sixties and early Seventies, not only because of the war he waged in Vietnam, but because he seemed intent on waging war against the counter-culture. He was the epitome of the "uptight square" whose misunderstanding of youth was so prodigious that, in the early hours before a Washington protest rally, he visited some protestors who were camped in a park and astounded them by venturing to discourse about college football.* He was not the least admired man in our poll, but he ties for second-to-last with Nelson Rockefeller and George Wallace—just a fraction higher than last-place Charlie Manson.

When Woodward and Bernstein dug up the facts that led to the revelations collectively referred to as Watergate, Woodstock Na-

---

*Of our political activist group, 49% disliked football in the Sixties and 22% didn't care. Only 29% say they liked the sport, so Nixon *did* have a chance of striking up a football conversation with almost one out of every three demonstrators—but it was doubtful under those circumstances.

tion identified strongly with this pair. Revenge against Nixon had been achieved at last. Not surprisingly, those who had been political activists in the Sixties identified more strongly with the two reporters (57%) than those who had not been active (35%).

"1. They revived the sense of 'us against them,' the people vs. government. 2. Proved that justice could be served under our system: 'we' could prevail. 3. Influenced my current choice of occupation." (Researcher-writer, 25, female, New York)

"Tricky Dick" was finally ousted. It may not have been the revolution some in Woodstock Nation had hoped for; in fact, it was widely hailed as proof that "the system works." But it was nonetheless a triumph to see the old nemesis tripped up by a couple of young guys, one being a long-haired former rock critic.

"Their Watergate exposé made it much easier to convince people that Nixon was a creep and had to be gotten rid of." (Writer, 28, male, Illinois)

The Comedians

"Lily Tomlin is a woman who thinks for herself and gets what she wants out of life," says a Washington, D.C., clerk. Primarily popular among women (43%, to the men's 28%), comedian Lily Tomlin rated high because of an image of independence, consistent with Woodstock Nation's strong identification with the women's movement. She is more popular with the Sixties activists (40%) than with the nonactivists (29%).

"Lily Tomlin is the woman of the 70's—open, vulnerable, intelligent, satiric, vicious, and just plain brilliant." (Cartoonist, 29, female)

"She helped keep a sense of humor alive while raising consciousness." (Mental hygienist, 33, male)

Moreover, comedy seems to have captured the fancy of our group much more in the Seventies than it did in the Sixties.

"I like comedians. I'm a rabid follower of most comedians on the tube or on the screen." (FM deejay, 29, male)

A 25-year-old Massachusetts teacher says that the main influence on his life in the Seventies was "comedy. As a force for social change, and pleasure, it has become as important to me as rock and roll."

Is comedy the new rock and roll? The patterns seem to be the same. Heavy drug users, the biggest fans of Sixties rock stars, show the greatest rapport with Seventies comedians. Chevy Chase, for example, receives a 28% positive rating from the former drug users, compared with 18% from those who never used the stuff. One woman comments, "Chevy Chase is, first of all, very funny, and secondly, he is a link to the 60's since he has a lot of the same feelings I do."

Even the chaos that Mel Brooks evokes seems to recall the "old days." Says one 30-year-old Brooks fan, "It's time for a return to total insanity."

Rock stars make up nearly half of the heroes in the Sixties; none at all appear as heroes in the Seventies, while comedians score big. This generation used to communicate through music, a direct outpouring of emotion; now the sense of generational unity is transmitted through words, humor. It is as though we have outgrown a more primitive mode of expression and matured to the point where at last we can verbalize. In other words, if we multiply the social indicators by the square root of Woodstock, add an ounce of Colombian, and divide by the number of signs in the zodiac, we find that we are all, like, uh, brothers and sisters on spaceship Earth. Can you dig it?

The Yaqui Way of Looking Out for Number One

The books of Carlos Castaneda, *The Teachings of Don Juan: A Yaqui Way of Knowledge* and *Journey to Ixtlan*, were best sellers in the Seventies and continue to be popular. They are about mysticism, magic, fantasy, mystery and drug-induced states of mind. A New York television producer, 33, explains (or, at least tries to): "He made me realize that my acid feelings and visions of all the many realities can be and are real if we allow ourselves to experience and see them!"

A San Francisco student and self-described "word processor"

says that Castaneda's "power of suggestion and inspiration lifted my spirit."

The cultist aspects of the books about the mysterious Mexican teacher Don Juan at first seem to be consistent with the counter-culture's fascination with mysticism during the Sixties. But mystics and gurus prominent during both decades, such as Swami Satchidinanda, Baba Ram Dass, Guru Maharaj Ji, and Maharishi Mahesh Yogi, are not among the most popular figures in our poll. Also, although Castaneda's greatest enthusiasts show up in the group of Sixties drug users (49%), he has many admirers (41%) among the political activists, too.

Perhaps all along the fascination has been not with mysticism in the religious sense, but rather with mysticism as magic, as a means of acquiring power. Many of the heroes of the Sixties were admired for projecting a sense of personal power that was based on deep inner awareness. Dylan, Baez, Lennon, Joplin all appeared strong because they were sensitive. King, a Baptist minister, was obviously inspired by deep religious convictions. So the idea that you can become a more effective person by getting in touch with your inner feelings—or, in the words of Don Juan, locating your "power spot"—carries over from the Sixties to the Seventies in the popularity of Castaneda's books. A factory worker in San Francisco describes the attraction the tales of Don Juan hold for him: "As the 'movement' evaporated and everyone became so introspective, the 'battlefield' moved inside also, and Don Juan's shamanistic stance of 'The Warrior' seemed to symbolize the kind of powers I desired to make life in America more interesting in the 70's."

A 33-year-old Atlanta broadcaster says that for him, Castaneda was "an early source of concept of personal power, multi-dimensional reality . . ."

And a retail clerk in Berkeley declares: "Castaneda taught me to be a warrior—the philosophy of being impeccable."

Russian Dissident

At first, the Russian novelist and dissident Alexander Solzhenitsyn seems not to fit in our Top Ten list. He is often associated with members of the American right wing, who repeatedly laud him for his vociferous anticommunism and use him as a warning to American radicals supposedly bent on replacing democracy with "Kremlin-style" government. In 1976, supporters of Ronald Reagan successfully lobbied to include Solzhenitsyn's name in the Republican party platform. But Solzhenitsyn's literary merits and political stance seem not to be the foremost reason for our respondents' admiration. He simply represents a Sixties-style rebel, a man who fought the system and thereby retained his individuality, not unlike McMurphy in Kesey's *One Flew Over the Cuckoo's Nest*.

"Even under the most repressive of political regimes, there are always some individuals who, disregarding their own safety, will stand up for what they feel is right." (Economist, 29, male)

"I was impressed by his tenacity, even if I couldn't buy his politics whole. I needed a model in lonely perseverance for the cold 70's." (Typesetter, 25, male)

"In *The First Circle*, he seemed to write of the best type of political civil disobedience and morality for our time. He seemed strong, although since leaving Russia he has disappointed me greatly." (Landscaper, 25, male)

Congresswoman from Texas

Congresswoman Barbara Jordan from Texas was an outstanding member of the House committee that deliberated on the Watergate scandal and the fate of Richard Nixon. Her dignity, intelligence, and eloquence impressed many people, but Woodstock Nation saw her as an independent, Sixties-style fighter. Her rating is highest (30%) among the activist group.

"Just total admiration for her. She could lead the world to Peace with her convictions. Too bad she'll be curtailed by the system." (Real estate salesman, 29, male)

"She proved to myself and the rest of the country that a woman could perform at the highest levels of power in a manner admirable by people of both sexes and all persuasions." (Store clerk, 27, female)

"I had kept in touch with her career since the middle 60's and I feel personal gratification at the impact she had in Washington, D.C. during Watergate." (Unemployed, 29, female)

"Small Is Beautiful"

Jerry Brown, the young Toyota-driving governor of California who shuns luxury and is planning his own space program, is naturally counted as a member of Woodstock Nation. Says an enthusiastic 26-year-old teacher in Ohio: "If anybody, he represents our generation working within theirs. He's seemingly honest and would make a great president."

A 35-year-old librarian says, "As governor of the state I live in, he influences my life to some extent. I admire his spartan lifestyle and the way he appoints women to high offices. His interest in space colonies is nicely futuristic, a hopeful adventure."

Approval of Brown's ability to "work within the system" for social change is essentially a continuation of the faith in the democratic process which this group invested in the Kennedys, McCarthy, and Nader. In fact, he attracts the same proportions as they do among activists, drug users, and women, representing Woodstock Nation's middle-of-the-road.

"Battling Bella"

Although she may go down in history as the woman who pointed her finger at Jimmy Carter, Bella Abzug made her mark during the Sixties as an antiwar activist and organizer of Women's Strike for Peace. In the Seventies—despite such negative press-conferred labels as "abrasive" and "stubborn"—she became a House representative with the support of many of the young people we surveyed, particularly activists (30%) and women (29%, compared to the men's 17%).

"I have always been an admirer of Ms. Abzug and after having the opportunity of hearing her speak, I am convinced she is not only in favor of women's rights but rights of all mankind." (Administrative assistant, 31, female)

"I worked with her and I saw it was possible to be in the system and make positive change." (Graduate student, 29, female)

"She is a woman asserting her strength." (Refrigeration mechanic, 32, female)

"Grits and Fritz in '76"

At the time this survey was conducted, President Jimmy Carter was riding high in the Gallup Poll (over 65% of the country approved of him). Since that time, the former peanut farmer has had, according to the pollsters, his "upticks" and "downticks." Still, Carter's counter-cultural appeal is obvious and deliberate; he is the first president to quote Bob Dylan and publicly wear blue jeans.* In 1976, 55% of our respondents (including 57% of the political activists) dutifully went to the polls to vote for him. Why? Those who admire him view Carter as someone who comes close to the Kennedy ideal.

"First time I've believed in a political figure since JFK." (Factory worker, 31, male)

"Basically same as JFK—came from nowhere—one of *my* people—voice of reason in an unreasonable world." (Unemployed, 34, male)

"He seemed to be the man to set the country back on track. Down to earth and one of us." (Letter carrier, 28, male)

Carter's biggest boosters are from the South, particularly his home state, Georgia, where people identify closely with him and his administration. A 37-year-old Atlanta journalist cites both Carter and U.N. Ambassador Andrew Young as his major influences: "I know both personally, and I think I know how they really feel inside and what they would like, and are trying very much to accomplish."

"He is southern, as I am, and I think he is a damn good President. He has restored my faith in politics." (Legal secretary, 25, female, Florida)

Evidently, despite a lack of regional distinctions elsewhere in our survey, some traditional regional pride exists in Woodstock Nation, although even a Yankee cab driver from Massachusetts

---

*Fulfilling Charles Reich's prediction in *The Greening of America* (1970) that we would someday have a bedenimed head of state.

can say, "When you see a good ol' country boy like Jimmy make it, it gives you confidence."

What links all of these people together is the fact that they are admired primarily for the ways in which they represent values of the Sixties. They are viewed in the Seventies from the perspective of the previous decade, and valued on those terms.

The newer heroes don't measure up to the old ones; the mold was broken. The most admired and influential personalities of the Seventies have much smaller followings than the heroes of the Sixties. Response to the ten most popular from the earlier decade ran from a high of 76% (the Beatles) to a low of 42% (Janis Joplin). The most popular figures of the Seventies, Woodward and Bernstein, top the list with only a 45% rating. In other words, *not a single personality* from the Seventies attracts the admiration of a majority of our respondents. It is revealing that, although the Sixties heroes have lost popularity in the Seventies, most of them are still more popular than those of the Seventies.

No new heroes have yet appeared who can articulate the aspirations of Woodstock Nation as it matures, and possibly none will. This generation still seems to be seeking in its newer heroes the qualities they found admirable in the Sixties. But perhaps a generation picks its heroes only once, early, when people are seeking an identity. The early heroes become the sentimental favorites, to the exclusion of newer faces. The heroes grow and change with the generation until they both pass into history. In this way, personalities come to represent entire decades: Charles Lindbergh and F. Scott Fitzgerald in the Twenties, Bette Davis and Ernest Hemingway in the Thirties, Frank Sinatra in the Forties, Elvis Presley in the Fifties. In each of these lives there is a reflection of how each generation sees itself.

The heroes of the Sixties are people who articulated the challenges of the era; they defined the need for political and cultural change in America. Those who agreed most with this message were, as we have seen in this chapter, those heavily involved in politics and drugs. The next two chapters examine why, during the Sixties, smoking a joint and carrying a picket sign were—and always will be—part of what Woodstock Nation is all about.

101

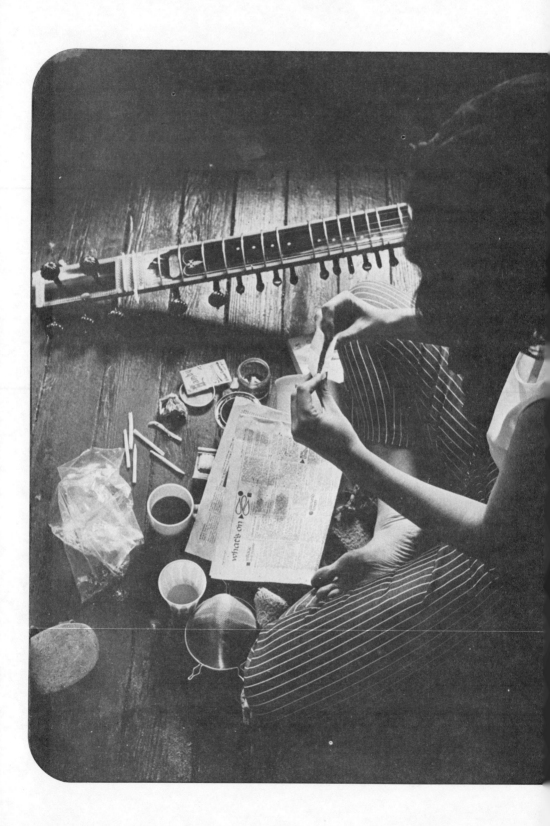

4
Drugs

"Whatever sublime feelings the
person on LSD *imagines*, the
fact is that he is out of his head.
He can't function in a normal way.
He couldn't play chess, make
a bed, run a cash register."

**—HARRY J. ANSLINGER,
former head of the Bureau of
Narcotics & Dangerous Drugs**

If anybody was drug-crazed in the Sixties, it seems to have been the press. The press *loved* drugs. Endless amounts of air time and column inches were devoted to drugs. As early as 1957, the press was glamorizing drugs with a story in *Life*, cover-lined "Great Adventures III: the discovery of mushrooms that cause strange visions." The table of contents read: "Secrets of the 'divine mushroom'; vision-giving mushrooms are discovered in a remote Mexican village by a U.S. banker who describes strange ritual and effects of eating them."

By the mid-Sixties, you could score a drug story in just about every newspaper and magazine in the land. The *Saturday Evening Post* carried a two-part cover story called "Drugs on Campus" by Richard Goldstein.* His cross-country research revealed some strange rituals. He found out, for instance, that at Shimer College, "Scissors is code for marijuana. 'Can I borrow your scissors' means 'I want to buy any pot you can sell me.' 'I need a haircut' means 'I want to turn on with you.' "

Goldstein turned up some real hep cats, too, to let the squares know what was really happening: "Mike, a student on the University of Illinois campus in Urbana, speaks while high on pot and beer. 'The new high is digitalis. It takes you up and brings you down again like a rocket. It makes pot feel like cotton candy.' "

And *Saturday Evening Post* readers were made knowledgeable on drug matters by Goldstein's invaluable tip that "aspirin and cola make a dandy high."

But nothing could top the psychedelic issue of *Life* magazine

*May 21, 1966.

105

that came out on September 9, 1966. The big story this time was psychedelic art—light shows, posters, and paintings. There on the cover, for millions of readers to contemplate in dentists' offices, was a whacked-out, bearded, half-naked freak wearing refractor glasses, bathing in brilliant halos of a light closely resembling Crayola red-orange. The issue was nothing less than a full-color advertisement for LSD.

No wonder parents were freaking out! No wonder they locked up the medicine cabinet! No wonder they looked at you funny when you said you had a headache and needed an aspirin!

The press whipped the public into a frenzy over drugs, creating an atmosphere in which even celebrities like Pat Boone became drug experts. There are currently circulating over one million copies of a book in which the clean-cut crooner cautions: "Those who experiment with narcotics can become hopelessly addicted for life, become mindless vegetables, may even die. Some authorities claim that *one 'trip' on LSD* may affect four generations of children born afterwards!! And, of course, we know that some children born to LSD users have had exposed spines, two heads, and other gruesome physical deformities."*

In the late Sixties, the FCC ordered all radio stations to screen the Top Forty carefully for songs with drug references. Examples of songs to be rejected were given, including "Puff, the Magic Dragon" (marijuana), "Yellow Submarine" (barbiturates), "A Whiter Shade of Pale" ("mind-bending characteristics of the psychedelics"), and Brewer and Shipley's "One Toke Over the Line" (which Brewer did admit was a "cannabis spiritual"). This wave of anti–rock-and-roll McCarthyism (Joe, of course) finally subsided when the FCC was petitioned by one Mrs. Madeline S. Large to rescind the order because radio stations wouldn't play her antidrug recording, "No Thanks, Mr. Pusher," written by her 11-year-old son.†

But then again, Woodstock Nation was selling the squares as much drug baloney as they would buy. Timothy Leary gave LSD its greatest push when he told *Playboy* magazine, "In a carefully

*_A New Song_, 1970.
†Joe Kane, "Dope Lyrics," _High Times_ magazine, March 1978.

106

prepared, loving LSD session, a woman will inevitably have several hundred orgasms." He warned that America "will be an LSD country within fifteen years."*

The *East Village Other* was printing headlines like "Can the World Do Without LSD?" (The answer was no.) And, of course, how could any Sixties debate be complete without a metaphor from the counter-cultural bard? "LSD is a medicine—a different kind of medicine," said Dylan. "It makes you aware of the universe, so to speak; you realize how foolish objects are. But LSD is not for groovy people; it's for mad, hateful people who want revenge. It's for people who usually have heart attacks. They ought to use it at the Geneva Convention."†

"Better living through chemistry" was how one psychedelic poster wryly put it. Trust in the goodness of marijuana, LSD, and other "consciousness-expanding" substances was expressed in the maxim of the "Fabulous Furry Freak Brothers," Gilbert Shelton's popular comic strip: "Dope will get you through times of no money better than money will get you through times of no dope."

For some of our respondents (13%), taking drugs for the first time defined the very beginning of the decade. It was a risk—breaking the law, defying society, doing strange things to your mind and body. As one respondent puts it: "I remember we were very furtive in '66. We got high in a friend's basement, knowing that not only cops and parents would disapprove, but even most friends."

Back in the Sixties, very little was known about the subject. Attitudes ranged from "A person under the influen e of marijuana can get so violent that it takes about five policemen to hold him down" (Harry J. Anslinger) to "A vote for mental health is a vote against good times" (the San Francisco *Oracle*).

As late as 1969, even the most informed observers of the scene had to admit they had very little information to go on. Dr. Kenneth Keniston wrote:

> For example, we do not know how most drugs affect the human mind, and this is as true of aspirin as it is of LSD. Furthermore, with regard to

*Theodore Roszak, *The Making of a Counter-Culture*, 1969.
†Art Spiegelman and Bob Schneider, *Whole Grains*, 1973.

107

marihuana, the drug most widely used by students, we still know almost nothing about basic drug effects, since the active ingredient of marihuana has only been available for research since the summer of 1966. Nor do we know for sure what proportion of students use drugs . . . . And remarkably little is known about the psychology and sociology of drugs on campus.*

GETTING STONED

Because getting high on illegal substances was indeed a voyage into the unknown, the first drug experience is remembered vividly by our respondents. Recollections of the time, the place, the people, the music, the strange effects and emotions create a sort of time machine:

"Five friends got in a circle on the floor with the black light posters, et al, and passed a joint. We all felt deliciously anti-establishment. Anyway, the grass was cut with acid so I experienced a high I have never since reached on grass."

"A girl in my English class turned me on with some hash in a corncob pipe with aluminum foil with pinpricks in it. Paranoid— 'Reefer Madness'—we bought Country Joe and the Fish album, locked the door, turned off the lights, turned up the sound, got stoned. It took a while to get high."

Some people, particularly in the older age bracket, discovered drugs when they mingled with hipsters on the beatnik scene in the early part of the decade.

"In 1960 my high school history teacher took me to the Five Spot in New York, then back to Thelonious Monk's 'pad' where we got stoned."

"In 1961 in Greenwich Village. Met people in a coffeehouse who had 'reefers.' Went back to their 'pad' and smoked."

The largest percentage (20%) of the people we surveyed first tried drugs in 1967, the "Summer of Love." During the next two years, nearly 29% of our respondents had their first experience with drugs. About a third of them were turned on by friends.

"In 1967 I went back to the apartment of a man I'd met that

*Helen H. Nowlis, *Drugs on the College Campus* (introduction by Kenneth Keniston), 1969.

108

same night. He turned me on to grass—I loved it. I also lost my virginity and don't remember a thing about it."

"First tried grass with my best friend. Was pretty naive and had just found out he smoked; my first reaction to this was a turn-off. Then I asked to be turned on—OUT-A-SIGHT!!"

"1968—grass—I was wearing a purple cape and the guy I was with said my arms looked like white birds rising out of it—that made me giggle a lot."

"I was a freshman in high school and this asshole named Brian, my next-door neighbor, said 'try this, it expands your mind.'"

The music was integral to many people's experiences:

". . . listening to Stravinsky and Charles Lloyd."

". . . Sgt. Pepper, or was it the White Album?"

". . . Bob Seger and Sly & the Family Stone."

". . . before going to hear Shocking Blue, Pacific Gas & Electric, and Country Joe & the Fish."

". . . Steppenwolf."

". . . Jimi Hendrix."

". . . the Rascals."

". . . Beatles, Doors, the Byrds."

". . . on Telegraph Avenue, Berkeley, in the Blue Cue pool room. The Jefferson Airplane was playing 'White Rabbit' on the sound system."

". . . New Year's Eve, 1965–66, Berkeley, California. 'Rubber Soul' played as I stepped in front of a mirror and 'flipped out!' experiencing God and the Universe."

Sometimes the first drug experience was with substances other than pot or LSD.

"I was sniffing glue in 1965 in an abandoned barn with a bunch of friends. Became a regular thing for a couple of years."

"I copped Robitussin and experienced the dream state."

A few of our respondents were introduced to the drug experience courtesy of the U.S. Army. "In the Republic of Vietnam—'ya wanna smoke some marijuana?' 'Sure!' That's it, 50¢ reefers and I got as high as I've ever been."

Others took a completely counter-cultural route. "I had run away to a commune and was 'turned on' to marijuana there."

One man learned to smoke marijuana by way of an ancient

American culture: "In 1958 I was working for a friend on his father's farm. His grandmother was Indian. She showed us pot. So I tried it."

The drug scene often coincided with political activity. A 27-year-old lab technician in New York describes the scene: "1967. The Pentagon demonstration. I got turned on by a friend in hotel beforehand. We ditched the grass for fear of being busted at the demo, but when we got to the Pentagon steps everyone was passing joints."

People often got stoned for the first time when they were in college—exactly as parents feared:

"In 1962 I was new to college. A friend turned me on and put head phones on me and a fire in the fireplace. I loved it."

". . . in the dorm room listening to the Stones."

". . . in the dorm room listening to Led Zeppelin."

". . . in the dorm at Yale with about 15 people who had to pretend they were stoned even if they weren't."

Almost as often, however, the little dope fiends were "turning on" right at home under Mom's and Dad's noses.

"First got stoned in my brother's room at home in 1967. We smoked a reefer, listened to Dylan, and talked all night. I liked it. My first reaction to being high was 'Why is this stuff illegal?' "

"In 1968 on 18th birthday. Got high in my folks' basement while they were away. Three friends and I laughed ourselves silly."

"Older brother and stoned hippie friend, hash in my garage, music and laughing at mother afterwards."

"I began my first trip in my parents' living room in suburbia. They couldn't understand why I was suddenly so entranced by the electrical fireplace logs. That was my first psychedelic light show."

"My brother turned me on at 14 in 1967. I counted all the M&M's in my mother's candy dish and separated them into colors."

The first time our respondents got stoned, it was usually with a group of people. A 30-year-old Kansas City man recalls: "In the fall of 1968, I was finally coaxed by some girlfriends to try grass. I was the very last holdout in my peer group. I came in my pants, and spent the rest of the afternoon making them promise not to leave me behind as we tripped up the street."

"At a quiet gathering in 1968 with a few close friends and several acquaintances. I was in a bad mood because one friend had hurt another. Harold wanted to sidetrack me, and offered half a cap of Purple Kathy's psilocybin. Lovely. He stayed close but not all over me all evening, throwing me mind trips I could do. I didn't get around to smoking grass until much later."

"With several of those sweethearts of Sigma Chi. After several consecutive nights of trying, we finally got me high—Mickey Mouse and the whole gang were there and it was beautiful!"

"You're never gonna believe this but the first time I got stoned was on a camping trip with the Boy Scouts. No shit. True story!!"

"The group experience and the ritual of using drugs," as one respondent notes, were "more important than getting high."

And with the drug lore came attitudes, opinions, figures of speech, politics, a whole outlook on life. The counter-culture was passed, hand to hand, like a burning joint.

"Got high for the first time with some guys who worked at the same pizza place I did. They lived in a place that looked like a picture of drug havens in *Life* magazine. I was fascinated."

"In 1967 a San Francisco hippie arrived in town, fell in with my college group in Alabama, and doled out grass from a bag the size of a loaf of bread. As a matter of fact, it was wrapped in a bread wrapper. The first time I got stoned we sat in a car and made animal noises."

TRIPPERS, HEADS, AND FREAKS

With all that was being said about drug-gobbling hippies, and with all the inane things hippies themselves said about drugs, it's no wonder that in August 1968 the late Mayor Richard Daley of Chicago ordered a round-the-clock guard posted at all the city's water treatment plants. He really believed that the Yippies would carry out their threat to dose the drinking water of Chicago with LSD during the Democratic National Convention.

How many of us believed our own propaganda? We put the question to Woodstock Nation:

	% of Total Who Agreed Completely	% of Total Who Disagreed Completely
In the Sixties, did you think that a good dose of LSD in the water supply would be good for everybody?	13	54

The 13% of our group who believed in the supposedly messianic qualities of LSD constitute a large enough group (130 people) to have carried out a mad scheme like the one proposed by the Yippies. But they were definitely in the minority. In fact, 42% of our respondents never tried LSD in the Sixties, 13% never used marijuana, and just as many people drank beer regularly during the Sixties as smoked hashish (17%). As for harder stuff, 40% never tried speed (amphetamines) and 83% stayed away from heroin. To find out how widespread drug use was in Woodstock Nation we asked the following question, and got the following results:

HOW INVOLVED WERE YOU IN THE SIXTIES DRUG SCENE?

	% of All Respondents
Totally involved	27
Somewhat involved	37
Wasn't interested but used drugs if they were offered	17
Had nothing to do with it	17

PURPLE HAZE

Counting those "totally involved" (the heavy drug user group) and those "somewhat involved," 64% of the people we surveyed confess to experimentation with drugs. So not everyone in the counter-culture was touched by reefer madness, but the majority was. Judging from the accounts, the effects of marijuana, LSD, and other psychedelics were unpredictable.

112

"It was around Christmas. I was at a friend's apartment and someone brought grass over. At the time, I swore I wasn't really stoned, but I could not explain why the Christmas tree lights were blinking in perfect time to 'Inna Gadda Da Vida' which was on the stereo."

"I laughed a lot. Stared at a tree."

"A friend turned my husband and me on with a pipe packed with grass. We were lying on the floor listening to the Doors and Cream and I distinctly remember 'crawling inside the music.' "

Many of our respondents report that during their first drug experience it was difficult to feel the effects.

"The grass burned my throat and I couldn't figure out why it was supposed to be that great."

"Little or no reaction. I felt like a fool."

And several report that they didn't enjoy it at all.

"I was violently opposed to marijuana up until 1968 when I finally gave in to my persistent boyfriend who kept telling me it was so much better than drinking. It dazed me and I found myself throwing up in his front yard. I don't remember why I smoked it a second time."

Generally, however, drug users remember their first drug experience as a good one.

"In 1968 I bought a dime of hashish in the alley behind the Blusette, a rock club in Baltimore. Then we sat around and smoked it in a car. I think I laughed a lot."

"The first *good* pipe I smoked in 1967. I cut school, got *wrecked* (the reds were redder and the blues got bluer) with this white guy in the football field across the street. Went to Metropolitan Museum, freaked out, fell in love with New York in October."

"I got stoned the first time at a 1968 Who concert in Washington, D.C., the night Johnson said he wouldn't run for office. The concert turned to madness. Constitution Hall will never be the same!"

Of all the drugs consumed by Woodstock Nation, LSD was the most unpredictable. Many tales circulated during the Sixties emphasizing its dangerous effects. People on "bummers" reportedly walked in front of moving traffic, committed murder and mayhem, and jumped out of windows, thinking they could fly.

Also, there was the problem of "bad acid," concocted by the counter-culture's Dr. Frankensteins from speed, strychnine, arsenic, Drano—everything but LSD. Our respondents did indeed have some terrible bummers, which many classify as their "worst Sixties experience."

"Getting caught on acid by my parents. I had put pillows in my bed and snuck out in the middle of the night. Came home at dawn—every light in the house was on, my parents all psyched up for the big confrontation, asking questions like 'Are you a virgin?' and crying because I'll never know the joy of a 'first kiss.' "

"Freaking out at the Fillmore at the Santana, James Gang, and Catfish concert."

"Being at a party where someone had dosed all the drinks with acid and watching close friends freak out—and being of very little help myself (stoned also)."

At last we can finally sit down and sort it all out. Did people have a good or bad time on LSD? It turns out that while 33% of our respondents had LSD bummers, 54% say they "had a wonderful acid trip" during the Sixties. For many, it was their "best Sixties experience."

"A thousand-microgram acid trip at Esalen with Tim and Rosemary Leary and the World Family Commune. At one point, we were all in the hot baths together, holding hands in a circle, chanting 'OM.' I got so high I had an orgasm. It was like fucking everyone in the pool simultaneously."

"Being on mescaline in Yosemite and realizing how much I loved my close friends, how I was 'one' with nature and every person, and that being gay was a wonderful thing to be."

STAYING STRAIGHT

What about the people who say they were not *at all* involved in the drug scene during the Sixties? They were a small minority (17%) of the total number. As a group, they were—and continue to be—distinct in many ways.

Non–drug users tend to be older. While nearly half (48%) of the drug users are in the youngest bracket, only a little over a third (35%) of the non–drug users are that young. Respondents from

114

the oldest age bracket make up only 12% of the drug users, while twice that many (24%) were non–drug users during the Sixties. Apparently, the taboos against drug use were felt more strongly by people who came of age early in the decade.

About half of the non–drug users say they thought it was extremely important during the Sixties to abstain from all drugs except liquor. Half of the non–drug users say they were occasional drinkers of hard liquor, though they steered clear of most drugs. Yet, only a third never tried grass at all, while 23% smoked grass occasionally, 22% tried it once or twice, and 9% of the non–drug users say they smoked grass frequently during the Sixties—proving that it was possible in the Sixties to use the stuff and still have "nothing to do with" the drug scene.

Why did some people decide against using drugs? For some it must have been a matter of politics. About a quarter of the non–

CONTRASTING ATTITUDES OF NON–DRUG USERS AND DRUG USERS OF THE SIXTIES

	% of Non–drug Users	% of Drug Users
College dropouts	21	47
Did postgraduate work	45	18
Were political activists in the Sixties	8	37
Political views in Seventies		
Moderate	25	13
Liberal	28	37
Radical	18	27
Conservative	7	2
Apathetic	8	16
Called cops "pigs" in the Sixties	40	88
Still call cops "pigs" in the Seventies	27	47
Are working today in professional jobs	43	35
Are working today in skilled crafts	2	10

drug users say they held positive attitudes toward such politically conservative figures as Barry Goldwater and Lyndon Johnson. Very few of the non–drug users were political activists during the Sixties, and as a group, they tended to be less involved with the counter-cultural style, more involved with "straight" society in general. There is a big difference between the two groups' attitudes on such matters as respect for authority and career choice.

The fact that people who didn't use drugs very much were more likely to stay in college and go on to graduate school should not necessarily be construed as evidence that drugs lessen ambition or ability. Rather, we are looking at two kinds of people—those who chose conventional social mobility, and those who preferred alternatives. As time went on the distinctions blurred somewhat: not all the non–drug users continued to abstain from drugs in the Seventies. About two thirds of them eventually succumbed to the pleasures of pot-smoking. Nevertheless, this group continued to share very little with the rest of the people we surveyed. As a 28-year-old secretary in Atlanta remembers, it was difficult, "trying to have friends and be sociable in the late 60's without smoking grass and drinking to excess and sleeping around." The drug experience of the Sixties formed important bonds between people. Not having participated in the drug scene of that time places one on the very fringes of Woodstock Nation.

THE WOODSTOCK PHARMACOPOEIA

At this point it is important to clarify exactly what drugs were being put to recreational use during the Sixties. Which were the favorites? How often did people take them? (See chart opposite.)

The answer is surprising, considering the popular image of the supposedly drug-crazed counter-culture. The majority of people in Woodstock Nation—no matter how they classified their involvement in the drug scene—did not use any substance other than marijuana regularly or frequently, and most people never sampled the full range of hip highs. The exceptions that prove that rule are LSD and mescaline—psychedelics that just over half of our re-

116

spondents tried at least once; amphetamines, which 59% used at one time or another (probably just before exams); marijuana and hashish, which very few *didn't* try.

Even among those who say they were "totally involved" with the Sixties drug scene, drug use was not extreme (see chart, page 118). Everybody in this group smoked grass and hashish. Almost everybody took more than a couple of LSD trips. Nearly half carried on extended experiments with LSD. Aside from these exploits there was some dabbling in the other substances, none of which acquired great followings. Of our heavy drug users, 41% tried heroin at least once, but less than 7% were regular users.

The dividing line during the Sixties between those in the drug scene and those outside of it was LSD—the acid test of the counter-culture. The universal bond, however, was marijuana.

DRUG USE IN THE SIXTIES AMONG WOODSTOCK NATION AS A WHOLE

Drug	% Who Used Regularly or for Prolonged Periods	% Who Used Frequently	% Who Used Occasionally	% Who Used Once or Twice	% Who Never Used
Acid (LSD)	14	12	19	12	42
Cocaine	2	4	14	16	62
Cough syrup	1	4	16	21	56
Downers (barbiturates)	3	6	15	18	56
Glue	1	1	2	7	87
Grass (marijuana)	43	19	18	6	13
Hashish	17	23	26	10	21
Hashish oil	4	6	14	16	58
Heroin	2	1	3	9	83
Mescaline	5	13	19	17	45
Opium	1	3	12	24	58
PCP (angel dust)	1	1	4	13	78
Peyote	2	3	11	19	65
Quaaludes	1	2	7	10	78
Speed (amphetamines)	11	9	22	17	40

DRUG USE IN THE SIXTIES AMONG THOSE "TOTALLY
INVOLVED IN THE DRUG SCENE"

Drug	% Who Used Regularly or for Prolonged Periods	% Who Used Frequently	% Who Used Occasionally	% Who Used Once or Twice	% Who Never Used
Acid (LSD)	45	26	19	6	3
Cocaine	6	10	29	26	27
Cough syrup	2	8	16	28	45
Downers (barbiturates)	10	14	25	27	24
Glue	2	3	5	18	72
Grass (marijuana)	84	11	4	—	—
Hashish	42	37	16	3	1
Hashish oil	10	13	22	21	31
Heroin	7	1	11	22	59
Mescaline	17	34	27	15	7
Opium	4	9	33	34	20
PCP (angel dust)	2	4	12	26	56
Peyote	6	8	24	33	29
Quaaludes	5	5	15	17	59
Speed (amphetamines)	27	20	29	16	9

"PSYCHEDELICIZE SUBURBIA"*

Whatever your involvement with drugs was during the Sixties, it was difficult to avoid the cultural effects of the drug scene. It affected the way people talked (Wow! Groovy! Outasight! Ego trip!). It influenced the way people dressed (bell-bottoms, granny glasses, paisley shirts). It gave rise to new food products ("Purple Zonkers") because of the stoned craving for "munchies." The drug culture even affected play, and unstructured games like Frisbee became popular because stoned potheads couldn't be bothered with rules and traditional team efforts.

To those who were totally involved in the drug scene, day-to-day life in the Sixties was in many ways different from everybody else's.

*Popular button, c. 1967.

118

ATTITUDES TOWARD DRUG USE DURING THE SIXTIES

Thought it was extremely important to:	% of Drug Users	% of All Respondents
Always have a stash	62	26
Know a dealer	67	32
Be a dealer	19	7
Be around people who liked the same drugs	63	29
Be high all the time	33	12
Be high frequently	56	22
Be high just once in a while	57	31
Turn other people on to drugs	51	20
Turn the world on	36	15
Turn parents on	14	6

"Always have a stash" was very important to the dopers, and this supply, if you were clever, was inaccessible to inquisitive police—or greedy guests. One respondent says he kept "devising more and more elegant hiding places for the acid."

Perhaps it was the lure of adventure, intrigue, or, for some, just plain greed that led 19% of our dopers to consider dealing dope an extremely important part of their lives during the Sixties. As one respondent puts it, "Living in the Village in Toronto, doing drugs and selling them was my best Sixties experience. The cops never bothered you there. It was all freaks. Two years of fun." Although only 19% seem to have been dedicated dealers, it seems that dealing was a definition of being "totally involved" in the drug scene, since 83% of the "totally involved" at one time or another sold drugs, compared to 42% of Woodstock Nation as a whole.

One of our respondents relates that her best Sixties experience was "trading a kilo of dope for a 1951 Packard Ambulance that picked us up hitchhiking. By the end of the ride, they had our back-pack full of dope, and we were behind the wheel of their museum piece."

Like drinkers who are offended at the presence of teetotalers, dopers preferred the company of dopers. Being with other people

119

who liked the same drugs was extremely important in the Sixties to a majority of the drug users. One recalls, "I didn't like being around people who weren't high when I was." This is the kind of feeling that led to the instant community formed whenever somebody lit a joint.

Half of our dopers considered it extremely important to turn other people on to drugs during the Sixties, and a little over a third were bent on "turning on the world," while some even wanted to turn on their parents.*

The bond formed by drugs during the Sixties is a constant theme voiced by our respondents, often wistfully. "Camaraderie among friends during early grass days, 1966, and all the playfulness" is how a respondent describes his best experience of the decade.

EIGHT MILES HIGH

Part of the kinship was the secret language of rock music. This is a concept so elusive that less than a decade later it is practically lost. Yet, it was an important part of the zeitgeist, a mystery that only initiates into Woodstock Nation could really grasp. In fact, 43% of all our respondents believe, more or less, that the music of the Sixties can be understood only by those who have had the drug experience.

The FCC was right! Rock music *was* speaking in drug language to millions of turned-on "heads." Sometimes it was blatant, as in the Jefferson Airplane's "White Rabbit," which urged us to feed our heads. Other songs were more subtle, using rhythm, composition, and style to communicate. It was a new kind of rock 'n' roll that coalesced in San Francisco around 1965 and was dubbed "acid rock"—a term which "could be taken to mean *enhancing*, as well as *inducing* psychedelic transports."†

Sixty-seven percent of our respondents—including 89% of the

---

*And 26% felt at the time they filled out their questionnaires that it was extremely important to "turn on the people who give surveys (discreetly)" which may account for the fact that along with their questionnaires, some respondents mailed the authors small quantities of something that looked and smelled like pot.

†Lillian Roxon, *Rock Encyclopedia*, 1971.

120

drug users—enjoyed acid rock (73% of the youngest group, compared to just 50% of the older people). This means they listened to such groups as the Thirteenth Floor Elevators, Grateful Dead, the Doors, Jefferson Airplane, Steppenwolf, Electric Prunes, Count Five ("Psychotic Reaction"), Blues Magoos, Magic Mushrooms, Blue Cheer, Big Brother and the Holding Company, Seeds, Chocolate Watch Bank, Quicksilver Messenger Service, and Strawberry Alarm Clock.

A great number of respondents remember the music as being part of their *best* Sixties experience.

"We were on some mushrooms and just sitting around when someone put on George Harrison's electric music. It was the best. Nothing has ever come close."

"The night when my partner in crime and our ol' ladies got stoned on a 30-joint nickel, and first heard 'Beggar's Banquet.' I was totally blown away."

"I was tripping on LSD at a White Panther political meeting with loud rock 'n' roll blasting in the background. Best time I ever had."

With stoned precision, one man remembers the afterglow of the Woodstock Festival: "Walking at sunrise with the woman I was to marry away from the Airplane, after a night of Creedence, Janis, the Who, and Sly. It was a four-mile walk."

And then there was Jimi Hendrix, the quintessential Sixties concert artist, "Mr. Sixties himself," as one respondent says. "Music, sex, and drugs all in one," says another. People who were heavy drug users admired Hendrix the most (66%, as compared with 39% of the respondents in general). Their perceptions of Hendrix sum up the entire experience of acid rock:

"Admiring Jimi and exploring his style allowed me to dabble in simple electronics, play guitar, listen to *dynamite* stereo sets, meet my first husband, cut school and get high, go to the Fillmore East and Electric Lady Land." (Unemployed, 25, female, New York)

"He was a symbol of freedom and expression. He lived out his fantasies and invited us along. He was a good musician and brought art into rock music and pleasure in my life." (Artist, 26, male, Washington)

"His music was my head-trip and reinforcement for the things I was imagining and shaping in my own mind." (Teacher, 25, male, Tucson)

"I admired him because he was so free and powerfully sexy and expressive and tender, and was influenced to see the world differently (Are *You* Experienced?)" (Student/part-time psychologist, 26, male, California)

"His music seemed the perfect score for the play my life unfolded." (Exterminator, 29, male, Pennsylvania)

In the Seventies, just 36% of Woodstock Nation still enjoyed acid rock (enthusiasm had dropped also among the dopers, to 46%). This loss of fans may have been caused partly by changing styles, but when some of the biggest stars disappeared into that great light-show in the sky, for some respondents it was the end of acid rock, the end of the decade.

"The Sixties finished with the deaths of Jim Morrison, Jimi Hendrix and Cass Eliot, ushering in a change of music."

"The deaths of Fred Hampton [Black Panther leader], Janis Joplin, and Jimi Hendrix was when it was all over."

PARANOIA STRIKES DEEP

There was a practical reason why drug use created an automatic kinship: It was against the law. This greatly contributed to the us-versus-them, squares-versus-hippies, young-versus-old character of the times and became a badge that Woodstock Nation would wear almost belligerently.

Discussing the fear engendered by participating in the dope culture, one respondent writes, "I don't like buying or smoking dope unless the other people are dear friends. I have never felt comfortable since the 60's talking on the phone."

Many people shared this fear of speaking freely on the phone— "I was panicked that if I said anything on the phone about drugs I'd get arrested," reports another respondent—and it turns out that they weren't far wrong: "They tapped my phone in Canada and now my husband is wanted. The charge is conspiracy—with no pot found."

There was a strong suspicion of surveillance, and 26% of the heavy drug users were convinced that the FBI was reading their mail. One person says he "used codes for drugs when on the phone or in letters."

Evidently, there was good reason to be fearful.

"Some hash was found in my mailbox by the mailman, somehow, which led to the police and hassles."

"It turned out that the FBI had been watching us throughout my first summer of grass. They actually took the trouble of catching a dozen of us (we were lifeguards at Fire Island) and taping our confessions. We weren't busted though."

The pleasures of the drug experience were continually tempered (or perhaps heightened) by the fear of getting caught.

"My next-door neighbor for a year was head of the local SDS unit. Smoking dope with him was never entirely free from paranoia, because of his high visibility and commie-traitor image."

"I was generally afraid of police and because I handled drugs in a small town had good reason to be. Amphetamines caused me to be paranoid sometimes."

The persistent fear that accompanied drug use caused for some respondents their worst moments of the decade.

"The second time I smoked pot, we elected to park by the high school. Bright. A cruiser spotted us, and I tried to drive away, but he pulled us over. The trooper recognized my name, discovered my uncle was a cop and let us off with a warning to 'stick to Marlboros.' My pipe had fallen through a hole in my pocket and was running down my leg as he talked. I was scared shit my parents would find out. They never mentioned if they did. Some kids thought I was a narc after that. Oh, well."

For those not so lucky to have a cop for an uncle, getting busted for drugs was the worst experience of their lives during the Sixties.

"Busted for pushing and held in jail for ten days until my father could raise $10,000 property bond. Meantime, almost was hurled off the 3-story tier in the cellblock by an irate convict who did not believe I didn't have a cigarette. Bummer!"

The punishments for drug users were often severe, and many prominent counter-culture figures were persecuted in a political manner by the government, under the guise of enforcing the drug laws. To set an example, the leader of the White Panther Party in

Ann Arbor, John Sinclair, was given a ten-year sentence for the possession of two joints. One of the worst experiences of the Sixties for some people was "watching my friends get busted and go to jail for a harmless plant."

THE BAD NEWS

Along with the many reports of wonderful acid trips and hilarious communal pot parties come tales that are not so pleasant. The bad acid trips, the hard drugs, the fear, and the busts ruined people's lives; in some cases, virtually ended them.

"Drugs ruined my health, ruined two marriages, ruined my career, amplified all of my run-of-the-mill neuroses to psychotic proportions."

Only 3% of our respondents used heroin regularly or frequently, and they testify to its ill effects:

"I have a police record, a bad discharge from the army, lost a good job, woman, and have become in the aftermath of kicking, bored, depressed, and sometimes paranoid of social contact."

When the rest of Woodstock Nation was exploring freedom, some could not.

"I did felony time for drugs, so I lost lots of personal freedom from them."

Some are still paying a penalty.

"I got a little loose. Finally I was given 25 years in Virginia State Pen, which is where I am now."

In all of Woodstock Nation, 31% "knew personally two or three people who died from drugs during the Sixties." Of those who were "totally involved" in the drug scene in those days, the number of people touched by drug deaths was dramatically higher (51%).

"A classmate OD'd on heroin. That became a symbolic bad experience of the 60's."

"After an Easter reenactment of Calvary, a friend on LSD took his own life."

For a few, it's an endless bummer.

"A friend of mine completely lost his mind on acid. He never

124

has been the same since. Really what we called fried, if you know what I mean."

"LSD ruined my life. After a nightmare acid trip in '67, I began suffering acute anxiety attacks and schizophrenic episodes. Have been hospitalized several times and am currently living with my parents in almost total seclusion."

And one of our respondents actually verifies a rumor that ran wild during the late Sixties: "Staring at the sun on some bad acid (speed-laced), I was blinded for a week. Gradually the blindness turned into a large black spot which covered whatever I focused on. Then it began to get smaller and smaller over several months. Eventually it disappeared completely. After about a year I could see normally again."

The fact that so many of our respondents counted drug experiences as both their best and worst memories of the Sixties may explain the depth of feeling members of the Woodstock Generation hold for that decade. The sense of tragic loss is never far from recollections of giddy and childlike exultation. The fact that Woodstock Nation saw so many friends busted, wasted, and dead from drugs helps to account for the way this group perceives themselves as "survivors."

THE GENERATIONAL EXPERIMENT

Looking back on the Sixties, and all those unpredictable highs and lows that drug use seems to have caused, we don't wonder that a few of our respondents told us they now are repelled by drugs:

"Abuse of drugs in the 60's kept me from realizing my potential as a human being, although I think they have made me more expressive artistically."

"Pot hindered my maturation because I hid behind a constant high. By recognizing and modifying my dependence, I've made progress (even if minimal) toward . . . you know, I'm still not sure where I'm supposed to go."

"I'm starting to get suspicious of it. I mean sometimes I use it to avoid things or people."

"Sometimes I wonder if LSD killed some of my brain cells."

Do these findings indicate that Sixties veterans regret their generation's involvement with drugs? The majority (66%) of our respondents disagrees with that idea; in fact, most people agree that the results of the drug experiment were mostly positive. One respondent reports that drugs have influenced his life "totally. They made me a more relaxed and aware person. Integrated my personality more. Brought me into contact with people I would not ordinarily have met."

One fourth of all those who were frequent users claim that drugs have in some manner deepened the thought process and expanded the consciousness.

"Mescaline taught me how limited our 'categories of understanding' are—I believe I have greater tolerance of (if not appreciation for) chaos than I used to: i.e., I'm not completely freaked out by change."

Among the respondents in general, many claim that the drug experience has made them better people.

"LSD, mescaline, and psilocybin had tremendously beneficial results in putting me in touch with myself. My world perspective became more religious. These things being accomplished, psychedelics themselves decreased in importance."

"Drugs helped me to see how the world really is and to know myself better. I gained confidence to speak up about things I thought were wrong."

"Drugs made me more open, less uptight. I like myself better."

A few people cite specific ways in which the drug experience has changed their lives.

"I reformed due to LSD insight after two years of stealing (lobster, underwear, dresses, suede coat, etc.). My God!, I say now."

"Drugs somewhat emphasize certain events in one's life and in the process of being stoned I might solve problems differently."

"Drugs helped me cut my alcohol intake."

"During my few (light) mescaline trips (20–30) over two summers, I made major decisions—changed careers, left a job—went back to college for second time for a second career."

In Woodstock Nation today, drugs, particularly pot, have been integrated into daily life.

"Sometimes my apartment smells funny. I've got to watch the dog and cat (they eat dope). Be a bit discreet when my Mom visits. Include stash money in budget. Spend money on Oreos a lot."

"They have become a central part of my lifestyle. Much of my activity centers around obtaining and consuming drugs."

It may be that drugs—LSD, marijuana, other psychedelics—have, in themselves, brought these people the insights that they say changed their lives. But drugs have always been available, and it would be misleading to credit the chemical process with the kinds of cultural change that have occurred since the Sixties. For Woodstock Nation, drugs were primarily a medium by which the counter-culture was learned and spread. And the old sense of kinship lingers on.

"I feel a certain kinship with others in my office or friendship circle who get high."

"I have a hard time dealing with people who don't use it and are down on it."

And the antiestablishment sentiment common to "heads" persists today.

"I felt like an outsider, a rebel. I still haven't gotten over this. I still divide people into 'straight' and 'hip.' "

"I am contemptuous of the entire drug law enforcement establishment in this country. My taste in music and entertainment has been directed by the 60's drug scene."

"Acid confirmed my pacifism and turned me more to the Mystical Path, opened up the gates of memory of previous lives and confirmed my suspicions about the Establishment, thus placing me permanently on the fringes of society."

Perhaps the best summation of the long-range effects of marijuana and LSD is offered by the person who reports, "I no longer iron my button-down shirts." If that isn't enlightenment, what is?

WHEN THE MUSIC'S OVER

The authors of this book confess to having taken their share of drugs during the Sixties—well, one took more than his share. But during the Seventies, it has always seemed that we had no time for drugs. One of us quit smoking pot altogether around 1972 (claiming to be a graduate of "Contact High"), while the other will indulge if a joint comes her way at a party. We have enjoyed shoveling someone else's expensive cocaine up our noses, and we fully indulge our tastes for bourbon, rum, tequila, and beer. But don't ask us the price of grass; we haven't bought any in years. As for LSD, the only trip we're interested in is Florida in the wintertime.

We have reduced our drug usage, and, as it turns out, so has the rest of Woodstock Nation. "We always used to get stoned before going out to a party, movie, dinner," writes one woman, "but now we need more energy and concentration and don't generally smoke at parties because we have found we actually enjoy people much more with a clear head—no dope, no booze, nothing!" In every category, drug usage has decreased dramatically for everyone, including those who in the Sixties were "totally involved" in the drug scene.

DRUG USE THEN AND NOW BY THOSE "TOTALLY INVOLVED"
IN THE SIXTIES DRUG SCENE

	Used Regularly or for Prolonged Periods		Never Used	
	Sixties	Seventies	Sixties	Seventies
Grass	84%	59%	1%	13%
Hashish	42	16	1	13
Acid (LSD)	45	2	3	41
Speed	27	5	9	50
Mescaline	17	2	7	48

Many articles were published during the mid-Seventies charging that one reason why Woodstock Nation had become so "quiet" was that this generation had switched drugs, from psychedelics to downers like Valium and Quaaludes. It may be that some people were plunging themselves into apathy on these chemicals but *not* the members of Woodstock Nation: in the Seventies, 65% never used downers, 71% never used Quaaludes, 79% never used Valium more than once or twice. Nor has the "angel dust" (PCP) plague (if there is one) hit this group: 87% never touched the stuff.

Alcohol use has increased slightly among our respondents. About one third say they are drinking a lot more beer, wine, and hard liquor in the Seventies than in the Sixties, and a third say they are drinking a little more. The drinkers are mainly in the youngest age bracket. Those who are *not* drinking more beer, wine, or hard liquor today than they once did are chiefly the oldest respondents. This is part of an overall trend within this group to forego tripping upwards, downwards, or sideways as they grow older.

Cocaine attracted great public attention during the late Seventies. Rock stars, Hollywood idols, politicians, and executives were all rumored to be tooting "blow" through rolled-up C-notes. But of our respondents, 68% never used cocaine more than once or twice in the Seventies. With 48% of its people making less than $10,000 a year, Woodstock Nation could hardly be expected to afford such chic tastes.

These media-promoted notions—that everybody is snorting coke, everybody is taking Valium and Quaaludes—are all obfuscation. The truth is much simpler and makes more sense than all the conjectures that have been spun around the question of what happened to all the "heads."

"I SMOKE POT AND I LIKE IT A LOT"

"My husband and I use grass daily, the way some people use alcohol or tobacco, to unwind. We do not drink or smoke tobacco. Occasionally (once or twice a year) we do psychedelics (psilocybin) when we can get them. We seldom go to parties where we know there will be booze, boozers, and thick tobacco smoke."

Not everybody we surveyed is so selective about parties, but most of Woodstock Nation considers marijuana its drug of choice. Of all the substances experimented with during the Sixties, most have been discarded in favor of pot. In Woodstock Nation, 42% have been smoking pot regularly or frequently, consistently through both decades, and at the time of this survey, 72% were smoking at least occasionally.

"I do a little grass now and then with a friend to help blow the bullshit out of my mind from work. To get laid back and stoned with a friend is one of the few sanctuaries left in life. You know, when you just can't handle the bullshit anymore."

There are approximately 16,000,000 pot smokers in America,* and a May 1977 Gallup poll showed that 35% of all Americans have taken at least a puff or two.

Pot smoking has lost much of its counter-cultural status. Today there are fat, glossy magazines devoted entirely to dope, carrying advertisements for "exquisite jeweled hash pipes complete with velvet pouch," monogrammed rolling papers, solid gold coke spoons, "pot isomerizers," mink-covered stash boxes, "hand-sculpted pewter roach clips," and "do-it-yourself magic mushroom cultivation kits." The ads represent a multimillion-dollar industry in dope paraphernalia—or "lifestyle accessories," as some merchants prefer—that convenes for annual trade fairs at the New York Coliseum. "This Christmas give an alternative gift," advises a full-page ad in one dope journal. "Give something that complements that special lifestyle of your friends and lovers. . . . Patronize your alternative gift shop. Small, independent business people serving you since the 60's."

The furtiveness that once made pot smokers such an exclusive club is disappearing as the drug laws are reformed. In several states cops hand out the equivalent of a traffic ticket for what used to put people in jail for years. In New York City, lunch-hour crowds often linger on the sidewalk, openly passing a joint around before going back to the office. Even *Newsweek* has taken note of a group it calls the "New Bootleggers," reporting that:

> America's marijuana farmers have developed a quality domestic product that is challenging imports. Many users say Maui Wowee, Kona Gold and Big Sur Holy Weed provide a better high than Colombian pot. . . . Domestic farmers are reaping higher prices, too. Mexican grass sells for $150 to $350 per pound, while the California brands can fetch as much as $3000 a pound on the streets of New York or Chicago. . . . Says Monterey narcotics agent Ed Warner: "We've found marijuana farms in the Los Padres National Forest, Big Sur and on the Hunter Ligget Military Reservation."†

*National Institute of Drug Abuse, 1977.
†October 30, 1978.

So the smoking, cultivation, and dealing of pot has become as much a part of middle-class American life as Tupperware parties or family cookouts. The National Organization for Reform of Marijuana Laws has mounted an extensive lobbying campaign, and its conservatively dressed lawyers buttonhole congressmen in the same smoke-filled rooms where votes are traded for dams, highways, and tariffs on Japanese wristwatches. With 84% of our respondents in favor of decriminalization of marijuana, it is likely that pressure for reform of marijuana laws will intensify.

All of this may appear to be a betrayal of the Sixties counterculture, a retreat from the days of "heads versus feds." But that is a superficial reading of the situation. According to our respondents' comments, it was not the drugs themselves that were so important, but what they represented—and marijuana represents a kind of freedom. It is one of the few products that is still totally unregulated and untaxed. Sold outside the legitimate marketplace, pot is priced according to supply and demand in the only free economy left in this country. Perhaps pot's appeal—like that of CB radio, mopeds, and hang-gliding—is that it is outside the reach of a meddling government. Participating in the buying, selling, and smoking of marijuana continues to be an assertion of freedom and individuality, part of the "do-your-own-thing" ethic that is so fundamental to the politics of Woodstock Nation.

5
Politics

"You smash it—and I'll
build around it."

—JOHN LENNON

According to one fourth of our respondents, the beginning of the Sixties was signaled by events of political turbulence.

"Kennedy was shot."

"I got busted in 1964 in the Free Speech Movement at U.C. Berkeley."

"In October 1967, as a 16-year-old freshman, I witnessed the New York City police ravage a group of SDS members who were demonstrating peacefully at Brooklyn College."

From the civil rights movement of the early Sixties to the student power conflicts of the mid-decade to the antiwar movement of the late Sixties, it was a period of enormous political intensity for young Americans. If political struggle was, as Eldridge Cleaver once said, the "central event" of that era, how many in Woodstock Nation played a part in it? Who were the activists? And what did activism really mean?

THE NONACTIVISTS

Somewhat less than a third of the people we surveyed say they participated very little, if at all, in the political activities of the Sixties. Of this group of nonactivists, 75% say they were "concerned, but not directly involved" in politics, and 25% say they were simply "not involved." As we shall see, this meant they avoided demonstrations and other political activities, although not necessarily because they were unsympathetic to the radical causes of the time.

Only a handful (7%) of the nonactivists defined their political stance during the Sixties as "conservative." There were even some

(15%) who say they were "radical," while 16% say they took a "moderate" stance. Others (18%) say they were "apathetic," like the Kansas City man who declares, "Politics suck and they always will," or the television editor from New York who explains, "I was always too busy getting high."

But drug use was not a significant factor in drawing people away from political activism. The majority of nonactivists (59%) actually were not drug users. Only 21% of the nonactivists were heavily involved in the Sixties drug scene.

The largest percentage (42%) of nonactivists defined their political stance during the Sixties as "liberal." This includes the woman in Tucson who says, "I was too involved with my schoolwork to become overly committed to anything else." The fact that most nonactivists seemed to share this attitude of being "concerned, but not directly involved," while defining themselves as "liberals," tends to confirm the old definition of the liberal as someone who "does a little by not doing a lot."

THE SOMEWHAT-ACTIVE ACTIVISTS

Just over a third of our respondents describe themselves as having been "somewhat involved" in political activities during the Sixties. These people seem to have had more motivation than the nonactivists but were not willing to advance all the way to the barricades. As one woman puts it, "I knew things had to change and I wanted to be one of the changers, but I never felt totally committed to the radical lifestyle."

This group includes a large percentage of people whose attitudes were "radical," but who disagreed with the directions in which radical politics of the time were going. One man in San Francisco explains, "I hated what the radicals hated but disliked their methods of correction. I was ready to pledge allegiance if they should win." A New York public relations executive says, "I was unable to feel comfortable in a situation where my feelings did not match the intensity of the organizers. Also, there was the fact of their intensity, which may tend to promote apathy in some of us less motivated, more moderate types."

It seems that the "somewhat active" activists were the kind of people who, during the Sixties, might have attended a demonstration if it wasn't raining, or if they didn't have something more entertaining at hand, like pot. About a third of the heavy drug users (30%) fall into this category of political activism.

THE ACTIVISTS

Almost exactly a third of our respondents say they were activists during the Sixties. In this group, the majority (72%) say they were "very active," while 29% say they were "totally involved" in political activities during that decade. Three fourths of the activist group defined their stance during the Sixties as "radical." Just 22% were "liberal."*

It's immediately obvious that, for a "protest generation," this group has an overwhelming majority of members who, as one respondent puts it, were "really against the war, otherwise tagged along for the ride"—as these survey results show:

PROTEST ACTIVITIES

	% of Activists	% of Nonactivists	% of All Respondents
Demonstrated against the war	93	40	74
Marched for civil rights	73	11	43
Boycotted school classes	69	29	50
Demonstrated for women's rights	53	10	30
Sat-in for integration	41	5	20
Went on a Freedom Ride	8	1	5
Performed street theater	30	5	17
Went to Chicago demonstrations in '68	19	2	9
Carried a picket sign	84	16	49
Got tear-gassed	61	14	36
Got beaten by cops	31	6	16
Got arrested	40	22	28
Went to jail	31	17	22

*About 3% of the activists say they were "conservative," indicating that their political activism was focused on the Right of the political spectrum. Our interest, however, is in those involved on the Left.

Even within the activist group, there is a minority of hard-core politicos in the company of many more who were less committed.

So this is the "small, vocal minority" that was so often lambasted by conservative and timorous liberal essayists of the time. As small as the activist group was, however, its influence in Woodstock Nation was dominant. We have already seen that the counter-cultural style was strongest among heavy drug users and activists; in addition, the largest political allegiance among heavy drug users (45%) was to the activist group. Drugs may have been the medium through which the counter-culture was spread, but the basis of the counter-culture was political. It was called the Movement.

THE MOVEMENT

Many felt they were a part of it, some even imagined they were leading it, but never was the Movement definable in traditional political terms. A general description is offered by Raymond Mungo, speaking of his own little late-Sixties Movement group, Liberation News Service:

> It is impossible for me to describe our "ideology," for we simply didn't have one. I guess we all agreed on some basic issues—the war is wrong, the draft is an abomination, abortions are sometimes necessary and should be legal, universities are an impossible bore, LSD is Good and Good For You, etc., etc.—and I realize that marijuana, that precious weed, was our universal common denominator. And it was the introduction of formal ideology into the group which eventually destroyed it.*

This pretty much describes the white, middle-class Movement as a whole; especially accurate is Mungo's omission of racial or poverty issues, imperialism, capitalism, or any other -isms. These concerns were voiced by various activists, but they served as a coherent system of political belief for only a few. The rest of our activists fit the picture once presented by SDS leader Carl Oglesby: "Perhaps he has no choice and he is pure fatality; perhaps there is no fatality and he is pure will. His position is

*Raymond Mungo, *Famous Long Ago*, 1970.

138

invincible, absurd, both or neither. It doesn't matter. He's on the scene."*

Being on the scene meant action. The simplest definition of the activists we surveyed is that they are the ones who attended the most demonstrations.

ATTENDANCE AT DEMONSTRATIONS DURING THE SIXTIES

	% of Activists	% of Nonactivists	% of All Respondents
Attended none	3	48	19
1–5	18	44	39
6–10	27	4	18
11–20	21	1	10
20 or more	33	1	13
Traveled over 100 miles to attend a demonstration	63	7	35

The fact that 44% of all nonactivists attended at least one or more demonstrations and only 19% of all those surveyed failed to attend any during the Sixties shows that politics touched nearly everyone, whether they were involved in the Movement or not.† But among the activists, over half were present at more than eleven events, and the 33% who took part in over twenty protests represent the hard-core politicos.

What was it like to be there? A man in Madison, where street fighting was particularly fierce during the latter part of the decade, recalls that his best experience of the Sixties was "running in the streets chasing pigs." His worst experience was "running in the streets, pigs chasing me." And then there were all those chants that resounded like thunder in the urban canyons of "Amerikkka":

Ho, Ho, Ho Chi Minh,
NLF is gonna win.

*"Into the 70's: From Violence to New Values," *Time*, December 19, 1969.

†According to a 1970 Harris poll of college students around the country, 60% had attended at least one demonstration.

One, two, three, four,
We don't want your fucking war.
Two, four, six, eight,
Organize and smash the state.

Hey, Hey, LBJ,
How many kids did you kill today?

Hell, no,
We won't go.

Hey, hey, what's shakin'?
Today's pig
Is tomorrow's bacon.

One side's right, the other side's wrong,
We're on the side of the Viet Cong.

Big firms get rich,
GIs die.

Beep beep, bang bang,
Umgawa, fire power.

What do we want?
Peace!
When do we want it?
Now!

All we are saying
Is give peace a chance.

It was an unforgettable experience—the heart-thumping adrenaline surge one felt while moving amidst a crowd of comrades jamming a street for as far as the eye could see, brandishing banners and signs, marching through the heart of the city as office workers waved the peace sign from windows and helmeted cops on nervous horses trotted along the sidewalks. This was the Movement, fighting, as Che Guevara put it, "in the belly of the Monster."

Why did activists go to demonstrations? Some (8%) went in search of fun, adventure, and romance, like the California musician who says, "It was a good place to party, meet chicks, and get in on the action." Only 4% mention peer-group pressure, like the computer programmer from Illinois who admits, "I went to protests because everyone else did."

Nearly a third of the activists, though, believed that the mass gatherings were an effective way to accomplish their goals.

"There was strength in numbers. Also, I liked the spirit and the excitement, and it was nice to see I was not alone in my frustrations."

"I participate because I like to be with lots of people who share my feelings. Also, sometimes we get positive results. I go to all the pro-choice (abortion rights) demos I can."

"I thought it might do some good. It did. It made Nixon so paranoid he blew it with Watergate."

Another third went to demonstrations just because they believed in the cause.

"I wanted to stand up and be counted against the war, hate, racism, violence and Adolph Coors."

Those who didn't go to demonstrations in the Sixties had their reasons, too.

"I believed in the cause but found out the counter-culture leaders were assholes just like the people they were opposing."

"They are important in themselves—the notion of 'bearing witness'—but probably not very influential. And unless they deal with something you really care about, they're *so dull!*"

"I had other personal things going on. I wanted most of all to go to college—priority #1."

"I was an ROTC cadet. I was the epitome of the 'bad guys' on campus."

And some were afraid to put their bodies on the line.

"Fear of blood, cops (pigs), tear gas, and my parents taking away the car keys—all this kept me away."

People were wary for good reason. Some people's worst experiences of the decade occurred at demonstrations, where they came up against bad dreams like these:

"Getting clubbed at the Chicago convention. I cried because I didn't want to be a radical, an alien."

"Being yelled at at peace demos and grape boycotts."

141

"Getting clubbed by a Berkeley pig at Peoples' Park."

"Being hit over the head by police in Haight-Ashbury police-induced riot."

"Being tear-gassed at the 1970 Mayday Demonstration in Washington, D.C., against the war."

"My boyfriend was a medic at Yale during the Bobby Seale trial. He got his face kicked in by demonstrators he was helping. Ultimate paradox."

But the majority of the activists who attended demonstrations remember them as some of the best events of their lives.

"My best Sixties experience was at the Chicago 1968 Democratic Convention: I was overwhelmed. The collective friendships I formed and work I began that has gone on developing 'til now."

"Nixon's inauguration in '68. A counter-inaugural ball in a tent near Washington Monument. Phil Ochs was there. There were a bunch of us in a chartered bus from Boston. We met an older woman with a family while hitching in Washington. She gave us dinner and let us stay for the weekend. Everyone felt open, together, and united against the stupidity of Nixon."

As with the drug experience, what people seem to have enjoyed most about being political activists and going to demonstrations in the Sixties was the esprit de corps. A 26-year-old woman, now a film producer in New York, remembers her best Sixties experience as "a student strike in 1969. Real feelings of participation and community."

Obviously, the activists were in the front lines, but there was more to being in the Movement than demonstrating. From minimal forms of activism such as signing petitions to the flagrant waving of a Viet Cong flag, activists were the ones who were most involved.

One half to one third of the activists were involved in truly radical activities: 36% harbored a fugitive, 32% joined SDS, 37% were organizers in poor neighborhoods, 32% withheld taxes for political reasons. Typical of the 39% of the activists who chose their line of work according to political beliefs is the man who says, "I turned down a job with Bell Labs because of their contract with the Defense Department."

142

INVOLVEMENT IN POLITICAL ACTIVITIES DURING THE SIXTIES

	% of Activists	% of Nonactivists	% of All Respondents
Signed petitions	98	72	89
Handed out political leaflets	90	15	54
Boycotted lettuce and grapes	87	33	61
Put up political posters	86	14	51
Gave money to the antiwar cause	79	24	55
Gave money to black activist groups	52	10	30
Worked in a political campaign	78	17	51
Attended a teach-in	66	17	42
Raised money for the cause	62	7	32
Made a speech	60	14	34
Campaigned for Eugene McCarthy	55	13	36
Supported the Viet Cong	51	7	28
Ran the mimeograph machine in a Movement office	46	2	20

This is not to say that nonactivists and Woodstock Nation in general were unsympathetic to the aims of the serious politicos. Nearly three quarters of the nonactivists signed petitions and a third participated in the boycott of grapes and lettuce to aid striking farm workers. Fifteen percent of the nonactivists say they even went so far as to harbor fugitives.

But the true activism in the Sixties seems to have been more limited than is generally believed. For while most of the people who define themselves as Sixties activists were willing to put their bodies on the line at demonstrations, risk a taste of tear gas, and put up political posters, only a minority acted upon a strong, consistent ideology, such as that espoused by SDS. Of every three people you meet today who claim to have been activists "back then," perhaps one was seriously working to reform or revolutionize the American political and social system.

143

THE BIG FEAR

A former activist, now a lawyer in New York, recalls the feeling of fatalism that was prevalent during the Sixties, and seems—for some of us—so far off and unthinkable now. He refers to a common rumor: "I simply assumed that if there was going to be a crackdown, my friends and I would be rounded up and placed in the camps we thought they had ready for us."

A Chicago community organizer who was very active in the Movement puts it this way: "We actually believed it was a choice between fascism or immediate revolution. 'It's all coming down now, so choose sides.' The Weatherunderground was the logical next step for people who thought Amerikkka was on the verge of collapse and right-wing takeover."

The sense of impending Big Brotherism tinged political activism with fear. Even the smallest act of dissidence caused some people to hesitate. "Although I only signed petitions," says one respondent, "I was afraid my 'past' would come back and haunt me if I got a job where I needed a background check."

The anxiety filtered down to even the youngest activists, one of whom remembers "being paranoid, mostly in high school politics. Could you trust everyone in the meeting?"

Many people believed they were under surveillance. Half of the activists assumed to some degree that the FBI was reading their mail, and a third of Woodstock Nation as a whole was equally suspicious.

"I was popped a few times (Student Mobilization Committee, Vietnam demos, and integration sit-ins) and had a few confrontations. I always knew my phone was tapped."

"I was sure there was an FBI file of my protest activities."

"I saw men in trenchcoats taking pictures at demonstrations."

"I knew my phone was tapped, that I was known to the local police, that they would use any pretext to bust us. It drew people closer together; you had to rely on your friends more."

Feelings like these were not delusions. Well before Watergate, Nixon's enemies list, and the revelation in the Seventies of the government's "CoInTel" program to disrupt Movement groups, there was ample proof of the government's spying on private citizens. The intrigue often reached Mata Hari proportions, as one man recounts: "A girl I used to get stoned with had an affair with an older (and married) man who worked at City Hall in Boston, and he told her that they had files on me and several of my friends. Later, when I looked out my living room window and saw two cops going through our trash cans, I began to get pretty paranoid."

"At one point I carried a gun, because I belonged to the staff of a free university in the San Francisco Bay area which offered courses in everything, including communism, and we were in fact watched and harassed by a local right-wing group (with knowledge of city police). They bombed our cars, offices and homes."

In a way, the official persecution of radical activists produced more radicalism.

"I saw evidence of police conspiracy in late 1968, and learned of my own Red Squad dossier in 1971. I avoided symbolic arrests because of adolescent experiences with police. I was proud of associations with 'subversives.' "

"I rather enjoyed the idea of the government spying on me. It was a status thing."

But while the pressure may have helped to bring activists closer together and to reinforce radical behavior, it had unfortunate, divisive effects, too. The fear of informers, provocateurs, and infiltrators bordered in many instances on hysteria.

"I was at times thought of as a spy by the radical groups I was in. But there was a spy-of-the-month syndrome at work, lots of group paranoia," reports one ex-activist. For this man, now living in New York, his worst experience of the decade was "being personally rejected by the SDS group I was with for their thinking I was an agent."

The fact is, however, that the fear was often grounded in reality. After black leader Malcolm X was assassinated, it was revealed that one of his bodyguards was an FBI agent. In New York's East Village, nobody smoked more dope or was hipper than "Crazy George," who helped organize and lead a political fringe group called the "Crazies." After some of his comrades were arrested in 1971 for a bombing scheme (which he helped formulate), it was revealed that Crazy George was actually a police agent. In every radical community in the country, similar tales of betrayal are still recounted. A Tucson social worker says, "I was an active black militant and I know they have information on me. I was a member of a fraternity and one of the prospective pledges came out and told me he was assigned to report on me." And a broadcaster in Atlanta recounts this episode: "As a co-founder of a chapter of Vietnam Vets Against the War, I was busted and served a year in jail on a conspiracy charge. The 'evidence' came from a paid informer and provocateur."

Exactly how far the government succeeded in crippling the Movement through its use of informers and provocateurs is still not known, although more and more people have discovered, through the recently passed Freedom of Information Act, that Big Brother *was* watching them during the Sixties. It is certain, though, that fear and suspicion immobilized some people, discouraging them to the point where Movement politics began to seem as unattractive as the establishment they were fighting. For at least one activist, her worst experience of the decade was "seeing all the factionalism and backstabbing and more-revolutionary-than-thouism permeate the Movement."

WHY ACTIVISM?

Did activists risk life, limb, and jail because, as Raymond Mungo theorizes, they had "nothing to do and the prospect of holding a straight job [was] so dreary that they join[ed] the 'movement' "?* Was it, as Abbie Hoffman said, a case of "revolution for the hell of it"?

Most of the activists we interviewed would disagree. Nearly a third (30%) say they wanted to effect social change.

"I was outraged at the thought of 'coming of age' in the system as it stood. Oppression, capitalism, imperialism were very real."

This was true even of people who had no definite understanding of what changes they wanted.

"I wanted total transformation of our society; however, I hadn't read much about politics or thought things out."

*Raymond Mungo, *Famous Long Ago*, 1970.

146

But 21% of the activists explain their radical stance during the Sixties as having been a reaction to injustices, such as the respondent who cites "the poverty of black people amidst so much wealth." And 29% point specifically to, as one respondent describes it, "the grotesque injustice of the war in Vietnam." For some this meant a very personal sense of desperation in the face of onrushing events: "I felt a need to get in my two cents' worth before I got shipped to Vietnam and blown away."

The war led some people to examine other issues and conclude they were interrelated:

"First, it became clear that the Vietnam War was both morally and politically wrong. Then, that social justice and racial equality and sexual equality were all lacking. Then, that the changes necessary would require a revolution."

"The situation was so morally and politically bankrupt that only radical action (getting to root cause) could change events fast enough. One does not play parlor games when death and destruction become official policy of our government."

The belief in the necessity of rebellion or revolution was what motivated 23% of the activists. However far they wanted to push the barricades, the activists generally were responding to specific and immediate conditions that they had diagnosed as being wrong and unjust. As one respondent put it, "I could not understand why freedoms enumerated in the U.S. Constitution were deliberately and methodically disregarded."

This could not be called activism for the hell of it.

THE DRAFT

As the war became the central issue of the Movement in the mid-Sixties, the draft posed a ready target for activists. Over the war years, 27 million men became eligible for military service. Walk-in draft-counseling centers were a growth industry. The Resistance, a nationwide coalition of antidraft groups, was organized in 1967 and issued the call: "On October 16 we will hand in our draft cards and refuse any further cooperation with the Selective Service System. By doing so we will actively challenge the government's right to draft any American men for its criminal war against the people of Vietnam." That was "Stop the Draft Week," with its sit-ins, draft-card burnings, riots, and rallies, and the invasions of draft-board offices by resisters who poured blood on the files. The 1968 raid on the Baltimore County draft board in which 378 files were destroyed by Daniel and Philip Berrigan and the rest of the "Catonsville Nine," and the Boston trial of Dr. Benjamin Spock, Rev. William Sloane Coffin, and others all put the resistance on America's front pages. But it all came down to one very personal decision for every draft-age male. Should I go? Should I not go?

One respondent recalls the crucial moment: "The night of the first draft lottery, my girlfriend and I were listening to Bob Lewis on WABC-FM read the dates as he got them off the AP ticker.

MEN'S REACTION TO THE DRAFT

	% of All Males	% of Activist Males	% of Non-Activist Males
Avoided service through student deferment*	47	47	41
Lottery number never came up	30	26	29
Beat the draft through subterfuge	15	17	8
Was legitimately 4 F (disqualified)	15	15	18
Enlisted	12	3	7
Burned my draft card	7	14	2
Was drafted	7	8	7
Became a conscientious objector	5	9	2
Served in Vietnam	4	3	7
Fled the country	1	2	—
Went to jail	1	1	—
No answer	9	10	8

*Of the men we surveyed, 29% were in the youngest age bracket, which put them safely in high school during most of the draft years and gave them a legitimate student deferment.

148

Suddenly my heart stopped and my girlfriend broke down and cried—my birth date was the third to be pulled."

Nearly three quarters of Woodstock Nation's males sidestepped the question altogether. About half avoided the draft because they happened to be fulfilling the middle-class duty of attending college, and a further 30% "won the lottery." Outright resistance was rare, and it is interesting to note that more people in our group enlisted in the military than burned their draft cards. There were a minority who fooled the draft board into disqualifying them for service:

"When I took off my clothes at the induction center, my body was painted with psychedelic designs in Day-Glo paint. They knew I was nuts."

"I was going to be a conscientious objector, but my parents had a friend who was a psychiatrist and he wrote a letter to the draft board and they made me a 4F."

"I told them I was a faggot."

"At the physical, the doctor saw fake tracks on my arms, asked if I took drugs. I said yes, I was a junkie and couldn't wait to get to Nam because smack was so cheap over there."

A handful became conscientious objectors, a legal, socially acceptable alternative to military service. Exactly five of the men in our survey escaped the draft by fleeing the country. Three avoided the draft by going to jail. One resister says he simply "didn't register" (risking a ten-year jail sentence), and one says, "I was literally chased cross-country by the FBI for several years." Some resisters are still wary: "I won't write this down," says one respondent. "Who are you people, anyway?"

Four of the men we surveyed say they were deserters from the military. They joined over a half million who likewise went "over the hill" during the war.

Where it took a certain amount of risk and/or principle to stay out of the war—burning your draft card, deserting, becoming a CO—activists outnumbered others. Even so, most of the activists and Woodstock Nation in general were not draft beaters or resisters. Instead, the majority fell into the less radical category of draft avoiders, using the system to escape military service. This was largely a privilege of class, and Woodstock Nation took full advantage of it. Only 4% of those we surveyed went to Vietnam.

Out of the 27 million men throughout the United States eligible for the draft, less than 10% saw military service in Vietnam. Of those, 51,000 were killed, 270,000 wounded.* Although these figures do not include many members of Woodstock Nation, those who escaped the draft did not entirely escape the war. Draft researchers Lawrence Baskir and William Strauss have noted that "Vietnam was a crisis they all faced—whether in the barracks, on the campus, or in the streets. Unlike other Americans, most members of the Vietnam generation are reluctant to judge a man by his personal response to the war. They know that the labels—loser, coward, evader, deserter—are part of the tragedy of Vietnam."

WHERE DID ALL THE ACTIVISTS GO?

The Movement has, for the most part, disappeared from newspapers, television, and magazines. The cover stories, feature articles, and 90-minute special reports on radical activism and campus politics that used to advertise the Movement's existence have ceased, except for the occasional "where are they now?" retrospectives.

Has activism really died out? The press has written its obituary many times. In a story headlined "The New Campus Mood," *Time* magazine told us on November 18, 1966: "Most students, while unhappy about the war, seem weary of rehashing all the old arguments, and the issue is losing its emotional kick."

Because activism began on the campus, older and supposedly wiser observers in the media tended to regard it during the Sixties as something superficial that would come and go like any college fad. Paul Sann, a former editor of the New York *Post*, included in his book *Fads, Follies and Delusions of the American People* a chapter called "The American Campus, Then and Now." In a section titled "The New Revolt," he equated campus activism with goldfish-swallowing, panty raids, and telephone-booth stuffing: "The spring rioting did lose some of its popularity, at least for a while, as the Sixties wore on. For the alienated students there were new kicks. A 'cool' culture developed, geared to marijuana and such

*Lawrence M. Baskir and William A. Strauss, *Chance and Circumstance*, 1978.

150

mind-altering drugs as LSD and also marked, for the hippies, by an interest in religious pop cults."

Reporters, perhaps remembering their own college days, saw the campus revolts as something that would vanish with summer vacation or graduation. Perhaps because they were part of the establishment that was under assault, they instinctively dismissed the Movement by treating it as a childish tantrum that would soon pass, giving way to an acceptance of the status quo.

Were they right? Has there indeed been a shift toward apathy and conservatism in Woodstock Nation? We asked our respondents to indicate their political stance in the Sixties, where they stand in the Seventies, and why their political views have either changed or remained the same.

About 9% told us they were more apathetic and selfish in the Seventies:

"I now realize that the individual can only act successfully for himself. I am now totally apolitical."

"Today I have no hope of being instrumental in making any change and even wonder about the possibility of change other than by evolution or as a result of a major disaster. I'm more selfish and concerned with my own survival."

"I'm into the human condition in a smaller, more personal way. I've turned my focus from the 'solid' realm to more spiritual concerns."

A few of these people expressed a conservative view with a tinge of racism:

"My liberalism has been tempered somewhat by a creeping hatred for third world causes."

"I'm in it for myself. Give me money and keep out the Negroes."

Just 2% said they had been apathetic through both decades:

"I think politics is crooked and the system is impossible. I believe in doing what you can for those you know."

Twenty-eight percent said they have moved away from the left— from radical to liberal, or from liberal to moderate. Most explained they had simply grown older, more "mellow" in the Seventies:

"I've mellowed somewhat since that time—the war ended and

151

primarily my concerns now relate more toward the ERA and women's status in society."

"Perhaps it is that I now have a family depending on me, and while I still feel a lot of change is necessary, the largest immediate problem (military-industrial) is resolved. Now we must get on to other issues, like saving the earth before we kill ourselves off."

"Vietnam is gone. The King is dead. I am still aware of oppression, capitalism, imperialism, but the mood has changed. All this laid-back shit."

Many respondents show a continuing awareness of political problems in America, and still use the ideological language of the Movement ("military-industrial," "women's status in society," "people in motion around issues," "oppression," "imperialism"). But they find that their lives have changed. Or else they have found other ways of effecting social change.

"I have the same basic radical view of politics and culture, but am involved in more peaceable work toward it and a much more peaceable lifestyle."

Others, however, have sized up the situation and decided that there is little they can do.

"I see little possibility of changing things. I think that much of what I wanted in the Sixties might be good for me and some people but not for most people."

"What's different today is that, despite the fact that the war is over and that small steps have been taken toward social justice, racial equality, and sexual equality, I'm cynical. I still believe a revolution is a must, but I no longer believe there's a chance of that happening in my lifetime. And I'm a whole lot less willing to put my body on the line."

"I still feel the same, but feel more powerless to do things on a large scale. So I combat inflation, dishonesty, pollution, etc., on a personal level. Grow organic foods, move toward self-sufficiency and mutual dependence with friends. Things like that."

In addition to this feeling of powerlessness, there is also fear. For many people, the day in 1970 that National Guardsmen shot four students to death at Kent State University in Ohio was the day the Sixties ended.

152

"Kent State really finished it. Not just because of the common metaphor. It chilled a whole nation of freaks."

Perhaps the examples of the Weatherunderground bombers, blown to pieces in the New York townhouse where they were preparing explosives, and of the Symbionese Liberation Army, wiped out in a 1975 gun battle with police, frightened people from radical activism.

"I used to feel it was particularly important to show one's feelings and solidarity with the Movement, which was widespread and positive—now it is scattered, dangerous and terrorist-oriented."

"There is more of a feeling of hopelessness—that things are headed downhill—more plastic, more violent, more dangerous—I cannot and will not take risks now."

Some members of Woodstock Nation today have too much of a stake in the status quo to feel like changing it.

"Things have calmed down today; I am older and making a living within this society."

Of all the people in this survey who say they have shifted to the right in the Seventies, 37% are former Sixties activists. Of all the people who indicate that their radical stances of the Sixties have remained the *same* in the Seventies, 64% are former activists. In other words, more activists have held onto their radical views than have abandoned them.

A little over half of the Sixties liberals have retained the same political views. And 11% of Woodstock Nation say they have moved *farther left* in the Seventies. Of these new radicals, 26% had been activists in the Sixties. Why?

"Although tough politics ended the war sooner than it would have otherwise, it still continued at a devastating rate. The economics, stagnation, social problems and doomed programs are part of the ongoing legacy of the 1960s. They have *not* gone away, but only taken new forms and require new and continued radical action if progress on our front is to be worthwhile."

"How can a person decide to believe in violence, indifference, and apathy instead of living for peace, love, and equality? It is impossible that my lifestyle change."

153

"The U.S. still picks and chooses heads of state by assassination, corporate power still controls the country. In fact, one of the differences between the 60's and 70's is now they give us even less because they have less to placate with."

"I've spent a lot of time exploring different left groups. I became a feminist in the 70's. I would describe myself more or less as an anarchist and a feminist."

"My outrage over ignorant drug laws has spurred my general political radicalization."

"As conditions in the U.S. and world continue to deteriorate, I become more radical because the present system offers no workable solutions to the problems we face."

This contradicts the general picture of activism projected by the press. "Today," reported *U.S. News & World Report* on March 27, 1978, "many former radicals or dropouts have become entrepreneurs ... making the climb up the corporate ladder or getting ahead in law, advertising, architecture and other professions." CBS-TV's Morley Safer strolls along Telegraph Avenue in a *60 Minutes* segment on April 30, 1978, making the rather narrow observation that Berkeley was "once the scene of many battles, [but now] there seems to be little here that's counter about the counter-culture." The implication is, of course, that activists of the Sixties have given up, become apathetic, and blithely accepted the status quo. Former SDSer Todd Gitlin says of this kind of reportage: "Hype feeds on hype. The noisy 1960's were far out, the silent 1970's are far in ... the media obituaries are partly expressions of wish, partly sighs of relief, partly arguments against resurrection."*

Obviously, the people who once made up the Movement are still around, and many still hold the same views that motivated them during the Sixties. Half of those who have become more radical during the Seventies are in the youngest age group, showing that the activist ethic of Woodstock Nation continued to be influential past the turn of the decade.

The shift away from the left involves 37% of Woodstock Nation, while 29% have stayed radical or moved farther left. Of the

*"SDS Around the Campfire," *The Nation*, October 22, 1977.

154

CHANGES IN WOODSTOCK'S POLITICAL VIEWS:
SIXTIES TO SEVENTIES

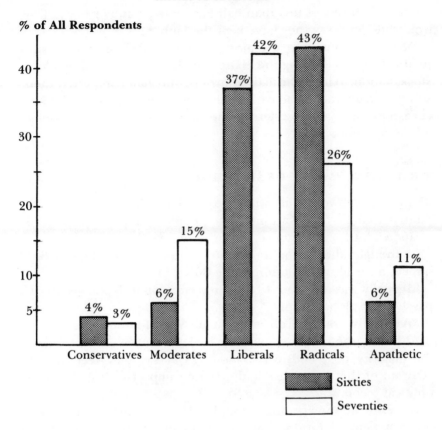

% of All Respondents

Conservatives 4% / 3%
Moderates 6% / 15%
Liberals 37% / 42%
Radicals 43% / 26%
Apathetic 6% / 11%

Sixties
Seventies

SIXTIES ACTIVISTS IN THE SEVENTIES

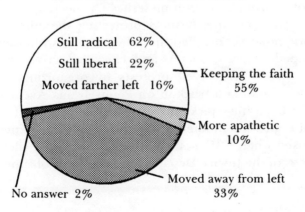

Still radical 62%
Still liberal 22%
Moved farther left 16%

Keeping the faith
55%

More apathetic
10%

No answer 2%

Moved away from left
33%

activists themselves, less than half have moved away from radical-ism, while 55% say they have kept the faith.

Does this constitute a major political shift? Not really, since political activism during the Sixties involved only a third of Wood-stock Nation. Within the activist group, only half committed them-selves to truly radical activities. This was—and remains—the hard core, a group that defenders of the status quo still have to regard as a time bomb.

THE LASTING IMPACT OF SIXTIES ACTIVISM

"I hoped we would all wind up working for each other—for mutual benefit. No war, no rich people, no poor people, no weapons, lots of acceptance, caring, and love."

"I thought there'd be an economic depression followed by, I hoped, a socialist revolution in the 80's."

"It really was a dream, I had some crazy apocalyptic vision of a psychedelic global utopia."

"A socialist rock 'n' roll state. That's what I hoped for."

Although the utopia some were looking for never materialized, the majority of Woodstock Nation (73%) say they feel that the activism of the Sixties has had a lasting impact on the American political scene.

Demonstrations are one example. Although the average num-ber of demonstrations our respondents have attended has dropped from 7 in the Sixties to only 4 in the Seventies, with even the activists averaging only 6 demonstrations in the Seventies, compared to 13 in the previous decade, the movement's favorite method of focusing attention on issues has been appropriated by everyone else. Recently, farmers protesting the administration's agricultural policies encircled the White House with their tractors and stampeded goats, sheep, and chickens across the Capitol steps. Truck drivers staged protests by organizing nationwide convoys and holding a truck-in on Pennsylvania Avenue. House-wives have been busy picketing state legislatures for and against the Equal Rights Amendment. And, in 1978, many Sixties activists were amused when FBI agents gathered for a mass silent protest on the steps of the Justice Department in support of superiors who had been indicted for illegal tactics used while investigating Sixties activists. The fact that public demonstrations have become so much a part of the political system is attributable to Sixties activists, who not only revived the Boston Tea Party tradition but also stimulated a new sense of individual power.

"As farmers and libbers have proven, the right to assemble peacefully will never be infringed again, thanks to Chicago, Kent State . . ."

"The minorities, women, gay, and other movements will not ever sit back and let the corporate majority dictate to them completely as in the past. But this needs constant work and dedication to keep the extreme right or left from running this country (or world?)."

"People now know they can change government policy and events directly. The politicians also know it, as does the press. . . . Rural farmers are now committing 'civil disobedience' with tractors. The lesson may have been subconscious but it was learned."

"People are more aware of the strength of the power elite and not quite as complacent as they were before. They are more suspicious and less likely to believe everything they are told."

Of course, the Movement did not accomplish everything its participants hoped it would. An Arizona woman points out that "basically, the U.S. still carries out imperialistic policies in relation to other peoples (even the native people here)." But most of our respondents cite concrete gains:

"Youth got the vote."

"The Civil Rights Act."

"Nixon got booted out, Carter got elected, there is more communication between groups (rednecks and hippies)."

"The gay rights movement is burgeoning and vigorous. The women's rights movement has a pending amendment to the Constitution. The damn war is ended."

"Involvement of large groups of people in political movements. 'Grass roots' political awareness. More sensitivity of politicians concerning quality-of-life issues. Environment. Consumer protection. Family planning."

"Freedom of Information Act, restriction of activities of FBI, CIA, and more integration, ERA."

157

"Blacks lobby more effectively, women's rights are getting started, and Abbie Hoffman has disappeared."

And a 28-year-old Florida man speaks for many respondents when he says, "I think 'we' proved that 'America, right or wrong,' is bullshit and will be bullshit henceforth. I think leaders are more responsive because of that." Of course it may be true that, as one woman suggests, "The influences are subtle, since the people of the 60's and early 70's are carrying the basic attitudes with them into politics and business. The real impact might not be felt for another 20 years." But right now, in Woodstock Nation, there is a feeling of power well-exercised, of confidence, of victory.

It's not necessary to go back over all the old battles and ten-point programs and nonnegotiable demands of Movement days, trying to figure out if the "revolution" was "won" or "lost." It doesn't matter where the old leaders are today, or what heresies they're committing. Many people believe that Sixties politics worked, that their actions were important, that they affected history. These people are still around, working, changing, bringing their ideals and methods into every area of American life. As a woman in Berkeley sees it: "The 60's lit a fuse that's just now detonating."

6
Sex

"All I know is that these
fucking kids are getting more
than we ever did."

—JOE, IN THE MOVIE "JOE"

"The more I make revolution, the more I want to make love." So went a graffito that appeared on the walls of Paris during the student uprising there in spring 1968 that paralleled the uprisings occurring on college campuses all across America. There was definitely a sensual atmosphere around the Movement; pressed together with all those hundreds and thousands of other marchers and demonstrators, people were physically making a political statement. Small wonder, then, that such mass exercises in heavy breathing would lead to a more private kind of activism among those who believed in making love, not war.

"We're not just eating and sleeping together," a Detroit coed told *Life* in 1968. "We're protesting the war together."

The popular image of Woodstock Nation's love life during the Sixties is captured perfectly in Dale Gordon's previously discussed *Hippie Sex*, the cover of which promises, "FREE SEX . . . PROSTITUTION . . . LSD . . . FLAG PARTIES . . . MAKE LOVE NOT WAR . . . MARIJUANA . . . BONDAGE . . . HOMOSEXUALS." The author declares in his introduction that the book will discuss "Love-ins, sex orgies, communal living, the 'hang loose' attitude of the hippies." Sixty-two percent of our sample considered themselves hippies during the Sixties, and it's instructive to compare their attitudes and experiences with the "professor's" frenzied stereotype.

WAS THERE A SEXUAL REVOLUTION?

When asked if they felt during the Sixties personally involved in a sexual revolution, 28% of the people we surveyed said no. One man takes the historical view: "People have always made love

163

whenever they could. New chemicals (the pill) and freer attitudes simply increased the available outlets for sexual expression. Eighteenth-century France is one place to look to see that there was really no sexual revolution in the 60's."

A woman explains that she didn't think she'd been involved in a sexual revolution "because my girlfriend, who *was* involved, slept with 45 guys and I've still only slept with 6." And another woman says, "I didn't have sexual relations until 1968, and until 1971 it was with the same person."

But having sex with a lot of people was not necessarily considered a sexual revolution. A Texas accountant says, "I would not term my experiences 'revolutionary,' just pleasantly promiscuous." And according to another man, "If a sexual revolution is fucking a lot, then I did. If it incorporates things like the rights of women, I'm not sure if my involvement meant a damn thing."

This kind of thinking led 21% of our respondents to say they were "not sure" if they had been involved in a sexual revolution. There has always been some uncertainty about what constitutes a sexual revolution, and whether or not one really happened in the Sixties.

"I might have behaved the same way with or without a media-publicized 'sexual revolution.' "

But half of the people we polled are quite certain that they personally experienced a change in the sexual atmosphere during the Sixties. These people tend to be the ones who were most active in the counter-culture.

WHO FELT PERSONALLY INVOLVED IN A SEXUAL REVOLUTION IN THE SIXTIES?

	% of All Respondents	% of Activists	% of Non-activists	% of Drug Users	% of Non-Drug Users
Involved	49	63	41	64	28
Not involved	28	19	38	15	51
Not sure	21	16	21	21	19

THE FIRST TIME

"Too Much Sex On Campus" complained a 1966 headline in the *Ladies' Home Journal.* This may or may not have been the case, depending upon your upbringing or your appetite. The truth is that during the Sixties, college was the setting for most of Woodstock Nation's "first time." This is clearly shown by the fact that the average age at which our respondents lost their virginity was 18, the year when our largely college-educated group left home and became freshmen and freshwomen. But was this something new? One man comments, "I was just being the adolescent that I was ... might've been getting laid but it was pretty much in the spirit of my father before me who was just another suave Joe College getting 'his.' "

What does appear to have been a new development was the tendency for people to have sex at an earlier age. While 21% of respondents 32 to 37 years old waited until they were at least 22, only 7% of those 25 to 27 years old waited that long to have sex. If there was a new atmosphere of open-mindedness, then it certainly allowed younger people to experiment with sex, as shown by the fact that 19% of those born between 1950 and 1952 had sex at 15 or earlier—nearly twice as many as those born before 1950.*

There was, according to some of our respondents, a certain amount of pressure to experiment with sex at an early age. A New York designer says she felt at the time that "virginity became an embarrassing state." "I was still kind of young," says another woman, now employed by the army, "but I knew that being 16 and still a virgin was bad news." The result was that younger people during the Sixties generally had more opportunities to engage in sex, or as one man puts it, "I got laid more than my older brother."

*The increasing acceptability of premarital sex has been a national trend. Robert Wuthnow reports in *The Consciousness Reformation*: "Between 1969 and 1973, the proportion of persons in national Gallup polls saying premarital sex is wrong dropped from 68% to 48% ... significant in light of the fact that somewhat similar questions in 1937 and in 1959 had shown no change during that period." Wuthnow also cites Gallup figures showing that the nationwide percentage of college students with premarital sex experience rose from 51% in 1969 to 63% in 1971.

165

Sex without marriage was an experience that many respondents cite as revolutionary.

"I slept with men and did not feel guilty about the fact that I was unmarried and having sex."

"I had pre-marital intercourse and would not have done it five years earlier because society had not yet permitted."

"I decided not to 'save it' until I was married."

"I lost my (so-called) virginity (I think it's a dumb patriarchal concept) to a total stranger (male) in a free clinic. (Yes, in the clinic!)."

THE LOVE LIFE OF WOODSTOCK NATION

"There was the time all the girls got naked one summer day by the river and we painted them fluorescent and flower power ... Fun!!!"

"I spent 3½ hours with 21 bikers from a club in Virginia (it was the first time I met them—I later became club Mama). Everyone earned their 'red wings' and then stood in line while I balled them all. Pretty weird. But I enjoyed it. Don't think I could do it today though!"

"I attended a psychedelic wedding reception with lights, drugs and nudity, all my private parts exposed. Literally, I was in a new world."

"While I was living in a commune in San Francisco, all of the inhabitants of the house were sleeping with each other interchangeably."

"I once took a course in marriage at the Berkeley Free School and after three lessons it turned into an all-out orgy. I left."

These people (not counting the one who left) are probably the orgiasts to whom the author of *Hippie Sex* was referring, but they are in the minority. Only 20% of Woodstock Nation were ever participants in a sex orgy. Yet there does seem to have been some basis for the notion that hippies dispensed "free sex." It turns out that 54% say they had one-night stands with people they didn't care very much about. A 30-year-old Alaska woman explains, "As a former loose-loined lass, I guess I was involved with treating sex

166

as something not to be taken too seriously—the old, 'if it feels good . . .' "

"I tried out having sexual liaisons with people I expected no future commitment with. I think that women before the Sixties generally had sexual encounters with people they hoped to form lasting relationships with only."

"People were freer about sex. I remember sleeping wtih strangers very light-heartedly, in groups of more than two."

In 1967, Lewis Yablonsky, a professor with real credentials, made an expedition to the hip worlds of the East Village and Haight-Ashbury. He observed that: "Hip sex is not 'free love.' Many 'untuned-in' sailors, students and 'dirty old men' who gravitate to the hip community for sex become angry when they are rejected by the love children. Sex is not free—one must be resonant to the feelings of the potential sex mate. For people fully tuned-in, sex is 'free,' plentiful, and from all reports, a 'groove' (great) in the hippie world."*

Although Yablonsky sounds a bit like Malinowski among the Trobriand Islanders, his report happens to be confirmed by our findings. One female respondent describes it this way: "I really liked the way if a person looked like a head, you could smoke dope and make love with no hang-ups, 'cause you were all part of the same persuasion. It really cut down on all the dating bullshit."

How much of the sex that went on during the Sixties was of the kinky variety the press so often twittered about? Well, it's obvious that some people were looking to experiment with unusual kicks. A popular Day-Glo poster of the era showed a series of love-making positions (suitable for double-jointed gymnasts) taken from the Oriental sex manual called *The Kama Sutra of Vatsayana*, and both the poster and the book were common fixtures in hip pads. How many tried to duplicate every position in the *Kama Sutra* (both literally and almost literally)? Just 17% of our respondents say they did.

Exactly how much sex *was* going on? If our respondents' memories serve them well, it seems that the average number of sex

*The Hippie Trip, 1973.

partners people had during the Sixties was 12. Women had a slightly lower average of 11. The fact that women almost matched men in their sexual experimentation marks a departure from the old double standard. (See table opposite.)

But how much bed-hopping actually occurred? Of our respondents, 17% had sex with more than 20 partners. The majority, 53%, had less than 11 partners, and there were 28% who had sex with only 1 to 3 partners.

"I had more relationships in one year (1969) than I did in the previous five years," says one woman.

The consequences of promiscuity were sometimes unfortunate. About 15% of Woodstock Nation contracted venereal disease. And 26% report they acquired crab lice. If you were involved in the sexual revolution, you were much more likely to be visited with these afflictions; 20% of the sexual revolutionaries caught VD (compared with only 6% of those *not* involved), and 35% caught crabs (while only 12% of the uninvolved were itching).*

Close to 14% of the women surveyed say they had an abortion during the Sixties. The proportion is slightly higher (19%) among those women who felt they were involved in a sexual revolution. The rate might have been even higher had it not been for the new form of chemical contraception. "I left home and got on the birth control pill my first semester at college," comments one woman. "My friends and I considered it very IN."

The liberating effects of the Pill may account for the fact that somewhat more women than men (52%, compared with 47%) believe they were involved in a sexual revolution. A woman recalls the experience of "going to Planned Parenthood for the Pill, along with most of my girlfriends, and cutting school to do so." Another woman describes the changes that occurred in her life: "I, a nice Catholic girl, Latin Honor Society, Junior Catholic Daughter of the Year from Grosse Pointe, Michigan, minor in theology, a virgin at marriage, began to use the Pill, have extra-marital affairs, and fantasize open marriage."

But was it all just physical? Wasn't this supposed to be the "Love Generation?" Doesn't anybody mention love?

---

*A-200, a popular remedy for crabs, was the only nationally sold product to advertise regularly in the underground press.

168

The answer is yes. Not only did 73% of the people in Wood-stock Nation say that during the Sixties they fell in love more than once, but 76% followed the advice of the Steven Stills song to "Love the One You're With." One woman rhapsodizes: "I was in love with everyone! Men, women, all were equally capable of love for me and I for them. I still have some of those feelings left, but I find it hard to love people with the openness of the 60's. It seemed we were all involved in a feeling of loving everything. Maybe it was the drugs, but it was a wonderful feeling."

BODY COUNT—PROMISCUITY IN THE SIXTIES

	All Respond-ents	Males	Females	Activists	Non-Activists	Drug Users	Non-Drug Use
Did not have sex with anyone in the 60s	15%	12%	17%	9%	21%	2%	34%
Had sex with:							
1–3 persons	28%	26%	30%	20%	33%	18%	39%
4–10	25%	27%	22%	27%	20%	27%	12%
11–20	13%	15%	11%	18%	9%	18%	5%
21–50	10%	10%	11%	14%	9%	17%	5%
51 or more	7%	7%	7%	10%	5%	15%	—
Average number of sex partners	12	12	11	15	10	19	5

"In 1967 I drove to the beach in my 1950 hearse with a couple friends. I met a boy who had just come back from India, or so he said. We smoked that incredible hash he had. I loved it. Then we fucked."

Are pot, hashish, and LSD aphrodisiacs? It's not exactly a medi-cally proven fact, but 57% of all the people we surveyed (users and non-users alike) are inclined to agree that "drugs improve sexual pleasure." It was the heavy drug users who felt most like participants in a sexual revolution. They averaged the largest number of sex partners during the Sixties (19, compared with everybody else's average of 12). Apparently, the drug scene at-tracted people who were naturally more adventurous and willing to break conventions. And it is likely that the worn-out come-on line, "Come on up to my place and have a drink," was superseded

169

by the much more effective, "Come on up to my place and smoke a joint." It didn't always turn out so well for everyone involved, as one woman relates: "When I was a senior in high school, I was turned on by my junior boyfriend. It was the only time I ever blacked out completely (to the Mothers of Invention). I thought I was being raped."

And then there was the experience of one sorry fellow, who recalls: "A friend of mine from the army came over and we smoked hash. I got zonked and he balled my chick (he got beat up!)."

But the majority of heavy drug users (66%) are inclined to believe that drugs improve sexual pleasure. One woman told us, "I enjoy getting stoned and do so often. Grass has made me more sexually attuned and able to enjoy it more." And another woman states that her best experience of the entire decade was "fucking on mescaline!"

Drugs may not have caused the sexual revolution—but they obviously helped.

THE HIPPIE AS HOMOSEXUAL

When Peter Fonda and Dennis Hopper walk into the southern roadside joint in *Easy Rider*, the rednecks snicker at the bikers' long hair. "Faggots!" they taunt. War resisters and protestors were often labeled "peace creeps" by detractors, implying that there was something perverse and unmanly about opposing the Vietnam War. Abbie Hoffman, in *Revolution for the Hell of It*, describes a scene in the police station after a 1968 demonstration in New York City: "In the back room three cops are working over one demonstrator who has his arms handcuffed behind his back. They beat him for a good ten minutes with fists and clubs . . . . They call us 'scumbags' and 'fairies' . . . and one says, 'You pull dese guys' pants off and they ain't got no pecker, just a little piece of flesh.' It sure seems they got this sex hang-up."

All arguments about political position and sexual preference aside, let it be noted that just 2% of our sample say that their sexual preference during that decade was gay, and 6% say they were bisexual. For these people, the sexual revolution often involved (as a 35-year-old teacher from Texas puts it) "coming to grips with my own homosexuality."

"I had to confront my gay side and realize I wasn't a freak, and that it's a matter of human rights. I took part in the sexual revolution by writing pro-gay rights manifestoes, articles, and a book."

"Being gay in itself was revolutionary. Also, in the late 60's I began sleeping around more in an effort to see if love and sex could truly be separate. I began sleeping with friends with the idea that sex could be an extension of friendship. To me, anyway, this was revolutionary."

"I got involved with several different types of people, both emotionally and sexually. Learned what sex was all about, learned how to pick up a guy. I met a guy out at a lake skinny-dipping, and told him he was the most beautiful guy I had ever seen. Two days later he kicked me out, but that was cool because I told him I would stay as long as he wanted me to."

Increased personal tolerance for sexual experimentation during the Sixties is what some people cite as evidence of their involvement in a sexual revolution. A woman who indicates that her sexual preferences have always been "straight" says, "I had more sexual experiences with varied men and had an affair with a man and a woman. I felt good about it. No guilt."

There is evidence, though, that as liberating as the Sixties were, homosexuality did not really become acceptable until the Seventies. In the latter decade, compared with the former there are twice as many people (5%) who say their sexual preference is gay, and the same is true of bisexuals, who increase from 6% in the Sixties to 11% in the Seventies.

"In the 60's I began to readily lose my sexual inhibitions. Yet, accepting the fact that I was gay—long after I came out—came much later. Perhaps it's still coming."

"I was not really that sexually active, except with my girlfriend, until I turned gay. By then the 60's were over."

171

THE PHONY REVOLUTION

"The rebels of the 60's are adrift in a sea of permissiveness," warned *Time* in a 1964 cover story on "Sex in the U.S." But in many ways, the Sixties were an era of repression. Lenny Bruce was labeled a "sick comic" and repeatedly arrested for obscenity. *Eros* magazine, tame by the standards of the late Seventies, was also declared obscene and its publisher, Ralph Ginzburg, sent to jail. Linda LeClair, described in the press as "Barnard's Kiss-and-Tell Girl," revealed in 1968 that she had been living off campus with her boyfriend for two years and was promptly suspended for violating the university's *in loco parentis* rules. Colleges still had curfews, separate dorms for men and women, and limited visiting hours that were strictly supervised by "floor monitors." High schools enforced dress codes that prohibited blue jeans, tight skirts, clinging sweaters and—in some cases—those shiny patent-leather shoes that could possibly reflect a girl's underwear. Underground newspapers faced numerous legal challenges for printing "obscene" cartoons by Robert (Mr. Natural) Crumb, Spain (Trashman) Rodriguez and others. And on his television show, Ed Sullivan (who introduced the Beatles to America) refused to allow the Rolling Stones to sing the original version of "Let's Spend the Night Together." Instead, they sang "Let's Spend Some Time Together."

"People talked about being liberated," comments one of our respondents, "but it was in part an effort on the part of the media to titillate the straights. Most people were fairly uptight."

But what about the rise of Hugh Hefner, the self-proclaimed leader of the sexual revolution, whose *Playboy* magazine changed the image of sex in America in 1958? By 1964, his magazine had a tremendous circulation, with 68% of its readers between eighteen and thirty-four—or so an article in *Newsweek* reported on January 6, 1964. However, Woodstock Nation wasn't buying it. The counter-culture seems to have felt that Hefner and his *Playboy* philosophy were part of the establishment they were rebelling against.

"Month after month," wrote former SDS member Jeff Shero in

172

the underground *Austin Rag*, "Hugh Hefner in the Playboy philosophy beats the tired dog of puritanism. . . . The real Playboy philosophy, however, appears throughout the magazine in the cartoons, photos, and advertising. This advertising-promoted view of sex is so blatant and sterile that one would think it would be taken as a joke."* While this may seem like an extreme reaction, in our list of newsmakers Hefner himself scored only 12% in the "admired and influenced by" category. Those who had been most impressed by him during the Sixties were in the oldest age group, and his influence on males was 20%, as compared with 3% among females.

To find the real sexual revolution, we must look beyond the *Playboy* philosophy, to the actual experiences of the men and women within Woodstock Nation.

SOMETHING HAPPENED

There *were* real changes in the sexual atmosphere during the Sixties. Even some of the people who say they were not personally involved in a sexual revolution during that time admit that sexual behavior was somehow different from what it had been before. One woman comments: "There was a lot of sex pressure and an atmosphere of promiscuity. I was not directly affected, but was conscious of the atmosphere and perhaps less afraid of sex than I would have been had I been 19 in 1957."

Without a doubt, the widespread availability of the Pill had an impact on people. Women mentioned this fact more often than men.

"I knew that once I started the pill I had what I felt was to be almost limitless freedom in sexual practices. I knew this was a radical departure from the woman's traditional role as the reluctant, worried participant. I forgot about VD and how casual sex would fuck up my head."

There was also a relaxing of racial and class barriers. The civil rights struggle and the great obsession with youth invested racial minorities and the young with romantic appeal. As apolitical an

*"Playboy's Tinseled Seductress," *The Austin Rag*, October 10, 1966.

observer as fashion designer Rudi Gernreich—the man responsible for the topless bathing suit—told *Fortune* magazine in 1969: "Haute couture doesn't have the same meaning any more because money, status, and power no longer have the same meaning. Now fashion starts in the streets. . . . That's why I watch kids." Some sons and daughters of the white middle class define their personal sexual revolution as the opportunity to cross racial and class barriers in their sexual affairs.

"I was able to openly have a relationship with a black man."

"I slept with a black girl at the age of 18."

"My first love affair was with a sexy, Jewish woman-of-the-world (and me an uncircumcised gentile!)"

Something was obviously going on. Many respondents report they weren't sure what it was, or how to act. One 25-year-old woman (who came of age in the late Sixties) says, "I was trying to figure out what was going on in the regular sense."

Others timorously explored the new possibilities. "I was so hung up!" reports another woman. "But I did (God help me) have . . . you know, pre-marital sex!"

But the experience most frequently mentioned by men is one in which women made the first move.

"I got propositioned by an older woman in Golden Gate Park while listening to Janis Joplin."

"At a concert once some girl walked up to me and grabbed my balls, took me in the bushes, blew me and left. Never got her name."

In reality, these men are describing their own sexual revolutions in terms of the new freedom of women to find sexual satisfaction.

"I finally got a chance to score the foxiest chick I knew. When the big moment came, I jumped on her and pumped a few times, got off and jumped off. She called me an asshole, set out to teach me how she wanted her sex. I received 'oral instructions' and have never forgotten them. I'd like to thank her again."

"Three aggressive women sexually attacked me at a commune in Madison, Wisconsin, simultaneously getting me off and explaining feminist dialectic."

Women agree that the freedom to make their own choices—

174

even the freedom to lecture men on feminist dialectic—was what the sexual revolution was all about.

"I felt much more freedom with men and more comfortable with men, partying and having sex, getting high, or whatever I wanted to do."

"I could pick up a guy and take him home with me for one night, and it was my choice. I was in control and I didn't feel he would think I was a 'slut.' My men friends could accept my right and desire to do the same as them. Actually, I think many men never got that far."

"I had no guilt or second thoughts about having sex for sex's sake. If it felt good, I did it, and if someone excited me I'd make sure we ended up in bed."

"I had several different lovers during the last years of my marriage (my ex-husband still doesn't know that). I was able to have these experiences on my own—and that's what was most important to me."

As a man from Kansas City comments on his questionnaire, "There has been an enormous change of perception of women's (and of course men's) roles."

Certainly, the women's liberation movement was not an invention of the counter-culture. Even as this country was beginning, Abigail Adams was politely reminding her husband at the Constitutional Congress to "remember the ladies." But the women's movement of the Seventies had its roots in the Sixties. Was this because the contradictions between ideals and practice were so blatant?

The civil rights struggles emphasized the *idea* of equality, yet Stokely Carmichael declared publicly that "the only position for women in SNCC is prone." The student-power campaigns sought to make the universities more democratic, yet the student leaders were mostly male. In fact, the proportion of women activists in our group (39%) is significantly lower than the percentage of activists who were men (61%).

The culture itself was not particularly supportive of women. Rock and roll music was supposed to be liberating, but the Rolling Stones were singing "Under My Thumb." Underground newspapers expressed outrage against the system's exploitation of workers for profit, yet the pages were often crammed with advertisements for X-rated movies and massage parlors. Communes formed with the intention of creating an alternative to bourgeois life, but women were still doing the cooking, washing the dishes, harvesting the herbs, rolling the joints, taking care of the kids. The entire counter-culture was founded on the principle of "do your own thing," but too often, women discovered, this applied only to the men. The relaxation of sexual prohibitions seems not to have been so "liberating" after all. "Women couldn't say no without being called frigid or hung-up," complains one woman.

Another says: "Guys just refused to take NO for an answer any more, so you gave in because you got tired of hassling and giving reasons not to—but you didn't get much out of it. The word for it is 'submission,' for no really good reason."

In a landmark 1970 essay entitled "Goodbye to All That," feminist Robin Morgan wrote: "It hurts to understand that at Woodstock or Altamont a woman could be declared uptight or a poor sport if she didn't want to be raped."

This essay, in the New York underground newspaper *Rat*, uncovered a kind of counter-cultural Watergate, as Morgan enumerated a list of men prominent in Woodstock Nation and detailed their various acts of antifemale behavior. It was a breakthrough for a movement that had obviously been a long time coming, and a warning, too:

"Goodbye to Hip Culture and the so-called Sexual Revolution, which has functioned towards women's freedom as did the Reconstruction toward former slaves—reinstituted oppression by another name . . . Goodbye to a beautiful new ecology movement that could fight to save us all if it would stop tripping off women as earth-mother types and frontier chicks . . ."*

The change had been taking place for some time, but even so, many men were hit hard by the women's liberation movement. As one male respondent sadly explains:

"Women's lib changed the whole (if you'll excuse the pun) ball game. I was a strike-out champ."

*Thomas King Forcade, ed., *Underground Press Anthology*, 1972.

How did Woodstock Nation react to the women's movement? The truth is that men's enthusiasm for it lags somewhat behind women's. For example, while 83% of the women we surveyed agree completely that abortion is every woman's right, 73% of the men feel the same way. But men and women agree to a very large extent on matters relating to the rights of women. In fact, the consensus of support for the women's movement parallels the consensus during the Sixties on the war issue, and today the values of feminism are as widely accepted in Woodstock Nation as pot-smoking and the "do your own thing" ethic.

ATTITUDES TOWARD WOMEN'S RIGHTS

	% Who Agree Somewhat or Completely	% Who Disagree Somewhat or Completely
It's okay for a woman to initiate having sex.	93	4
It's okay for a woman to ask a man out.	94	3
Abortion is every woman's right.	85	9
Magazines like *Hustler* exploit women.	66	19
Women should be passive while having sex.	6	83

This was the real sexual revolution. The wild, orgiastic sexuality that is so often associated with the Sixties was largely a fantasy of those outside the counter-culture. It was wild sometimes, but according to the people we surveyed, not that wild—and what was wild was nothing new. More often, Woodstock Nation was a warm, slightly confused place where people really tried to mean it when they used the word "love." The sexual revolution and its context within the counter-culture are summed up perfectly by a woman who describes a truly radical experience: "Sleeping in a bed in our commune one night with four other people (two men, three women) and *not* having sex."

7

The Seventies

"I knew the 60's were over
when Bambu started putting
the universal price code on
packages of rolling papers."

—A RESPONDENT

Whatever happened to the Sixties? Some say they ended the day the music died.

"When the deaths of Joplin, Brian Jones, and Hendrix occurred, I felt very sad. It seemed that this was an irrevocable ending of an era."

"When the Jefferson Airplane became the Jefferson Starship, the 60's were over."

"At the Atlanta Pop Festival II, July 1970, while watching the crowd, I noticed a forced feeling of doing Woodstock again."

"It was all over in 1973 when they wouldn't have any more Blues and Jazz Festivals here in Ann Arbor."

"The 60's were over when concerts weren't as much fun, and I moved to Brownsville, Texas, where I think the 60's never began."

The fact is that people who grew up in the Sixties don't get as excited about current music as they used to. As one respondent expresses it: "The music doesn't get me off. The Stones haven't done anything since 'Let It Bleed,' so now I'm into jazz and am very negative about world survival."

Jazz actually has jumped in popularity by nearly 50% (with the youngest people surveyed showing the strongest preference for it). If world survival depends upon rock and roll music, then we may be in trouble; the percentage of people in our group who like rock dropped from 87% in the Sixties to 73% in the Seventies. *Rolling Stone* magazine, which took off on the big wave of Sixties rock and was once regarded favorably by 50% of our respondents, is now popular among only 34%. It's not that people have suddenly begun to dislike rock and roll (most of the defections are now registered in the "neutral" column), but rather that they simply aren't as fond of the new music as they were (and in some cases still are) of the old.

For example, acid rock (like LSD) had fallen out of favor from a positive rating in the Sixties of 67% to only 36% in the Seventies. But our respondents did not contract disco fever as a replacement—just 29% danced the Hustle (compared to 84% who danced the Twist in the Sixties), and even fewer people liked discotheques in the Seventies (26%) than in the Sixties (35%). Not only is disco rejected, but the new wave of Seventies music called Punk Rock also gets thumbs down; only 11% of those we surveyed liked it. One respondent comments: "I feel that the music was a powerful vehicle for propagating the concepts of the Aquarian Age. It's disturbing to me that popular music has deteriorated so. I feel that the quality of the music is an indicator of the consciousness."

The change in music was mentioned by 7% of the people in response to the question "When, for you personally, were the Sixties over?" But political events were cited by 22% as having marked the end of the era.

"The 60's ended with the election of Nixon in 1968, and Kent State and Jackson State slaughter of students in 1970."

"It was over in Miami Beach in 1972 when I was gassed repeatedly during protests at the Republican Convention. It made me give up hope of non-violent change."

"The sixties ended sometime between the prison uprising at Attica in 1972, and the appearance of the Symbionese Liberation Army."

"When Rennie Davis and Eldridge Cleaver lost their minds, the 60's were finished."

"The 60's were over at the end of Vietnam and Watergate."

But the largest number (32%) of the people we surveyed date the end of the Sixties from the moment they found themselves working, marrying, and settling down in various ways.

"The Sixties were over when I put on a tuxedo to get married in a hotel (May, 1971)."

"The 60's thing ended for me about 1972, when I quit the MC club and my first child was born."

"In 1972, when I got busted for drugs and had to get married, or go to prison—the party was over! Had to start re-evaluating my life and what drugs had done to me."

"Probably in late '72. I was just married and suddenly felt responsibility. My marriage didn't work, however—I'm now divorced; but now I feel responsible for *me*. And that's good."

"When I came home from bumming around Colorado to get a regular 9 to 5 job again—'73."

"1975 when I got my Ph.D. and couldn't get a job."

"When I left school in 1975. After college, it was all over."

"In 1974 when I moved back to the town I grew up in."

"When I returned from a psychedelic tour of Europe, Africa, and the Middle East to the rather sobering atmosphere of Houston, Texas, of all places."

"Dec. 18, 1969. Ah yes, flunked out and had to leave many good friends, memories, and a terrific girlfriend. Went home to sell shoes and face the draft. The party was over."

"About 1972, when I went back to wearing make-up, started wearing platforms, and realized—lo and behold—I have to work for a living."

"When I took a full-time job making swimming pools in 1969."

"By the winter of 1972, when I was pretty well-established as a teacher, in psychoanalysis, and not using drugs any more."

Does this mean that the Sixties were nothing more than a giant sock hop, a nationwide orgy of adolescence to be quelled by pimple creams and time? The answer, for some of this generation, was undoubtedly yes. But the changes in style, music, and living situations that people point to as turning points were never what Woodstock Nation was really about. Our respondents have demonstrated that the most visible features of the counter-culture—the clothes, the style, the music, the rituals—were symbols of deeper values and ideals. And the respondents who mention personal ideals and inner values are the 14% who say the Sixties *never* ended.

"For me personally the 60's are alive and well inside me and always will be. I internalized the good of the 60's and left behind the bad."

"They aren't completely over for me yet. My ideals are the same. Also, most of my friends are in their early 20's and I'm reliving it with them."

"I like to think they're not over—many of my values of the 60's I still think are good. Unfortunately, our society won't let me live exactly as I'd like to. More demands and pressures often make you lose sight of things. The 70's really came to me this year because I had a baby—and in some ways had to stop being a kid myself."

"In a certain sense, I still don't feel that the 60's are over. The spirit, the sense of community remains with all of us who were part of it—even the business executive gets stoned—in some sense we are all connected, therefore—even today, and even if it's with and through drugs and not, alas, through love."

"Those who know me well seem to feel the Sixties have *not* ended for me yet; I have begun to feel retarded as my continuing social activism bounces off my contemporaries' mellow apathy."

It seems that when veterans of the Sixties look around them, they see many changes from one decade to the next. Yet, looking inside themselves, things haven't changed much at all.

DID THE SIXTIES DIE?

Did the Sixties die or didn't they? Our coroner's jury has to reach a verdict without having a body—and there's some question of whether it was murder or suicide.

The Burn-Out Factor

"The kids burned themselves out destroying other things," declares journalist Garry Wills, using a mechanistic approach. For him, the Sixties were a semierotic temper tantrum fed by negative energies that ran out in the Seventies. "With nothing left to confront, the movement did not exist—fell into post-coital lassitude. Fires burn themselves out; one can't stay passionate forever—which leads to a new sentimentalism of the young, tears shed for the tear gas days, for glad cries about offing the pigs."*

*"The Sixties," *Esquire*, October 1973.

184

Doesn't this explain why the Seventies appear devoid of political activism? Isn't it plausible that drugs, sex, and violence engulfed young people and destroyed their idealism? The Burn-Out theorists love to cite the example of Altamont, the disastrous free concert given in December 1969 by the Rolling Stones to cap a nationwide tour—a concert that left three people dead, 300,000 fans depressed, and the press mourning the demise of the counter-culture. A dispatch from Liberation News Service headlined "End of the Age of Aquarius" declared that at Altamont "a generation was stripping itself naked."*

Some individuals (we know a few personally) may have overdone it, burning their joints at both ends, or whatever. But our survey has not turned up a generation of bomb-throwing, Dionysian dope fiends. Two thirds of our respondents *were not* political activists, and those who were destroyed little more than the soles of their Frye boots while marching in demonstrations. Two thirds of our respondents *were not* frequent users of drugs, and those who were report, for the most part, soft landings. And the sexual revolution had less in common with Nero's Rome than with the 1920s suffrage movement.

As for the idea that Altamont was the counter-culture's apocalypse, very few respondents even mention it, although a handful (5%) were there. Mick Jagger's devil will have to look elsewhere for sympathy.

The Big Sell-Out

"Everyone wanted to save the world and mankind so sociology and psychology bloomed with good-hearted people who wanted to work within the system for change. But there were so many BA's and BS's in soc. and psych. that they got swallowed up in the system trying to make a decent living. I have several friends with these degrees who are handing out food stamps and doing investigation for Welfare. Helping to save the world? Hardly. But that's what happened to the brotherhood dream of the Sixties—eaten up by the harsh realities of the Seventies."

*Thomas King Forcade, ed., *Underground Press Anthology*, 1972.

185

The Kansas City computer operator who offers this explanation believes in the Big Sell-Out. The idea is that counter-cultural and political activists of the Sixties lacked complete commitment to their goals and ideals, so that at the first opportunity to join the establishment and make money, they just shrugged their shoulders and climbed aboard.

People frequently use this theory to explain why so many veterans of the Sixties are today gainfully employed, maintaining bank accounts, houses, mortgages, credit cards, and families. Also, it seems to account for haircuts, three-piece suits, and the disappearance of most of the counter-cultural style.

This might make sense if our respondents, particularly the political activists, were making fat incomes in the Seventies—but they weren't.

COMPARATIVE INCOMES IN THE SEVENTIES

Per Year	% of Activists	% of Non-Activists	% of All Respondents
Under $8000	38	30	34
$8000 to $9999	14	13	14
$10,000 to $14,999	27	30	27
$15,000 to $19,999	11	13	12
$20,000 to $24,999	5	7	6
$25,000 or more	4	5	5

Whether in reality the answer is yes or no, 84% of our respondents perceive themselves in the Seventies as *not* having "sold out."

The Media Killed the Sixties

In his questionnaire, an Atlanta broadcaster complains, "The media exploited and distorted the counter-culture, which was and is a very real phenomenon," and 43% of our respondents agree. If the Sixties were murdered, then perhaps, some suggest, the perpetrators were the media.

"The media destroyed the counter-culture by over-exposure."

"I would say that outside of the underground press, media

186

didn't have a lot to do with creating the feeling of the 60's. But the straight media brought about its demise."

It would be difficult to prove that the press and television committed what might be called decacide. For one thing, the murder weapon usually cited is overexposure, or repetition—precisely what most advertising agencies use to sell their ideas to as many people as possible. In fact, some of our respondents have already testified to being "turned on" to the counter-culture in the first place by magazines, newspapers, and television. For another, complaining about media distortion places one in suspect company, as an Illinois legal assistant notes: "I felt the media reflected the 60's as they were. The gripe with the media was Nixon and Agnew's, not ours."

The Depressed and Disillusioned Crowd Theory

This is one of the most popular explanations of what happened in the post-Sixties period and is so widely accepted as truth that all a magazine writer has to do is toss off a few lines that obliquely allude to it, as one film critic does at the end of a less than enthusiastic review: "But like the dreams of the 60's that [the protagonist] mourns, one wishes it had all turned out better."*

Behind this theory is the idea that the Seventies were a reaction to the previous era, and a deliberate return to apathy. "The Seventies don't exist," opines Howard Junker in *Esquire*. "We agreed not to have the Seventies because we'd been had by the Sixties. Too much hype. Too many dreams abused."†

The assumption here is that the hopes and dreams of the Sixties were shattered in the Seventies, and that lofty goals rose sadly beyond reach. Signs of defeat are read into everything. As Junker tells it: "The perfect Seventies symbol was the Pet Rock, which just sat there doing nothing. . . . It was good to be laid back. As if narcolepsy weren't an ever-present danger, Quaaludes became the key drug."

This supposedly accounts for the notion that the Seventies were

*David Ansen, "60's Hangover," *Newsweek*, February 8, 1978.
†Howard Junker, "Who Erased The Seventies?", *Esquire*, December 1977.

apathetic, a "return to the Fifties," and so boring that people dedicated themselves to decadence and trivia, disco dancing, art deco furniture, cocaine, and *Star Wars.* In other words, after the serious Sixties, the frowns turned upside down into "Have a Nice Day" smile buttons.

This theory—and the answer to the question of whether the Sixties are dead or alive—depends on whether or not veterans of the Sixties are truly the sad bunch of failures and quitters they are assumed to be. Have things really turned out so differently than was hoped? What actually were the dreams of the Sixties that, some say, have been so abused?

DAYDREAM BELIEVERS

Many bold plans were announced to the world by the dreamers of Woodstock Nation. In the midst of the cultural warfare of the Sixties, the idea of the alternative society—a kind of hip promised land—was widely endorsed. Half of the people we surveyed (52%) believed during that time that it was possible to establish a viable alternative culture in America.

To some this meant simply going back to the rural life, settling in a self-sufficient commune with a family made up of close friends. To others it meant pushing for a sort of cultural nationalism, or even a popular uprising against "Pig Amerika," complete with barricades and guerrilla warfare. At the latter extreme were groups like the anarchist White Panthers in Ann Arbor, Mich., who modeled themselves after the Black Panther Party and declared that "our program of rock and roll, dope and fucking in the streets is a program of total freedom for everyone. . . . We are LSD-driven total maniacs in the universe."*

In the Sixties, the hopes and dreams of 14% of our respondents coincided with those of the White Panthers; as one told us, "I rather hoped for a violent revolution, followed by the deprivation of middle-class comforts to the wealthy like another depression with IWW and Ben Walker's army."

---

*Thomas King Forcade, ed., *Underground Press Anthology*, 1972.

188

And 11% had no hopes or dreams—"I lived for the moment, never looked that far ahead."

But for most of the people we surveyed, hopes and dreams for the future were fairly traditional. Some of the things they mention specifically are:

Peace—28% *

"A huge Woodstock Nation, worldwide peace and prosperity."

A new society based on love and human worth—19%

"My dream was the land would get cleaned up, you could do your own thing, it would be cool, and there would be no hassles I couldn't deal with."

Equal justice for minorities—10%

"I envisioned that a viable, broad, grass roots power base for blacks would be realized. I dreamed that black people's awareness would change from consumer to producer and eventually owner. I dreamed of real power at the polls and in the market place."

The majority, though, had less specific hopes for a better life in the Seventies. They say they imagined simply that "life would be better" in various ways.

"I hoped Bobby Kennedy would be President, that there would be peace and a government which was responsive to the people."

"I dreamed of a looser country, a more tolerant citizenry."

" 'What if they gave a war and nobody came?' I hoped to see a lot of useless professions just disappear and everybody doing really meaningful things."

"Decriminalization of marijuana. Equal rights for women. A sharing, non-possessive, communal lifestyle. Free love—non-possessive sex and love."

"I hoped there would be much emphasis on 'country living' with less traffic and more peace. I thought there would be more communes, less 'big city pitfalls.' "

*Our question was: "During the 60's, how did you envision things turning out in this country in the 70's? What was your hope? What was your dream?" Some people's responses fell into several categories, and 17% gave answers too varied to fall into any one category. For these reasons, the above percentages do not add up to 100%.

189

"I hoped that concern with spiritual harmony, and increasing flexibility, would inevitably grow as the 60's kids became influential in their communities."

"That a balance between socialism and capitalism could be found so that no one starved or was homeless. That blacks would be absorbed into the general population and have equal opportunity. More public works projects. No more wars. Legalized marijuana and mescaline. That life would become one long happy *Juliet of the Spirits* and *Black Orpheus* rolled into one."

These are not wildly extravagant visions. Some of the ideas—such as reduction of penalties for marijuana use, equal opportunities for women, racial desegregation—are slowly being realized. Americans have not fought any wars since 1973, or engaged in large-scale civil disorders since the Mayday demonstrations in Washington in 1971. Are the differences between the hopes of the Sixties and the realities of the Seventies that great? Do they really warrant the frequent downbeat evaluations of this generation?

WHAT DID YOU WANT TO BE WHEN YOU GREW UP?

The difference (or lack of it) between a vision and a reality is nowhere more evident than in cases of personal dreams. We asked people to think back and recall what they once envisioned themselves doing today.

A cadre of Sixties political activists (7%) say that back then they imagined themselves in the Seventies as full-time revolutionaries. The same percentage of the heavy drug users of the Sixties say they thought that by the Seventies they would be either dead, in jail, or in hiding. "My view of myself didn't include the notion that I would live to the ripe old age of 34—it was inconceivable."

For most of these people, the future turned out quite differently and, depending upon how they look at it, better or worse than they expected. Some goals, alas, were just this side of unattainable:

"I saw myself either establishing the Kingdom of God on earth or migrating to another solar system."

"I'd be the next Montgomery Clift."

190

Others were vague but definitely not mainstream: "Anything but a 9-to-5 job with two weeks vacation a year. I thought I would never get along with straight society."

And many respondents had dreams of living in the counter-culture forever.

"Utopia. Running away to a commune, away from my straight, awful parents. Buying a van with my sister and touring the country making films about hippy communes." (Publishing, 25, female)

"Being a rock star." (Attorney, 28, male)

"Finding a good lady, living in the country, some small-scale farming, raising some chickens and goats, part-time job for basics." (Tennis teacher, 29, male)

"I pictured myself with long hair, jeans, flannel shirt, with kids, animals, and lots of people living in my house. I'm on my second marriage, dress up a lot, have no kids or other people in my house besides my husband." (Programmer, 29, female)

"Anything but this. I honestly believed things would change. Now sometimes I feel as though the 60's were a figment of my imagination." (Electronics engineer, 32, female)

However, the largest percentage of our respondents (51%) say that back in the Sixties, they foresaw that a decade later they would be doing basically what they are doing today: working.

"Same as always—working for my food and shelter, rapping with my friends, running around with petitions and writing letters to editors and the government. Not giving up!" (Technical assistant in X-ray sales, 33, female)

"I dreamed of working as an artist, living on the land, forming trusting, loving relationships with friends, taking drugs legally." (Cartoonist, 29, female)

"I play drums and I saw myself making it in a big group by the 70's. It has not happened yet, but I keep trying." (Cabbie/part-time student, 26, male)

"Being the best teacher in New York City—Plato's intellectual mid-wife, etc. Having a great love affair, books, and records." (Teacher/graduate student, 25, female)

"Getting a fun job which included bucks commensurate with my talents." (Library assistant, 26, female)

191

"Being a self-employed jeweler and artist—becoming a total woman ... working within a community of people trying to achieve fulfillment." (Jeweler, 28, female)

"During the early and middle 60's I was hoping to be a doctor, accountant or businessman. In the late 60's I was unsure, but I wanted to do something more directly to help people and change society in some way." (Vocational evaluator with the deaf, 29, male)

"I saw myself traveling around Europe and later on settling down with a family. I never made it to Europe but I do have a family." (Wife and mother, 27, female)

"I felt I would be successful in some professional career with two sheep dogs and a house on the beach, or at least I would have a career as a rock star which would allow me to have two sheep dogs and a house on the beach." (Assistant manager, 29, male)

"Living forever in an academic environment—being an English teacher, spending my time reading." (Press agent, 26, female)

"I saw myself being a hip, dedicated, ruthless, honorable civil rights lawyer." (Counselor for juvenile delinquents, 27, male)

"Enlightening the youth of America in the public school system to explore their full potential and pursue intellectual freedoms." (Legal assistant, 26, female)

"Not that different from what I am doing. I'm still 'me.' I try to think I'm changing things within the system (although it's hard). I haven't sold out, I don't rip anyone off, I try to give others the power they need and deserve. My 60's plans for myself is the 70's so far." (Social worker, 26, female)

This testimony tends to contradict the image of a generation that, in the words of Garry Wills, "burned itself out destroying other things." It seems that the Seventies met the basic expectations that the majority of our respondents had for themselves and for society, mainly because those expectations were generally more modest than most people realize.

WERE THE SEVENTIES DIFFERENT FROM THE SIXTIES?

These are the differences our respondents note when comparing the two decades.

192

Less social experimentation—10% *

"There are virtually no external manifestations of discontent with society—attempts are made at fitting in, at conformity. Manifestations of alienation are no longer sanctioned."

"There seemed to be a period of experimentation, both social and personal. The 70's seem to be a period of either consolidation (positive) or repetition (negative) of the experiments of the 60's."

Personally, I'm feeling older, more mellow—14%

"The 70's seem a more rational, thoughtful, comfortable outgrowth of the 60's innovations without the non-negotiable demands and ultimatums that could be so inequitable and egotistical."

"Time marches on, but not everything changes. The 70's are different because we have grown up. Not that I'm not still idealistic in my goals and hopes, but I don't take setbacks as the *crashing* defeats that I used to think they were in the 60's."

Less political and social upheaval—16%

"Quieter. A lot of political activity gets no publicity so people feel there is not much an individual can join."

"There is not the same explosiveness, the same sense of urgency or upheaval as there was during the 60's."

"The sense of expansion, growth, apocalypse was very positive in the 60's. In the 70's it turned back toward 'big sleep' and toward the possibility of negative apocalypse."

People are more self-centered, introspective—18%

"People are trying to figure themselves out, not join a group for identity."

"We've gone from an other-center focus to self-centered focus. That bothers me a lot."

"The 70's seem to me a time to reflect and grow from all the lessons of the 60's experiences, and use them to help grow and understand myself. And find my comfortable space."

We're dealing with the real world now—23%

"The 60's were the beginning of a new way of thinking (not so

---

*Percentage of sample mentioning these ideas in response to the question, "How are the 70's different from the 60's?" Some mentioned more than one idea.

193

'new' but so subdued in the 50's). The 70's, for me, is a chance to practice what I've learned. The 60's were a new list of priorities, the 70's are my chance to make them work."

"My energies are more devoted toward establishing myself fully in a career that will permit me to fully realize the expressive potentials I discovered in the 60's."

Disillusionment—23%

"Most of us 60's vets have become everything we revolted against. The electricity has dissipated. And where is John Lennon now?"

"Rennie Davis is selling insurance, Eldridge Cleaver is a Jesus freak, Richard Nixon is a wealthy man, Disco is mindless, Students are amoral, Mediocrity is the norm, and Remember Kent State. It's enough to make you puke!"

Of these six major differences between decades, three are cited by a total of 55% of the people—feelings of getting older, of being more self-centered, and of having to be more practical; all are related to the usual consequences of adulthood. This finding is consistent with the large number who believe the Sixties ended when they married, settled down, took steady jobs. Most people, in other words, regard the difference between the two decades as the difference between being an adult and being an adolescent. This is a profound change; no wonder a new mood pervaded the Seventies, a mood slightly sad and wistful—"Ah yes, the Sixties. Riding a chopped Harley and being single again"—and in some cases, remorseful and bitter.

But if there has been less social experimentation and less political and social upheaval in the Seventies, is it because growing older has also meant becoming more conservative? Have this generation's values changed? Have we really become "everything we revolted against"?

If the answers to these questions are yes, then the Sixties were nothing more than a time of exuberant, youthful irresponsibility, irretrievably lost. But we have already seen that many people maintain links with the Sixties counter-culture: They continue to smoke pot and endorse the results of the sexual revolution; and even in such fundamental issues as politics, their beliefs are un-

194

changed. How then does one explain the notion, prevalent both inside and outside Woodstock Nation, of a substantive discontinuity between the Sixties and the Seventies?

THE PIVOTAL MOMENT

The key is in the way people react to the query, "Did there come a time when you consciously renounced your Sixties lifestyle?" A minority of 25% report that there did come such a time.

"I was sitting on a curb in the rain, tripping—looking at how scarred-up my feet were from not wearing shoes and realizing that rich people's feet never touch the ground."

A few gave up personal ideals in order to pursue more materialistic goals.

"I became disillusioned with the response in the film-making industry to my job-hunting and realized most of all I wanted to make lots of money fast."

And frequently there was some pain involved in the process.

"Leaving my motorcycle club was a wrenching experience—hard to describe to someone who has never been a scooter person (or biker)."

Most of the people who consciously renounced their Sixties lifestyle say it was mainly a matter of changing the way they looked, or their living situation.

"It meant shaving my beard, handle-bar mustache, Zappa hairdo, and registering to vote for the first time."

"I went from Dr. Scholl's to stiletto heels, brown rice back to hot dogs."

"Better living conditions—no more lentils! Nicer clothes—less obvious freak image—working more coherently for social change."

"The choice was between living in a crisis lifestyle (moving from one crisis to the next) or setting up long-range goals. I chose the second."

"It meant moving to the city, associating with older people, having more committed relationships, looking for a straight job."

"It meant I was going to stop taking drugs with unpredictable

195

effects, get married, and live a holy life! Needless to say I wasn't playing with a full deck."

Over half the men surveyed who previously sported long hair, beards, and mustaches became more clean-cut in the Seventies. Nearly 74% of the women shaved their legs (an increase of 14%). The number of women using makeup jumped from 41% to 68%. Jeans and work shirts continued to be enormously popular, but 61% (compared with 39% during the previous decade) were interested in "wearing good-looking clothes."

However, a majority of 70% say they *did not* abruptly rid themselves of the Sixties. Some have gradually adopted different modes of living, while others still live—and look—the way they did during the Sixties.

"My lifestyle has been gradually evolving out of the straight mainstream. I now live on a commune—have for the last five years."

Many who underwent a transformation have an almost defensive attitude about it, hastening to add that, while they may look and live differently, they continue to believe in the ideals and values of the counter-culture.

"I feel and felt no reason to renounce something that had a definite personal value."

"I still try to live my life as much as possible as I did then—still listen to pretty much the same kind of music, still get stoned (only grass), still have long hair (by today's standards). Only now I have responsibilities I didn't have then and I try to keep up with the times without abandoning my beliefs."

"There is no ending. I continually transform. There were thresholds, e.g. when I cut my hair, e.g. when I ran for office. There was no renunciation."

"I kept a lot of my 60's values. I gradually dropped or modified various aspects of 60's culture with which I was no longer comfortable, but most of my lifestyle is still modified 60's."

"As the 60's euphoria dissipated, the facts of my own aging and needs slowly moved me away from that lifestyle. But I must say that I am not still *that* far away from it."

"I've made a much more gradual transition from being a student in the 60's to being a professional in the 70's. This change

196

has not entailed dropping things like smoking dope or rock music, or transformed my politics from being left of center."

THE ISSUES TODAY

For most people, moving into the Seventies did not mean shedding the values and ideals formed during the Sixties. This fact is reflected in the issues that people say are of the most concern to them today.

ISSUES OF MOST CONCERN IN THE SEVENTIES*

1. Pollution
2. Limitation of nuclear weapons
3. Marijuana decriminalization
4. Corporate power
5. Passage of Equal Rights Amendment

Each of these issues represents the continuation of battles waged during the Sixties.

The mobilization of people in the Seventies around the issues of pollution and "no nukes" shows that the spirit of the Sixties Movement survives and thrives, even when there is no war to protest. Many of the Movement's protest tactics, such as civil disobedience, leafletting, and petitioning, are now being used to stop the proliferation of nuclear plants and industrial polluters.

The fact that marijuana decriminalization is pegged third on this list proves that Woodstock Nation has not forgotten its grass roots. While the heavy drug users of the Sixties are more strongly in favor of lowering penalties against pot use, the general interest in this issue shows the pervasiveness of the "do your own thing" ethic among our respondents.

The issue of corporate power has always been one of Ralph Nader's themes, and our respondents are still following his lead. While this issue is rated fourth by our respondents in general, those who were political activists rate it as their number-two concern (after pollution), showing that they continue to entertain a radical analysis of society.

*In order of percentage of response to each issue.

197

The only issue missing from this list that might have been there during the Sixties is the issue of black people's rights. It seems that many of the people we surveyed believe, correctly or not, that this is a battle that has largely been won. A social worker in Ohio comments, "Black people fought for and gained respect, as well as positive legislation. They have a voice and are no longer in the position of powerlessness they were in before the Sixties."

Even so, feminism and the passage of the Equal Rights Amendment are civil rights issues, and they are an outgrowth of the struggles for individual rights that occupied much of the Sixties. All of the issues, in fact, are components of a single theme: the right to individuality, the right to "do your own thing."

THE NEW ACTIVISM

"I am a full-time revolutionary maniac dedicated to blowing up the state," is how one person describes his present occupation. A few people (exactly 29, if the FBI is really interested) say they are "working toward violent revolution." Half of this group is composed of veteran activists.

But when our respondents were asked what they are actually doing about the issues that concern them most, the response breaks down this way:

RESPONSE TO POLITICAL ISSUES OF THE SEVENTIES

	% of All Respondents	% of Sixties Activists
Talking and thinking about issues	36	27
Working within the system to make changes	27	28
Working toward peaceful, gradual revolution	16	24
Working toward violent revolution	3	6
Not doing very much	14	8

The hard-core half of the activist group still sees itself as actively involved in effecting social change, working both from within and from without the system. And nearly half of the total number of people surveyed also see themselves as working to change the world. One example is the 30-year-old college professor in Kansas City, who says, "I'm still rebelling and trying to change society now. Instead of throwing bricks, I'm chipping away from inside. I'm still bent (as opposed to straight) but now they label it 'eccentric professor.' "

Another example is the 31-year-old graduate student in Michigan who has shed the style of the counter-culture, but not the substance. "I have not changed my opinions about non-violence and the need for change and still carry much of the best of the 60's with me. On another level I do not use drugs any more, live in a house with a nuclear family and spend money with some enjoyment."

THE LOSS OF STYLE

It seems, then, that the Sixties did not die. There is no corpse, but rather a pile of discarded bell-bottoms, a strand of love beads, and a few handfuls of shorn-off hair. According to the people we surveyed, the Sixties *live* (although often in disguise). One working woman says, "I went into business in an area where your appearance and lifestyle make a difference. So my appearance and lifestyle are more conservative now. However, deep inside many of my feelings are still influenced by the 60's."

The style has changed, but the attitudes and outlook, for the most part, have not.

However, for some women, the Seventies have meant *more* than a change in style: Feminism has offered them a chance to realize the individualized Sixties ideal of "doing your own thing." Two women comment:

"Wouldn't be caught dead in a mini-skirt, and I decided I was through with sex without commitments (i.e. being a free lay)."

"I was tired of eating rice, or not eating, sewing patches on my jeans, wearing blue jeans that were always dirty and too long, and having to say 'yes' to sex to prove I was liberated."

It is important to note, though, that the stylistic changes have not been altogether drastic. Don't overlook the fact that natural body odor had more devotees in the Seventies than in the Sixties, nor that there was a slight increase in the number of people who like armpit hair on women—all of which corresponds with the continuing popularity of the "natural look," a symbol of integrity in the Sixties. Also, while half of the men who had long hair in the Sixties visited the barber in the Seventies, the other half still sported long hair.

Nevertheless, changing styles are the most visible sign of changing times, and the abandonment of Sixties style has deceived people—both inside and outside the counter-culture—into thinking it represents a kind of retreat, or even a defeat. Some of those who continue to hold on to the old styles, tastes, and values tend to believe they are alone in doing so.

"My present lifestyle is a direct outgrowth of the one I formed in the 60's. My ideals have changed very little, but I feel like an anachronism."

"My friends accuse me of living in the 60's. I have long hair and wear large earrings and bell bottoms, and the sight of red lips, nails, and short hair, on both women and men, doesn't turn me on."

In the Seventies, the widespread lack of visual reinforcement of Sixties values could only have contributed to the feeling of disillusionment expressed by 23% of the respondents. "I don't feel the same togetherness with others as I did then," says a 27-year-old woman from Texas. "Then, right or wrong, I felt like I knew who my friends were."

The loss of the counter-cultural style has frequently been ascribed to its commercialization and subsequent assimilation by mainstream society. But if anything, the commercialization helped spread the counter-culture among people who were sympathetic to the ideas the style symbolized. The real reason the style lost its importance in the Seventies was that it was no longer useful. A 33-year-old New Yorker says, "The styles of the 60's no longer have much symbolic value. They're mainly good for nostalgia. The important values I related to in the 60's remain true for me, although how to achieve them seems increasingly complex."

200

As we've noted earlier, the style functioned as a means of political protest for people who had been denied access to the normal political process. A sure sign that the process has yielded to change is that the counter-cultural style has largely been discarded.

WHAT IT ALL MEANS

Observers of the post-Sixties period too often perceive the counter-cultural and political movements of the Sixties as having been more radical than they really were. Because of this misconception, impossibly high goals are set for this generation—as often by critics outside the counter-culture as by the dreamers within. The true believers were inevitably due for a letdown in the Seventies, just as the critics were bound to say "We told you so."

The results of this survey consistently show that the majority of Woodstock Nation was far less radical during the Sixties than most people thought—this generation was made up of experimenters rather than crusaders. What is more, they were not poor people, nor Marxists, nor people new to this country. Woodstock Nation was always populated by the sons and daughters of the American middle class.

Feminism, environmentalism, and political activism are firmly based in American social and cultural traditions. The "do your own thing" ethic that inspires pot smokers is not so far from the rugged individualism that inspired frontier settlers in early times who moved as far away as they could from taxes, politics, and bureaucrats. The counter-culture was based on *traditional*, not radical values, so it is no wonder that the counter-culture was so rapidly absorbed into the American mainstream. As one person puts it: "What was far-out in the 60's is far-in in the 70's. The psychedelic, sexual and political revolutions have been absorbed by society but not smothered. What the 'straight world' couldn't even swallow in '67 it is digesting right now in '77."

And it is the middle class that has benefited most from changes that have occurred. It is as if an expanding middle class had discovered that it needed more freedoms, more rights. While the counter-culture of the Sixties used its outrageous clothing styles

201

as a form of political protest, it was also an assertion by middle-class people of their right to "do their own thing." It was a symbolic battle with practical applications. In the post-Sixties period, factory workers on assembly lines sport long hair and beards. Office workers wear bell-bottoms. There is no blue collar and white collar, but a complete rainbow of collars. The executive and dockworker look alike in leisure suits. The ultimate triumph of the Sixties unisex style was the pants suit, which allowed women to be as practical-looking on the job as men.

With its emphasis on self-fulfillment, the counter-culture was never bent on destroying society, but on making it more responsive to the individual. Once many corporations realized this, they relaxed their dress codes and encouraged employees to take up jogging and tennis or practice transcendental meditation. This is not to say that a change in clothing styles has erased alienation or corrected its causes, but it has made middle-class life easier to take.

For the emergence of the counter-culture was partly an instinctive reaction to modern alienation, a remedy for the twentieth-century illness that killed the Great Gatsby, caused the death of the salesman, sent Jack Kerouac searching on the road, and created the rebel without a cause. As a result, the men in the gray flannel suits have been transformed into the Fabulous Furry Freak Brothers, and the lonely crowd into a rock festival. And when, in 1978, socialite Gloria Vanderbilt placed her name on the backside of her "personally designed" blue jeans, she was actually signing a treaty of surrender.

A continuous line can be drawn from the best-selling book *Roots* in the Seventies to the Pop Art of the Sixties to Kerouac's celebration of the American landscape in the Fifties. The goal all along has been a return to traditional American values. To a great extent that goal has been achieved, the result being a kind of cultural unity that Americans have not known for decades. Long-haired country music stars like Willie Nelson have merged rednecks and hippies into one giant audience. A president was finally elected who was comfortable in blue jeans, quoted Bob Dylan (as well as Dylan Thomas), and liked rock and country music. The gap between hip and straight, once believed in by 59% of Woodstock

Nation, is believed in now by only 28%. And where 52% once believed in the viability of an alternative culture in this country, just 23% see that as a possibility now. Society is less polarized today, not because the counter-culture failed and the young people came home, but because the counter-culture won and America came home.

8
Looking Back, Looking Ahead

"I was so much older then,
I'm younger than that now."

—**BOB DYLAN**

If you were writing your memoir of the Sixties, how would you title it? And if you followed it up with your memoir of the Seventies, what title would you use for that volume? Some of the titles our respondents propose might eventually be Book-of-the-Month Club selections (or at least cheap paperbacks).

SIXTIES MEMOIR TITLES

"Rice Alley"—A Side Street in Saigon

Great Expectations

Silver Lamé Bell-Bottoms

*My Years As a Weekend Hippie, or Not All the Flowers
Are Worth Stopping to Smell*

The Death of Innocence

The Passive Decade of the Closet Radical

We Shall Overcome

College Struggles

Trying to Rebel While the Middle-Class Ties Keep Tugging

Don't Trust Anyone

The Best Years of Our Lives

Fear and Loathing in My Youth

Take It

If I Had Only Not Gone to Catholic School

The Bible (I do want a best-seller)

Looking for Heaven

It's Gone up to $30 an Ounce?

Looking for Earth

*How I Survived the 70's Without Being Made Part of the
Silent Majority—And It Wasn't Easy*

Survival

The Gradual Awakening of Another Cosmic Entity

*The Awakening—The Mind, the Body—Through
Philosophy, Sex, and Drugs*

On Becoming

Growing Up

Outside the Establishment from the Inside

How Not to Succeed in Business

Is There Life After 30?

Around the World on 80 Projects

Let's Get Out of Here

Getting There

*The Last of the Holdout Hippies, or Further Escapades
of the Underground Freaks*

It's Gone up to $60 an Ounce?

The nostalgia is difficult to resist. A 31-year-old California man
(who describes his occupation as "professional crazy") recalls an
incident that seems common to most of the people we surveyed:
"Several years ago, while reminiscing about the 60's on the telephone, a friend asked, 'Did you ever think then that you would
look back on those days as the best years of your life?' No, and I
do."

The vast majority (84%) report feeling nostalgic for the Sixties.
Sometimes, they get as sappy about it as the 34-year-old woman
who scribbles, "How do we get back to 1967? Please furnish time
machine! I'm crying as I write this."

Growing older and reminiscing about one's youth has tradition-
ally required the use of a handkerchief. And like members of other
American generations, many people who grew up in the Sixties
have some very traditional good times to reminisce about when
they remember their best Sixties experience.

208

"Winning the Garden State Baton Championship two years in a row."

"Being 'in' for one year in high school."

"My romance with the captain of drill team, star of school plays, etc. I was a nobody—never even had a real date when that all happened. I took him to prom, he wrote me poetry, etc. A dream come true."

"Giants defeat of Dodgers for National League pennant, 1962. Being awarded two scholarships the night of my high school graduation."

"August '66—I was 15½—our Scout troop went to Yellowstone for three days and then canoed down the Snake River for 100 miles. It was great to get away from the usual things. Great to be out in the wilderness, being with good friends, doing fun new things."

However, the traditional mixes with the unconventional.

"Scoring three touchdowns in one College Varsity Game. Singing at the Blues Bag at the Café Au Go Go in the Village."

For Woodstock Nation, the "good old days" were a decade unlike any other, a time when hippies were hippies, LSD was LSD (not horse tranquilizers), and grass was cheap. As the best experiences of the Sixties, people recall episodes that, for the most part, could only have been part of that era.

"I auditioned for and was accepted by the producers for the cast of the Hollywood production of the play *Hair*."

"Successfully picketing to wear jeans in school."

"Watching the lift-off of Apollo 11, one mile from the launch-pad."

"Selling underground newspapers under the influence of LSD in Haight-Ashbury to a Greyhound bus full of Chinese tourists."

"Delivering a Vietnamese woman's baby."

"The club runs—insane day after day blasts, unbelievable, rivalling the Romans, only we had more drugs and Harley-Davidsons."

"Seeing *Easy Rider*, then drinking cheap wine, on a very foggy Seattle November night and then having an evening of sex in a cemetery."

"1969—Woodstock-like solstice celebration in New Mexico with Hog Farm, Kesey, et al."

209

"I stayed in a place that had every drug I knew of, free, and there was a four-day festival outside, and we were naked and free—in our own world—no straights, no cops, just Peace and Love."

"I felt like I was just existing *until* I went to Kenya in the Peace Corps. There I discovered a simpler way to live, warm people and good dope. It was the highest (even without dope) experience of my life."

LIKE A ROLLING STONE

In the summer of 1969, the cover of *Life* pictured some hippies living in caves on the island of Crete. The youths in the photograph were deeply tanned, long-haired, free of clothing, and lounging languidly on the sunny rocks—kind of like one of those recently discovered Stone Age tribes that have no words in their language for "war," "hate," or "A-1 Sauce." The press had discovered that the hip scene was international, that young American long-hairs were roaming the globe—from Katmandu, Goa, and Tangier to Paris, London, Rome, and Ibiza—at the same time that hippies from other countries were extending the borders of Woodstock Nation. Nearly 22% of our respondents were bumming their way around other countries during the Sixties, and some remember it as the high point of the decade:

"Going to Europe and just living free in different cultures with all different kinds of people and beginning to trust myself as a survivor."

Even more of our respondents (40%) went traveling across the United States, with nearly 16% journeying to Haight-Ashbury during the 1967 "Summer of Love" (presumably with "flowers in their hair"). A common method of getting anywhere was hitchhiking, an experience that 73% had during the Sixties. Many—both men and women—remember both the feeling of a freewheeling lifestyle and getting to know people along the route as the best things that happened to them in those years.

"I took off hitchhiking from New York to San Francisco alone with forty cents and three cans of tuna."

"My best Sixties memory? Hitchhiking around the U.S.—fe-

210

male, 20, naive and yet unharmed, cared for, not approached by any negative experiences."

Not all women, however, found traveling alone so pleasant.

"My worst experience was hitching from Texas to Virginia in the winter of '69—freezing my ass off and almost being killed by a truck driver for not giving him a piece of ass," says a 25-year-old wrecker dispatcher from Texas.

"My worst memory of the 60's is sleeping with a truck driver who had picked me up hitchhiking," reports a 31-year-old wife and mother. "He said if I didn't he'd leave me on this 'nowhere' road—it was 3 A.M. and 20 degrees outside. He was a real bastard."

SEX AND THE SINGLE HIPPIE

While sexual mores were changing, there was often confusion and pain accompanying sexual experimentation. As some people remember them, the Sixties were a relatively repressive time.

"The 60's were not so liberated or hip—all the spokespeople from the counter-culture called homosexual men faggots. They were so homophobic," reports a 32-year-old graduate student. For one man, his worst 60's experience was "being caught by my lover's wife. I'm bisexual and we'd been together for three years secretly. He was a highly paid public figure. I was away at school. I wrote a graphic letter. She intercepted. She called my dorm and was a crying, threatening wreck. I'd just turned 19 and saw my whole life shot down. I saw a public trial and an ugly divorce, etc. I lived in terror for two months. They never got divorced and I've never seen him since."

For some women, sexual encounters, specifically rape, are bad memories that color their whole picture of the counter-culture: "I remember being broke and living on the street and being taken advantage of—being raped and strung out on speed—crying a lot—being ill because of the above."

And the illegality of abortion caused Sixties nightmares for men and women:

"I had a child out of wedlock and had to give it up for adoption. Abortion was not readily available. During and after the pregnancy I felt totally alone and became psychologically fucked up."

"I had an abortion on a kitchen table, followed by hospitalization in a psychiatric ward of a state institution."

"The worst experience was getting raided while my girlfriend's abortion was going on."

"WHEN I DIE I'LL GO TO HEAVEN, 'CAUSE I'VE SERVED MY TIME IN HELL"

The Vietnam War left its share of bad memories. Remembering his worst experience of the Sixties, one man declares, "I can't decide between boot camp and acne"; and a 30-year-old Boston man marks Vietnam as both his best and worst experience of the Sixties: "A real awakening, a throwing off of a lot of old stale ideas."

But this is not the common view; most others look back on the war with horror. A 33-year-old Atlanta man recalls "filling body-bags in Vietnam." And a 32-year-old Virginian remembers "watching and extinguishing in vain as napalm burned, to subsequent death, a Sgt. Guerrero in my fox-hole in Vietnam, in August 1966."

Women as well were directly affected by Vietnam. A 27-year-old New York teacher says her worst Sixties experience was when "I became a wife and a widow within four months. This plunged me into an awareness of many things. Vietnam had always been a reality for me but after losing my husband (the government did not recognize our marriage because it was done in an Apache ceremony the day he left for Nam), I began to question the motives and reasoning of our involvement there. It also prompted me to action."

CHANGING THE WORLD

Because most people feel that the political activities of the Sixties accomplished something, they have some very positive memories of their involvement in events that were historic.

"My best experience was the few weeks I worked to get signatures and money for the McGovern-Hatfield amendment to end

212

the war. I felt I was working within the system to do something productive."

"The best thing I did was donning a black armband and beret and leading the senior class on a protest demonstration against the war and the draft. (This action cost two of us a three-day suspension for organizing a potentially dangerous situation.)"

"Marching in the 1969 Moratorium in Washington, D.C., with one million other people. A wonderful feeling of commitment, brotherhood, and shared hardship."

"Oddly, I remember a sense of community in demonstrations. Watching Chicago through the night, close to tears and aware of power in the streets—and later, in a local 'riot' when a fellow hippie was jailed the kids mobbed the civic center, stopping cars for bail money, as groggy state troopers in T-shirts stood by with huge clubs."

"My best 60's experience was my parents coming to D.C. to get me out of jail. I had been to a demonstration. My father, who had been a drill instructor in the U.S. Marines, told me he thought what I was doing was crazy but he loved me for standing up for what I believed in and told me not to stop."

At the same time, however, the decade was marked by terrifying events. In addition to the assassinations and the war, many people's worst experiences came from being in the thick of political struggles.

"The worst was when I was trying to help someone who was being beaten up by Philadelphia police during an anti-Humphrey rally. A band was told to play louder to cover up the poor sucker's screams. As I stood with tears running down my face, Humphrey came along shaking hands. He grabbed my hand, which was flashing a peace sign, said, 'Yeah, peace to you too' and went on."

"Nixon's visit to New York City which provoked a massive antiwar rally which ended in bloody chaos with police on horseback brutally attacking marchers and innocent bystanders, overturning our P.A. truck, and beating those inside. Horrifying!"

"I got clubbed by a nazi San Francisco tactical pig. My spleen was amputated and three ribs were broken and I was falsely accused of inciting a riot. Four years later I got a hung jury on my million-dollar countersuit."

"I remember being stranded on the seventh floor with the draft board and the TAC squad. The elevators had been shut off. Eventually a camera crew from a local TV station came up the stairs, and I tried breathing again."

"The worst was the claustrophobia and near-panic I experienced in a large rally/march in D.C. My child and I were crying and choking from tear gas."

One person regrets most having been employed by the other side; her worst experience of the decade was "working at the Pentagon for one year."

GROOVIN'

If external events such as demonstrations and rallies are what some people remember when they think of the Sixties, personal experiences with sex and drugs are what come to mind for others.

"When I look back to the Sixties I remember getting laid in a rubber raft in the middle of a moonlit lake."

"Mona was a real fine chick. We had a fantastic time for several months. We were very real with each other. A 60's experience because I had way more self-confidence in the late 60's than before or after, and I met her the day after my first acid trip."

"My best 60's experience was getting laid for the first time while stoned. Getting laid for the second time while stoned. Getting laid for the third time while stoned. Getting laid for the fourth time while stoned."

"Getting very stoned for the first time. I enjoyed myself immensely while I was nearly choking to death, attempted to follow conversations and couldn't and listened to a friend talk about the immorality of going to Baskin Robbins while we were fighting a war in Vietnam."

"The best was eating acid and riding my motorcycle while wearing my red sunglasses up along the California coast—nothing like it."

"My clearest memory of the decade is of sitting on a mountainside in New Hampshire in October after ingesting a tab of mescaline. Shared with five good friends, a full moon, a windy day, and

214

two billion leaves (and my consciousness) changing color. That trip was so good that I never tripped again."

FLIPPING OUT

The Sixties was an era when people often acted as if they had lost all their marbles. Within the counter-culture, this was at times a pose, an extension of the Romantic idea that lunatics were close to God. From the days of the Beats (when poet Allen Ginsberg was briefly locked away in Rockland State Hospital and given insulin shock treatments), a certain amount of lunacy was encouraged. The drug experience was, clinically speaking, a temporarily induced schizophrenic episode, and many used it to achieve the mental state that British psychiatrist R. D. Laing extolled: "If I could drive you out of your wretched mind . . ."

The trouble was, some people actually did go crazy. They literally blew their minds on drugs, or "flipped out," due to circumstances that seemed way out of control. When people short-circuited on a Sixties overload, it was not at all "groovy," and the pain is remembered as the worst experience of the time.

"I went through a three-month period of total depression— probably brought on from taking too much speed for study purposes. (I was in college.)" (Media specialist, 27, female)

"Confusion! All the new values and ideas coming at once was more than I could cope with. My religious beliefs especially were challenged. I became angry and depressed." (Pastor, 32, male)

"Like in the Tibetan Book of the Dead, I had to confront and accept my own demons—my dark side. I became paranoid-schizophrenic (I went crazy), and I was always afraid. My journey back to Truth required such a departure from it." (Unemployed artist/ poet, 32, male)

"Ask my analyst—he says whatever it was he'd like to know too!" (Unemployed, 25, female)

BROTHERS AND SISTERS

Some of that craziness caused people to hurt each other. Experiences of mania, betrayal, and loneliness are recalled by several respondents as their worst moments of the decade.

"I was living in the East Village and I was beaten up by a crazy guy. When I called the police to get rid of him they told me 'that's what you deserve for living in the East Village.' " (Art gallery owner, 29, female)

"I was almost killed by a speed freak maniac who decided he loved me so much I had to die. He locked me into a room where he beat me for four hours." (Singer, 34, female)

"The day after my first acid trip was the worst. Two hitchhikers I picked up invited me to dinner. They gave me so much hashish that the world spun and I felt sick and believed they were witches and that I would pass out and wake up somewhere suspended upside down in some rite." (Animator, 28, male)

"In our zeal to help every living thing we took in people. One of them was super violent and had escaped from a mental hospital. It was a nightmare. We finally had to seek help from the Drug Intervention Center. The whole thing was impossible." (Unemployed, 28, female)

"A lover of mine moved to a religious commune and I found I was too skeptical to follow. Great despair and self-examination resulted." (Computer programmer, 25, male)

"The worst thing was when I realized that 'your friends' didn't always have the same values as you. I once thought everyone that got high was basically good. But after being taken advantage of, I lost my blind trust in hippies." (Unemployed, 25, female)

But the number of good experiences outweigh the bad. The bonds of friendship that existed even between strangers in Woodstock Nation were strong enough for people to address each other as "brother" and "sister." Being with other people in this kind of atmosphere was often the most memorable experience of the Sixties.

"I was the 'landlady' in this house where a lot of people lived and a lot more hung out 'cause of the food and the laughs and for a while before we moved on there were tremendous amounts of good feelings." (Library assistant, 26)

"I lived in a household of politico dropouts—'brothers and sisters'—which lasted about one year." (Mother/typist/cocktail waitress/gardener, 32)

"I remember living and being constantly high (stoned) with my

216

'family'—four of us hippies in a tenement three-room apartment in New York's 'East Village.' 1967—it was the 'Summer of Love' and, for me, PARADISE." (TV commercial producer, 27, female)

"The best was living in a commune and making music and doing things like a family. Having people who showed their love and support when I felt I needed it." (Deckhand, 29, female)

"Working in a summer camp in upstate New York, after a long hard day, drinking blackberry brandy, hanging out with the 'together' people and talkin' good people politics and ending the evening making love, with the Byrds singing 'Get Together' on the radio. Umm . . ."* (Clinical social worker, 26, female)

"Sundays at Milby Park—a park outside of Pasadena, Texas, where the freaks got together and talked, played music, smoked pot and sold dope—a large gathering every Sunday." (Nurse, 27, female)

"Living and working at The Park, an outdoor all-day concert that was held every Saturday in North Baltimore, Ohio. I lived there with a Vietnam vet and five other couples." (Managing editor, 25, female)

"Walking across campus with a bottle of wine in one hand, a joint in the other with good, funny friends and suddenly realizing no one wanted to stop us." (Chef, 26, male)

THREE DAYS OF PEACE AND MUSIC

And of course, there was the Woodstock Music and Art Fair, which began on Friday, August 15, 1969, and officially ended two days later, although many people stayed on in farmer Max Yasgur's fields for another week (some may be there yet).

Under the heading "Nightmare in the Catskills," the *New York Times* sermonized, "The dreams of marijuana and rock music that drew 300,000 fans and hippies to the Catskills had little more sanity than the impulses that drive the lemmings to march to their deaths in the sea. They ended in a nightmare of mud and stagnation that paralyzed Sullivan County for a whole weekend. What kind of culture is it that can produce so colossal a mess?"

*Too much blackberry brandy! "Get Together" was sung by the Youngbloods, not the Byrds.

217

But on the Monday after the festival, even the *Times* seemed to "go with the flow" in an editorial called "Morning After at Bethel." "Essentially a phenomenon of innocence," the editorial writer called it, "comparable to the Tulipmania of the Children's Crusade," and went on to quote the Monticello chief of police who said, "They were the most courteous, considerate, and well-behaved group of kids" he had ever dealt with. The *Times* concluded rather grandly that "comrades-in-rock, like comrades-in-arms, need great days to remember and embroider. With Henry the Fifth they could say at Bethel, 'He that outlives this day and comes safe home, will stand a-tiptoe when this day is nam'd.' "

The 17% of our respondents who were there *do* "stand a-tiptoe" when Woodstock is mentioned, claiming it was one of their best experiences of the era.

"My best 60's experience was being at Woodstock. I felt very much a part of a large group. I felt I had an identity and that I belonged." (Teacher, 28, female)

"*The* Festival. *Absolutely.* It took place closer to us—New Paltz—than to the village of Woodstock. We *still* call it 'White Lake' and felt it was a success because it was in *our* countryside." (Hotel manager/Aquarian Age minister, 32, female)

"Woodstock without a doubt! Such a carefree time—almost immersed in my own world there—could've easily forgotten about everything outside of Max Yasgur's farm land." (Secretary, 25, female, Florida)

"Woodstock was great—I just don't want anyone else to ask me how many naked people I saw there (I saw only one)." (Purchasing agent, 30, female)

"Woodstock of course, after which I left in a '46 Chevy for the Hog Farm and Phoenix for six months." (Letter carrier, 28, male)

Only two people register complaints about the event. A Wisconsin man says, "I went to Woodstock. I didn't get laid. I didn't get high. I got wet and grouchy." A "tinker and tunesmith" from Pennsylvania recalls a moment of stoned terror: "Incredible paranoia at Woodstock, first time at the big stage. 500,000 fuckin' people *all* lookin' at me!"*

*"That's funny," comments a friend of the authors' who was also at Woodstock. "I thought they were all looking at *me*."

218

Woodstock seems to have been both an end and a beginning. No better example can be found than the experience of a 36-year-old New York clothing retailer, who says the best thing that ever happened to him was "selling 45,000 ice creams at the Woodstock festival in 1969 and then going into business. For me, the end of the 60's changed my whole life."

"DON'T THINK TWICE, IT'S ALL RIGHT"

Were the Sixties worthwhile? Of all the people surveyed, 44% say they feel disappointed with the era—some because they missed experiencing it.

"Did anyone else feel 'out of the action' in the 60's or was I the only person who didn't march, protest, take LSD and deal dope?" (Unemployed, 26, female)

Others who experienced it miss the style.

"Where did it all go? I wish the music and the clothes and that whole crazy scene were still happening. Bring back Lothar and the Hand People!" (Dentist, 33, male)

Activists are slightly more disappointed about the Sixties (49%) than others, probably because they hoped for swifter and more significant political change as a result of the hard-fought battles of that decade.

"We all grow and change but the same injustices are still going on. The War, the FBI, the arms race, poverty, racial prejudice— and I never stop being aware of this." (Jeweler, 28, female)

But even so, more than half of our respondents feel the Sixties *were* worthwhile, despite whatever failures there may have been.

"Too many are disillusioned about the 60's. It was an awakening and like all awakenings it was groggy and stupid. It was disappointing but it was effective and should not be forgotten or denigrated."

"Just because the 60's were not all we hoped does not mean they failed to bring about change. The racial and sexual revolutions were profound. The political revolution mostly failed, but at least the war and the draft ended."

"May you live in interesting times" is an ancient Chinese curse. One person writes at the end of her questionnaire, "My kids should *never* have to go through a time like that"; only 13% of our respondents concur, although a frequent comment is that the Sixties were not easy to live through. The majority of people in Woodstock Nation have few regrets about the era. When asked, "Did you do a lot of silly things then that you now feel embarrassed about?", 73% say no.

"Hard times, but would not have missed it for the world." (Bricklayer, 32, male)

"I'm glad I lived through it. It brought me my friends, my lady and the ability to think quickly in crisis situations. I'm also glad it's over. It was heavy, ya know!" (Unemployed, 28, male)

"This country and I were both growing up. There were things we both had to go through to become better and stronger, to ourselves and others." (Phone clerk, 25, female)

"In some ways I wish the 60's were back. At least my leg would still be natural. People (older) ask me at times *if* I had it to do over again would I change it (drug-wise). Most certainly not. War-wise, yes, it's nonsense, people getting shot up for no apparent reason is a farce." (25, male, wounded in Vietnam)

"I wouldn't do it exactly the same but don't regret it either. Find the 70's more exciting as I get older. Like a lot of the changes that happened as a result of the 60's and 70's. Glad to have lived through these times." (Deckhand, 29, female)

"I grew up in one of the most exciting times of this century, only wish that the establishment now accepted in jobs folks who had unconventional backgrounds." (Political consultant/writer, 30, male)

"I thought the 60's were the most exciting era I can think of. It was exhilarating to be able to change the world a little, and to feel that the world changed me." (Publicist, 26, female)

THE FUTURE

We dusted off a tattered copy of the *I Ching* (unused since our last acid trip, ages ago) and sought an answer to the question: What's in store for Woodstock Nation? We tossed three coins. The resulting hexagram (it *really* "blew our minds," no kidding) was "T'ai/

Peace." The peace sign! Says the ancient hippie oracle: "The small departs. The great approaches. Good fortune. Success."

This positive forecast for the Eighties is in harmony with the mood of the people we surveyed. Most people have an optimistic outlook and are excited about the future. One respondent, a 31-year-old surveyor in Kansas City, tells us: "Back in the Olds one day I was doing acid and bummed with the war and my job. So I thought I'd leave the city and raise kids and goats and geese, and things. Now I have the land, the old lady's pregnant, and next year we'll be in the Ozarks. Peace."

PERSONAL FEELINGS ON APPROACHING THE EIGHTIES

	% of All Respondents*
Optimistic	20
Cynical	15
Worried	14
Excited	11
Confused	9
Encouraged	7
Serene	6
Frightened	4
Depressed	3
Bored	3
Other	10
No answer	5

*Percentages total more than 100% because some people marked two items.

Of course, some people are cynical about the future and some are worried or confused about what lies ahead, and certainly not everyone is heading for the Ozarks to live the simple life. But generally those we surveyed prefer to believe that because of the Sixties the future holds promise.

"A lot of things have changed for the better. People are more politically educated and open to progressive changes. There's still a lot to improve but I feel more confident that things will work out."

"The yearnings of the 60's have really matured in the 70's. I think there was a victory of the 60's."

221

THE "NEW NARCISSISM"

The Seventies were a time when many people sought self-improvement through various programs, such as Erhard Seminar Training, Transcendental Meditation, Rolfing, Primal Therapy, Smokenders, tap dancing, and you name it. A high proportion of the people we surveyed (43%) report having tried some course of self-improvement during the Seventies, but before we interpret this as a harbinger of increasing selfishness and navel-gazing in the Eighties, we have to ask, hasn't Woodstock Nation always been self-centered?

In fact, the majority (57%) say that even back in the Sixties, they were inclined to believe that "it's better to get my own head together than to try to change somebody else's." Many people see no contradiction between concentrating on self-improvement and social activism. One respondent puts it this way: "I think that, to paraphrase Jung, we each have to work on reconciling the schisms within ourselves before we can hope to be an effective force for social change, and I hope and believe that there is a lot of that going on in the 70's, preparing us for another decade of activism and change."

For the most part, however, our respondents are interested in liberal reforms, not radical change. The issues of most concern—the environment, nuclear weapons, pot, corporate power, feminism—although connected to the idealism of the Sixties, are consistent with middle-class interests. Poverty and racial discrimination do not concern Woodstock Nation as much—and if the distance between the haves and have-nots in our society becomes greater than it is now, if veterans of the Sixties become too complacent, an ironic confrontation could be the result.

THE COMMUNITY

Most of our respondents disliked suburbia in the Sixties (62%) and continued to dislike it in the Seventies (64%). Clearly, Woodstock Nation is seeking some other way of life.

222

Many observers perceived the communal movements and the experimentation with sexual relationships during the Sixties as antisocial trends. But based on the fact that at least a third of our mostly monogamous, middle-class respondents have lived in communes, it seems more likely that communities will be strengthened by people who are used to cooperative living.

If, like our Kansas City couple, a number of people head for the hills, then rural towns around the nation may find themselves in the same kind of growth explosion that affected suburban towns in the Forties and Fifties. New schools will have to be built, town services expanded and taxes increased.

Those who remain in the cities will transform the urban landscape. Already the Seventies have spawned a neologism— "gentrification"—to describe the movement of (mostly) middle-class young people into renovated industrial loft buildings or into decaying areas where old, quaint brownstones are cheap. The *Wall Street Journal* described this trend in an article headlined, "The Haight-Ashbury Turns into a Bastion of the Middle Class." Perhaps even more significant was the subhead, "San Francisco Hippie Haunt Undergoes 'Gentrification' and House Prices Soar." In the Haight-Ashbury district, for example, 24% of the residents earned more than $15,000 per year in 1977, compared with 15% in 1970.* These are the people who are turning defunct psychedelic crashpads into fine examples of period renovation.

This development is not without its problems, though. Already it has caused rent increases, a fact that dismays long-time residents. "What we need is a good riot to lower rents," one Haight-Ashbury regular told the *Wall Street Journal.* Added the coordinator of the San Francisco tenants' union: "I bristle at the word 'comeback' when applied to the Haight. A neighborhood is more than a four-color paint job."

Poor people who cannot keep up with the "comeback" may eventually be forced into other parts of the city, or out of the city altogether (perhaps to suburbia), thereby transforming cities into middle-class strongholds.

*Marilyn Chase, *Wall Street Journal*, July 24, 1978.

223

THE TROUBLE WITH KIDS TODAY...

You might not suspect that Woodstock Nation would view the upcoming generation with the same prejudices that older people of the Sixties had about them—but they do. "High schoolers today either have no idea how much our lives are manipulated by the government or they simply don't care to be bothered by others' troubles."

Not only are younger people regarded as ignorant and selfish, they are also accused of sacrilege, amoral behavior, and having too much fun! A Boston physician, 26, grumbles: "Getting stoned was supposed to be a mystical experience, leading to greater consciousness with regard to music, sex, or what not. You were supposed to learn and develop from it. We, the 60's generation, fought for the right to these experiences. The 70's generation, on the other hand, takes them for granted and just enjoys dope, sex, and cohabitation and so on purely hedonistically."

Yes, back in our day, *we* had to walk ten miles, barefoot, just to score a joint.

"Young people today have no goals," complains a Michigan pool-hall owner, 29, "no direction. We knew what was wrong and went to great lengths to change it. Now that it's changed there's nothing to strive for."

The trouble with kids today, explains a Texas carpenter, 35, is that they "are lacking the naive trust in one another that we had. They strike me as a hard bunch of loners. They have dope and sex but they don't have love or brotherhood."

"Today," observes a 30-year-old army man, "youth is either vicious (punk rock) or always mellow (Quaalude induced)."

A 25-year-old high school teacher in Michigan says that "the young people growing up today do not seem as unified as we were. An event like Woodstock helped to give us an identity and unity." And another respondent believes that "at the end of Vietnam and Watergate, apathy settled over the country like a moldy blanket and college kids went back to Villager clothes and worrying about grades."

It seems that projecting fears and self-doubts on younger gen-

224

erations is a tic acquired with adulthood. Although this survey did not include those unlucky souls born too late for Woodstock, SDS, and smoking banana peels, we do see indications that younger people are not, as some of us once called the unenlightened, "running-dog lackeys of the status quo." In a recent survey of college bookstores, a Washington *Post* reporter found, much to his surprise, that "Marx and Engels, and the literature of Marxian socialism, are not selling as well as they did in the 60's, they're selling *better*. From Berkeley to Boston, Austin to Ann Arbor, buyers agreed that sales in the 'Marxism, etc.' section had never been better. . . . 'It's not a faddish thing,' [one bookstore owner says] 'these people are real serious.' "*

Aging Sixties hipsters can put that in their pipes and smoke it.

THE WILD CARD

So far, we have been speaking mainly about the 69% of our respondents who say that they can more or less "fit into today's society while trying to change some of its worst features." For most of the people we surveyed, the salutary changes of the Sixties will allow them to live satisfactorily within a counter-cultural style of middle-class life, which is what they really sought all along.

But during the Sixties, there *were* young people who developed truly radical philosophies regarding culture and politics. The Port Huron Statement—the basis of SDS—called for a complete over-turning of the capitalist system in America, and at one time SDS attracted thousands of members.† Besides the political revolution-aries, there were the cultural revolutionaries who turned on, tuned in, and dropped out of society altogether, devoting themselves to drugs, mysticism, and communal living. Where are they now?

They are not only still around, but alive and well enough to answer questionnaires. They are defined, in this group, as the 26% who state that they absolutely cannot "accept a conventional way of life in society as it now exists." These people—whom we

*Garrett Epps, "Big Books on Campus: From Pynchon to Pirsig," Washington *Post*, October 1, 1978.

†According to SDS historian Kirkpatrick Sale, the organization's membership in 1967 was approximately 30,000.

call "Group X"—have very definite characteristics that separate them from the rest of their peers.

They are more committed to political radicalism:

	% of Group X	% of Everybody Else
Radical in the Sixties	57	29
Political activists in the Sixties	44	21
Supported the Viet Cong	41	17
Took stance in Sixties because they believed in revolution	22	8
Joined SDS in Sixties	19	10
Radical in the Seventies	49	10
Remained radical in both Sixties and Seventies	34	9
Concerned about issue of corporate power	31	15
Today working toward gradual revolution	28	8
Today working toward violent revolution	8	1

Group X tends to be more sexually unconventional:

	% of Group X	% of Everybody Else
Do not believe monogamy is important	23	13
Bisexual	16	7
Gay	8	3

They have been more involved in drug use, chiefly pot:

	% of Group X	% of Everybody Else
Smoked pot regularly in Sixties	49	30
Smoked pot regularly in Seventies	46	26
Have dealt drugs in Sixties	44	23
Have dealt drugs in Seventies	44	22

During the Sixties, Group X chose nearly the same heroes as everyone else, but with a slight difference. Group X, for instance, admired and was influenced by Abbie Hoffman to the same degree that the rest of our respondents admired and were influenced by Robert Kennedy. Moreover, they had higher regard for Abbie Hoffman than for Eugene McCarthy, and valued Jimi Hendrix and Timothy Leary more than George McGovern. In other words, while most of their peers looked up to politicians who wanted to reform the system from within, Group X admired people who were, in one way or another, outside the system.

Group X itself remains to a great extent outside the system; 49% are in the $8000-per-year-or-less category, and 44% admire Carlos Castaneda (whose *oeuvre* offers tips on alternative ways to achieve power and fulfillment).

More than everyone else, Group X has held on to the ideals and living styles of the Sixties. Nearly half (46%) report that they did not renounce their Sixties lifestyle because for them it is still valid.

In the Seventies	% of Group X	% of Everybody Else
Still call cops pigs	55	26
Cannot fit into a 9-to-5 routine	50	15
Believe it's possible to establish an alternative culture in this country	38	13
Believe in "straight" versus "hip"	36	19
Have lived in communes in Seventies	35	12
Feel alienated from the rest of society	28	6
Believe their lifestyles are different from everybody else's	24	7
Would sooner believe a story in Berkeley *Barb* than in *Time* magazine	21	5
Believe the Sixties aren't over yet	20	9

One person expresses the feeling this way: "Some of us are trying to keep the 60's alive and we *will* because to us it was more than an era, it is a way of living and perceiving life."

Group X is scattered across the country, in big cities as well as small towns. A particularly heavy concentration is found in Madison, Wisc., which serves as a good example of what Group X is all about.

Madison is a state capital and college town with a tradition of political radicalism that goes back to the nineteenth-century Populist Era. During the 1960s, the streets of Madison were the scene of massive antiwar demonstrations and fierce police-student confrontations. In 1970, the only recorded death to result from antiwar sabotage anywhere occurred when a professor was killed in the explosion of Madison's Army Mathematics Research Center. Madison was also the home of one of the first and best underground newspapers, *Kaleidoscope*. In 1973, a young antiwar activist, Paul Soglin, was elected mayor with the support of Madison's closely knit, politically energetic radical community.

Having taken power in Madison, however, the radical community has not ceased its political activism. *Takeover*, the collectively owned and operated newspaper that is a direct descendant of *Kaleidoscope*, plays up controversial issues facing the community, continually exposes scandals in government and business, and has been generally critical of Mayor Soglin rather than supportive. In other words, it doesn't matter *who* runs the government; Group X will always be a vocal opposition.

Group X formed the cutting edge of the counter-cultural and political movements of the Sixties. Most of Woodstock Nation wanted to end the war, or stop the draft, or give women and minorities equal job opportunities, or have the right to wear long hair and smoke marijuana; Group X wanted the world and wanted it now. This was a perfect, though inadvertent, bargaining posture for the movements of the Sixties, helping to force the acceptance of moderate reform.

Group X, though, continues to want the world and want it now. Any predictions about Woodstock Nation will have to count Group X as a wild card, for just as a small, vocal minority was in the vanguard of the Sixties, so, too, will they remain the movers and shakers of the future. Warns one Group X-er: "Us weirdos who survived the 60's and are coping with the 70's are going to hit big in the 80's. Watch out!"

WHEN WILL THE SIXTIES BE OVER?

"As long as there's a Grateful Dead, the 60's will never be over," declares a 25-year-old student from New York. That's one way to look at it. But at some point in the future the spirit of the Sixties will, alas, fade away. According to the findings of this survey, this has not yet begun to happen—at least in the minds of Woodstock Nation. And as far as we can see, that era will be with us for some time to come. Nevertheless, the Sixties will be over when certain changes occur.

Eight Sure Signs That the Sixties Are Over

1. When there is a return to conformity in fashion, and one or two styles dominate.
2. When Americans abandon public demonstrations as a means of social and political protest.
3. When a woman's place is only in the home.
4. When instead of many cults there is only one.
5. When marijuana becomes part of the government-regulated economy.
6. When Martin Luther King and Ralph Nader become obscure figures of American history.
7. When members of Woodstock Nation can't remember the first time they got stoned.
8. When the Grateful Dead are dead.

SOME FINAL COMMENTS

"I thought the changes of the 60's were good for me. I live the type of life I enjoy and dreamed of. I've gotten out of the Big City and into the Country. I feel I'm one of the generation of Woodstock who took the ideals seriously and have fulfilled them the best I can. I still have the everyday problems but I'm choosing my own destiny."

229

"The 1960's were a prerequisite experience leading, hopefully, to a meaningful change and maturation in human nature, and possibly, even to the next *evolutionary* step. 'Something' was set in motion."

"The 60's were an exciting time in which to be maturing; too bad there was a war going on. But it was that war that to a large extent united us; it was a catalyst just as the Beatles were. I'm proud to be one of the Woodstock Generation just as people in their late teens to mid-20's are undoubtedly proud of being in the disco generation. Despite everything, I agree with Country Joe McDonald (on his current album): 'Bring back the 60's.' "

"I'm extremely lucky to have lived through the 60's. Otherwise I might have ended up with some asshole job, a new car, a fat wife, and three screaming kids."

"What's the matter with all the single men—buncha chicken shits. They wanted to fuck me all right in the 60's, but now they're running scared, and I sure look the same. Maybe I don't sound the same though. But neither do they. . . ."

"My first night in Katmandu, Nepal, 1975, went looking for some hash. It found me and led me to a small pie shop which was blaring Jimi Hendrix and Grateful Dead. I later learned this street was called FREAK STREET. Something was significant about this—a world-wide counter-culture that had been propagated by the media on an international scale. That began in the 60's and it's still going on. But is there more to it than just the drugs, music and sex?"

"You have stressed the political aspects but my friends and I were (and are) involved in spiritual development and the occult sciences and in homesteading. You have not polled us on back-to-the-land activities or changes in religious directions, and for thousands of us freaks, *that's* what the 60's were really about. We play Arlo Guthrie records, not Patti Smith."

"Punk rock is good but it's not new. The free-form FM radio is gone, may it R.I.P., but I'll hope for a resurrection. Carter's a liar. Someone should develop 'underground disco'—getting rid of the dopey lyrics and cute riffs. TV is just as bad as ever. The cheapo performance cars of the 70's don't compare with the 60's muscle cars. Gas is a rip-off, takes the fun out of driving. Grass is better quality but prices are a joke, speed's hard to get, so's acid. I don't eat meat any more and luxury car owners are assholes."

"The spirit of the 60's should be kept alive. Not as some nostalgia trip or media road show but as an essential experience in trying to change society and grow as an individual."

"We live in interesting times, and have the privilege (or burden) of determining what is interesting about them."

"I've seen so many people laugh off the Sixties—how they've 'arranged' their lives so that they now have what their parents had. There was a lot of crap in the Sixties—too much dope, too much sex. But those years enkindled in me some new priorities and commitment to myself, my lover, and the people I do business with. I don't own a credit card; I never will. And the injustices of the 60's—I don't forget and they still anger me. More so—for they've gone on so long."

"I'm just hanging on until the social unrest breaks loose again. In the 70's I've travelled around picking fruit, working offshore, etc., looking for my brothers of the 60's; they must all be dead or in hiding. Is the party really over?"

"Hey, man—the 80's are going to make the 60's seem like a tea party—only I don't know which side will win—anyway, Forward to the Apocalypse!"

APPENDIX A:

The Questionnaire

THIS IS THE WOODSTOCK CENSUS*

With your help, through this questionnaire, we hope to find out what "The Sixties" meant to those who were part of it, and how the 60's Generation views itself today. Although these questionnaires will be kept anonymous, we are very interested in your opinions, so please consider your answers carefully. Your own personal feelings about the things described are what we're looking for. If some parts of what you read seem playful, that's because this questionnaire, although scientifically constructed, was as much fun for us to write as it will be for you to fill out.

1. During the 60's, how did you personally feel about the things listed below, whether or not you had direct personal contact with them? And, how do you feel about them now in the 70's?

	60's			70's		
	Liked	Neutral	Disliked	Like	Neutral	Dislike
Armpit hair on women.....	15%	36%	48%	21%	42%	36%
Acid rock	67	15	18	36	31	32
Astrology.........................	35	46	18	38	41	20
Black light posters...........	55	27	17	16	43	39
Being mellow	62	26	11	66	20	12
Being ambitious	35	33	30	55	30	12
Big Macs...........................	33	29	36	22	21	55
Capitalism	13	33	53	22	39	37
Cadillacs	12	21	60	10	21	66
Communes	53	36	10	33	49	15

*In tabulating the results of our questionnaire, we rounded all percentages off to the nearest whole percent. In some tables the percentages add up to more or less than 100. This is because some respondents gave more than one answer where appropriate, and some did not answer every question.

	60's			70's		
	Liked	**Neutral**	**Disliked**	**Like**	**Neutral**	**Dislike**
CIA	5%	29%	65%	3%	17%	78%
Communism	19	44	36	13	50	35
Discotheques	35	35	29	26	31	41
Eastern philosophy	46	44	9	47	41	10
FBI	7	24	68	3	20	75
Football	32	24	43	28	30	40
Foreign Aid	30	47	22	19	47	31
Gurus	23	45	31	13	43	41
Girdles	6	19	75	2	14	83
Going "bra-less"	73	17	9	71	20	7
Hard rock	76	12	11	51	27	21
Having a steady job	32	27	40	51	23	24
Hitchhiking	55	24	20	22	31	46
Indoor rock concerts	75	16	8	49	26	23
Jazz	36	41	21	63	25	10
Jeans	90	7	2	92	5	2
Kids	49	34	16	60	25	14
Light shows	68	23	7	45	38	15
Living in the city	53	21	25	53	21	25
Living in the country	59	28	12	64	23	11
Long hair on men	81	13	6	57	31	10
Make-up	22	30	47	24	35	39
Money	51	33	15	71	22	5
My parents	41	28	30	70	22	7
Myself	55	26	18	82	14	2
My job	28	36	32	54	28	16
Natural body odor	21	37	41	27	38	33
The New York Times	31	51	16	40	43	14
Outdoor rock concerts	79	14	5	56	26	15
Possessions	40	40	19	52	37	9
Rich people	11	42	46	13	53	33
The Rolling Stones	72	18	9	52	31	15
Rolling Stone magazine	50	42	7	34	48	17
Suburbia	11	26	62	8	27	64
Rock music	87	9	3	73	19	6
Soft rock	63	25	11	69	19	10

Transcendental Meditation	21	57	22	24	49	25
Underground newspapers	73	21	5	46	45	8
U.N.	34	53	11	23	59	16
Wall Street Journal	8	50	42	18	49	31
Wearing good-looking clothes	39	34	25	61	30	7
Work shirts	72	22	6	64	29	6

2. Imagining yourself back in the 60's, how would you have felt about the following statements? How do you feel about them now?*

	60's				70's			
	Agreed Completely	Agreed Somewhat	Disagreed Somewhat	Disagreed Completely	Agree Completely	Agree Somewhat	Disagree Somewhat	Disagree Completely
It's okay to work at a job you hate if the money's good	3%	18%	23%	48%	3%	20%	31%	39%
You find out what a person's like when you smoke pot with him/her	19	34	10	14	7	27	19	23
A good dose of LSD in the water supply would be good for everybody	13	16	10	54	3	6	12	72
Rock and roll is a revolutionary political force	27	30	11	20	8	23	19	31
Owning stock in a corporation is morally wrong	11	14	14	30	8	7	19	40
There are "straight" people, and then there are hip people	59	26	4	4	28	32	14	10
If there's trouble, the last thing you do is call the police	28	25	19	18	8	19	32	27

*An additional choice of "Neither Agreed Nor Disagreed" was originally given, yielding numbers that were statistically uninteresting.

	60's				70's			
	Agreed Completely	Agreed Somewhat	Disagreed Somewhat	Disagreed Completely	Agree Completely	Agree Somewhat	Disagree Somewhat	Disagree Completely
It is possible to establish a viable "alternative culture" in this country	52%	30%	4%	3%	23%	36%	21%	8%
It's better to get my own head together than to try to change everyone else's	31	26	19	9	52	25	8	4
Violent movies and TV shows can be entertaining	18	25	14	29	16	24	17	31
Rock stars are important people	30	31	9	9	11	23	18	17
I would sooner believe a story in the *Berkeley Barb* than a story in *Time* magazine	25	26	12	11	10	19	18	15
Johnny Carson is a dinosaur	25	11	13	18	27	13	12	19
In the general scheme of things, self-fulfillment is more important than success	65	21	4	1	67	23	4	1
I am completely different from my parents	49	29	10	5	20	31	29	11
Colleges should have stricter entrance requirements	7	9	23	30	15	22	15	21
Most black people in jail should not be there	17	29	15	11	11	22	24	13
My lifestyle is different from everybody else's	17	31	19	14	13	29	23	16
You can't trust anyone over 30	14	32	12	26	2	3	14	68
I feel alienated from the rest of society	27	40	10	10	13	30	20	19

My parents don't understand me	47%	31%	7%	6%	19%	27%	24%	13%
I will not work for or buy products from a company whose activities I do not approve of	49	28	4	2	39	35	8	2
I suspect the FBI is reading my mail	14	17	9	42	7	10	14	49
I'm suspicious of questionnaires	21	22	10	23	16	20	14	26

3a. For you personally, when did the 60's really begin?

3b. For you personally, when were the 60's over?

4a. What popular expression, or word, catch-phrase, or saying would *you* choose from the 60's to typify that whole era?

4b. What popular expression, or word, catch-phrase, or saying would *you* choose from the 70's to typify that whole era?

5. Name a book, or books, that you read back in the 60's that really influenced you.

6. Name a book, or books, that you read in the 70's that really influenced you.

7. If you had to pick one movie from the 60's that best expressed the feeling of those times, which one would it be?

8a. At some point, did there come a time when you made a conscious decision to renounce your 60's lifestyle?

YES   29%   NO   70%

8b. If you say yes, describe what this meant for you.

237

8c.   If you say no, please explain.

9.   It was widely believed during the 60's that the government was spying on private citizens and recent revelations about the FBI, CIA, and local police have confirmed this belief as fact. Can you describe how "60's paranoia" affected you?

10a. During the 60's, how did *you* envision things turning out in this country in the 70's? What was your hope? What was your dream?

10b. During the 60's, what did you see yourself doing in the 70's?

11.   How much of the 60's was real and how much was created by the media?

12a. Describe your best 60's experience.

12b. Describe your worst 60's experience.

13.   In the 60's did you

	Yes
Go to Haight-Ashbury during the Summer of Love	16%
Wear love beads	59
Play in a rock band	16
Play the guitar	33
Hitchhike	73
Go to Woodstock	17
Go to Altamont	5
Paint your car with bizarre designs	12
Get married	20
Get divorced	6
Have a child or children	10
Call cops "pigs"	73
Go from being a hawk to being a dove	45
(Men) Wear a Nehru jacket	14
Get regular physical exercise	57
Join ROTC	5

238

14.   In the 70's did you . . .

                                                                              Yes

"Sell out" 16%
(Men) Cut your long hair.. 30
(Men) Shave your mustache and/or beard........................ 17
Get into est, TM, primal therapy, rolfing
    or some other course
    of self-improvement 43
Vote for Jimmy Carter in '76 55
(Women) Wear make-up... 30
(Women) Shave your legs 33
Get busted.. 17
Carry a picket sign 31
Stop hanging around with the old crowd 43
Live in a commune... 21
(Gays) "Come out of the closet" 7

Do the Hustle... 29
Watch the Watergate hearings on TV 71
Feel nostalgic about the 60's 83
Feel disappointed about the 60's....................................... 44
Spend money on "art deco" 21
Read underground newspapers 73
Play in a rock band.. 9
Call cops "pigs" 40
Get into health food.. 64
Deal dope 34
Think Paul was dead 6
Quote Bob Dylan's songs 51

Refer to women as "chicks".. 38
Refer to blacks as "spades" 17
Refer to men as "cats" or "dudes" 40
Get married.. 33
Get divorced... 15
Have a child or children.. 16
Become more conservative in lifestyle............................... 49
Become more radical in lifestyle... 28
Continue the same lifestyle... 39
Get into punk rock 11
Get regular physical exercise 62
Join a consciousness-raising group..................................... 25

240

15. Which three of the following issues currently concern you the most?

Aiding Soviet dissidents	2%
Aid to Vietnam	2
Congressional corruption	15
Discrimination against racial minorities	18
Corporate power	23
Homosexual rights	12

Busing	3
Inflation	20
Judicial reform	6
Limitation of domestic nuclear use	17
Limitation of nuclear weapons	25
Marijuana decriminalization	24

Peace in the Middle East	14
Pollution	41
Population control	17
Passage of Equal Rights Amendment	22
Capital punishment	6
Poverty	19

Rape	17
Renewed ties with Cuba	2
Unemployment	19
Welfare reform	10
Energy crisis	2
Other (please specify	18

16. What are you doing about these issues?

Working toward violent revolution	3%
Working toward peaceful, gradual revolution	16
Working within the system to make changes	27
Talking and thinking about them	36
Not very much	14
Other (please specify)	2

17. Here's a list of names that made news during the 60's. Indicate how you felt about them then, and how you feel about them now.

	60's						70's					
	Admired and Was Influenced by	Admired But Was Not Influenced by	No Feeling One Way or Another	Did Not Admire But Was Influenced by	Did Not Admire and Was Not Influenced by	Who?	Admire and Am Influenced by	Admire But Am Not Influenced by	No Feeling One Way or Another	Do Not Admire But Am Influenced by	Do Not Admire and Am Not Influenced by	Who?
Woody Allen	16%	35%	32%	2%	9%	5%	36%	45%	10%	2%	6%	0%
Muhammad Ali	10	33	25	5	25	1	11	39	21	3	23	1
Neil Armstrong	5	37	34	4	16	3	2	26	44	3	19	4
Joan Baez	44	32	11	4	6	1	21	40	24	3	9	0
Beach Boys	23	33	24	5	13	1	11	33	32	4	16	1
The Beatles	76	15	3	2	2	0	42	37	12	3	3	1
James Bond	11	26	30	5	26	1	3	14	38	4	37	2
Lenny Bruce	24	19	32	4	7	13	29	34	23	3	7	2
Helen Gurley Brown	3	5	34	6	25	24	3	8	34	5	33	15
Lt. Calley	3	3	10	30	47	5	2	4	14	23	51	3
Cesar Chavez	32	28	20	3	5	11	27	36	20	3	6	5
Eldridge Cleaver	27	23	21	9	14	4	7	17	34	8	29	3
Walter Cronkite	13	22	44	7	11	2	14	25	40	6	10	2
R. Crumb	27	14	17	2	4	33	17	20	22	2	6	30
Adelle Davis	16	8	29	3	8	33	22	11	26	4	10	22
Angela Davis	24	25	19	9	17	4	11	26	34	5	19	2
Rennie Davis	18	17	25	5	8	23	4	9	36	3	22	23
Dave Dellinger	18	16	20	2	6	34	7	13	31	1	8	35
Bob Dylan	72	15	7	3	2	0	42	32	13	6	5	0
Jane Fonda	29	33	24	4	8	1	30	38	21	2	6	0
Betty Friedan	18	13	32	3	7	23	20	21	31	3	7	14
Kahlil Gibran	34	14	24	2	12	13	21	16	33	2	15	9
Allen Ginsberg	27	24	27	5	8	8	17	27	36	3	9	5
Germaine Greer	17	15	33	3	7	23	15	18	40	4	7	11

242

Che Guevara	22	22	25	5	13	10	14	26	32	3	15	7
Tom Hayden	26	23	27	3	7	12	14	25	36	3	9	9
Hermann Hesse	15	13	26	3	7	12	3	19	33	2	9	7
Abbie Hoffman	35	22	18	9	11	3	11	21	36	7	20	2
Jimi Hendrix	39	28	16	4	8	2	26	30	27	3	10	1
George Jackson	12	14	29	5	9	27	9	13	36	3	11	22
Lyndon B. Johnson	5	9	13	37	32	1	3	14	27	18	33	2
Janis Joplin	42	32	13	4	5	1	28	37	19	5	7	1
LeRoi Jones	11	14	30	3	6	31	5	14	38	2	7	28
John F. Kennedy	62	20	8	5	3	0	29	30	19	9	9	1
Robert F. Kennedy	47	28	13	5	5	1	28	29	24	6	9	0
Ted Kennedy	14	21	41	5	15	1	12	21	37	7	19	1
Martin Luther King	62	23	9	3	2	0	53	30	10	2	3	0
Timothy Leary	42	15	16	11	13	1	12	14	29	10	31	2
John Lennon	59	23	10	2	5	0	27	32	27	4	7	1
Charles Manson	2	2	6	22	63	4	1	1	6	19	69	1
Norman Mailer	11	15	40	7	17	6	6	15	38	9	25	3
Peter Max	23	28	25	4	10	9	8	20	41	3	17	8
Mao Tse-tung	20	20	32	9	16	2	18	26	32	7	14	1
George McGovern	40	25	16	4	7	6	18	30	33	4	11	2
Eugene McCarthy	43	24	18	3	7	3	14	27	37	4	13	2
Rod McKuen	16	14	26	4	32	5	7	12	33	3	37	3
Ho Chi Minh	17	15	34	10	19	2	13	18	39	5	9	2
Kate Millett	13	10	29	3	7	35	13	14	33	3	7	26
Joe Namath	7	21	30	4	32	5	3	18	36	3	36	2
Jim Morrison	31	26	23	3	6	9	16	22	38	4	9	8
Ralph Nader	49	24	15	3	4	3	47	25	14	5	5	0
Richard Nixon	3	4	9	30	49	2	1	1	4	30	54	5
Huey Newton	15	17	31	7	15	12	5	13	42	5	19	11
Ayn Rand	17	11	29	6	17	18	8	11	35	5	24	13
Hugh Hefner	12	13	26	14	31	1	7	11	30	13	36	1
Albert Camus	30	16	23	2	4	21	21	20	31	2	4	18
Jerry Rubin	35	19	19	9	11	6	6	12	43	5	25	5
Mark Rudd	19	15	23	6	8	25	4	10	40	3	15	23
Gloria Steinem	27	17	29	4	7	14	27	23	28	4	10	4
Dr. Benjamin Spock	33	21	29	5	7	1	19	25	35	5	10	1
Soviet Union	6	9	30	30	22	0	4	7	30	30	25	1
George Wallace	2	3	6	25	61	1	1	4	12	15	63	1
Kurt Vonnegut	35	19	25	1	5	12	32	27	25	2	6	4
Andy Warhol	21	23	28	7	14	4	14	20	36	7	19	1
Tom Wolfe	31	16	24	3	4	19	20	19	34	2	6	14
Malcolm X	27	18	28	7	14	3	19	19	37	5	14	1

243

	60's						70's					
	Admired and Was Influenced by	Admired But Was Not Influenced by	No Feeling One Way or Another	Did Not Admire But Was Influenced by	Did Not Admire and Was Not Influenced by	Who?	Admire and Am Influenced by	Admire But Am Not Influenced by	No Feeling One Way or Another	Do Not Admire But Am Influenced by	Do Not Admire and Am Not Influenced by	Who?
Fidel Castro	17%	19%	22%	16%	24%	0%	15%	21%	27%	11%	21%	0%
Barry Goldwater	5	8	13	19	51	1	3	9	24	9	50	2
Paul Goodman	13	6	22	1	3	50	8	8	25	2	2	48
Buckminster Fuller	23	17	27	1	3	25	25	21	25	2	4	18
Frodo	19	11	23	1	4	38	15	13	28	1	5	32
Marlon Brando	20	33	34	2	7	0	21	35	28	3	9	0
Elvis Presley	21	24	27	9	15	0	16	28	30	6	16	1
Kingston Trio	22	26	32	3	13	1	5	17	51	2	18	3
Audrey Hepburn	12	30	44	1	9	2	8	26	49	1	11	1
Sammy Davis, Jr.	7	24	34	3	28	1	4	16	35	4	37	1
Twiggy	9	14	40	9	25	1	2	7	54	3	27	3
Nelson Rockefeller	3	9	28	15	40	2	2	7	23	17	45	1
Stokely Carmichael	15	19	33	8	15	4	4	11	51	4	19	4
Simone de Beauvoir	13	12	33	1	4	32	16	16	34	1	4	23
Jean-Paul Sartre	30	16	29	3	4	14	23	20	34	3	5	9

18a. Of the people on the above list whom you admired and were influenced by, which one was the greatest influence on you in the 60's?

18b. Explain how.

18c. If you admired and were influenced by no one on the above list in the 60's, was there anybody else who influenced your life in a positive way?

18d. Explain how.

19. Here's a list of names making news in the 70's. Characterize your feelings about them.

70's

	Admire and Am Influenced by	Admire But Am Not Influenced by	No Feeling One Way or Another	Do Not Admire But Am Influenced by	Do Not Admire and Am Not Influenced by	Who?
Idi Amin	1%	2%	5%	22%	67%	3%
Bella Abzug	22	35	19	4	13	6
Anita Bryant	2	4	6	23	62	1
Charles Bronson	4	17	42	3	30	3
David Bowie	10	22	35	4	25	3
Howard Baker	4	13	32	5	20	24
Mel Brooks	28	40	18	2	8	2
Jerry Brown	23	32	27	4	8	4
Carlos Castaneda	34	15	26	3	7	13
Cher	3	16	32	5	41	1
Chevy Chase	22	36	25	1	9	5
Alice Cooper	5	17	38	4	32	2
Jimmy Carter	21	23	23	17	13	1
Rosalynn Carter	11	22	39	6	18	1
Archibald Cox	16	27	30	3	11	11
Baba Ram Dass	17	11	27	2	15	27
John Dean	6	14	27	16	32	2
John Denver	9	20	31	4	33	1
Werner Erhard	3	5	25	6	29	29
Julie Eisenhower	0	4	27	3	61	3
Sam Ervin	19	33	26	3	11	7
Larry Flynt	6	9	24	8	31	20
Betty Ford	10	32	35	2	18	1
The Fonz	9	21	41	3	22	2
Gerald Ford	4	16	33	12	32	1
Alex Haley	20	30	33	3	8	5

70's

	Admire and Am Influenced by	Admire But Am Not Influenced by	No Feeling One Way or Another	Do Not Admire But Am Influenced by	Do Not Admire and Am Not Influenced by	Who?
Patty Hearst............................	7%	8%	32%	15%	36%	1%
Halston..................................	4	8	31	3	16	36
Mary Hartman (Mary Hartman)...............................	16	21	32	5	23	2
Billie Jean King	16	38	29	2	11	1
Henry Kissinger	8	22	23	18	27	1
Kiss..	2	7	32	4	49	5
Erica Jong..............................	13	16	34	5	20	9
Barbara Jordan.......................	20	29	24	1	5	20
Elton John	13	33	31	4	16	1
G. Gordon Liddy....................	2	5	21	12	52	4
Lawrence Lipton	1	0	16	1	4	75
Linda Lovelace	9	14	36	7	30	2
Mary Tyler Moore.................	11	33	34	2	17	1
Marabel Morgan.....................	7	13	16	2	39	52
Ronald McDonald	4	3	27	9	50	5
Farrah Fawcett-Majors	3	10	26	7	51	2
Rev. Moon..............................	0	1	9	9	75	3
Bette Midler	15	35	31	2	13	3
Leonard Nimoy	15	30	35	2	10	6
The Osmonds	1	6	32	3	55	2
The Pope................................	3	8	36	6	43	2
Robert Redford.......................	10	37	35	2	12	0
Ronald Reagan.......................	2	5	19	3	59	1
Burt Reynolds	5	21	40	3	28	0
R2D2	16	25	32	2	11	12
Tom Seaver............................	3	20	42	1	11	21
Patti Smith.............................	10	16	32	2	15	22
Sylvester Stallone..................	13	31	36	1	11	6
Secretariat	9	28	41	1	11	7

246

Alexander Solzhenitsyn.........	26	36	20	3	7	6
Symbionese Liberation Army	5	5	15	20	51	1
Lily Tomlin	34	39	17	1	5	3
Bill Walton	11	21	33	1	9	22
Woodward and Bernstein	45	30	12	1	3	7
Raquel Welch.......................	5	20	47	3	22	1
Paul Williams	6	20	33	2	24	13
Andrew Young	15	30	28	4	11	10

20a. Of the people on the above list whom you admired and were influenced by, which one was the greatest influence on you in the 70's?

20b. Explain how.

20c. If you admire and have been influenced by no one on the above list in the 70's, has there been anybody else who influenced your life in a positive way?

20d. Explain how.

21. How politically active were you during the 60's?

Totally involved	9%
Very active	23
Somewhat involved	35
Concerned but not directly involved	22
Not involved	7

22a. Would you consider your political stance in the 60's . . .

Conservative	4%
Moderate	6
Liberal	37
Radical	43
Apathetic	6

247

22b. In the 70's, would you consider your political stance . . .

Conservative	3%
Moderate	15
Liberal	42
Radical	26
Apathetic	11

23. Explain why you took the political stance that you did in the 60's.

24. Explain what makes your political stance different or the same today in the 70's.

25. In the 60's, did you . . .

	Yes
March for civil rights	43%
Go to Chicago in '68	9
Join SDS	15
Consider yourself a Yippie	16
Carry a picket sign	49
Work in a political campaign	51
Get tear-gassed	36
Attend a teach-in	42
Support the Viet Cong	28
Boycott lettuce and grapes	61
Campaign for Eugene McCarthy	36
Join the Peace Corps	2
Hand out political leaflets	54
Sign petitions	89
Sit-in for integration	20
Work in Southern voter registration drive	3
Make a speech	34
Put up political posters	51
Go on a Freedom Ride	5
Run the mimeograph machine in Movement offices	20
Perform street theater	17
Raise money for the cause	32
Choose a line of work for political reasons	19
Travel over 100 miles to attend a demonstration	35
Go to jail	22
Get arrested	28

248

Get beaten by cops... 16
Run for elective office 8
Give money to black activist groups 30
Give money to antiwar groups... 55
Demonstrate against the war 74
Demonstrate for minority rights....................................... 49
Demonstrate for women's rights 30
Boycott school classes... 50
Harbor a fugitive... 24
Do organizing in disadvantaged neighborhoods.............. 19

Withhold taxes for political reasons 17

26a. Approximately how many demonstrations did you participate in, if any, from 1960 to 1970?

0	19%
1–5	39
6–10	18
11–20	10
More than 20	13

26b. Approximately how many demonstrations did you participate in, if any, from 1971 to the present?

0	41%
1–5	40
6–10	8
11–20	4
More than 20	5

27. Please explain your reasons for participating, or not participating, in demonstrations.

28. **(MEN ONLY)**
What did you do when you reached draft age?

Enlisted	12%
Served in Vietnam	4
Burned my draft card	7
Avoided service through student deferment	47
Got drafted	7
Obtained conscientious objector status	5
Fled the country	1

249

Went to jail	1
Beat the draft through subterfuge	15
Was 4F legitimately	15
Got drafted but later deserted	1
My lottery number never came up	30
Other	3

29. Do you see any lasting impact on politics in this country as a result of the political movements and activities of the 60's?

Yes	73%
Not sure	16
No	5

30. If you say yes, describe the impact. If you say no, or not sure, explain why.

31. At what age did you lose your virginity?

15 or younger	16%
16	10
17	14
18	18
19	13
20	10
21	7
22 or older	10

32. Describe your sexual preferences in the 60's and today in the 70's.

	60's	70's
Gay	2%	5%
Straight	84	80
Bi-sexual	6	11
Celibate	6	1

33. During the 60's, did you . . .

	Yes
Participate in an orgy	20%
Get crabs	26
Get VD	15
(Women) Have an abortion	6
Have one-night stands with people you didn't care too much about	54
Fall in love more than once	73
Try out every position in the *Kama Sutra*	17

34a. During the 60's, I felt personally involved in a sexual revolution.

Agree	49%
Disagree	28
Not sure	21

34b. Why do you say that?

34c. If you agree that a sexual revolution occurred in the 60's, give an example from your own personal experience.

35. During the 60's, with how many people did you have sex? And during the 70's?

60's		70's	
None	15%	None	2%
3 or less	28	3 or less	25
4 to 10	25	4 to 10	27
11 to 20	13	11 to 20	20
21 to 50	10	21 to 50	15
51 or more	7	51 or more	8

36. How do you personally feel about the following statements?*

70's

	Agree Completely	Agree Somewhat	Disagree Somewhat	Disagree Completely
My sexual partners were more numerous in the 60's than in the 70's	25%	8%	9%	46%
The man should be responsible for contraception	13	29	14	12
The woman should be responsible for contraception	17	33	10	7
Sex was better in the 60's than in the 70's	4	7	18	40
Sex is better in the 70's than in the 60's	35	20	6	8
It's okay for a woman to ask a man out	79	15	2	1
Men like women who play hard to get	4	25	24	19
There is such a thing as sexual perversion	35	29	11	8
Certain sexually-oriented films and magazines should be banned	14	16	16	41
Magazines like *Hustler* exploit women	38	28	9	10
Magazines like *Hustler* should be banned because they exploit women	7	9	19	49
There is no such thing as sexual pornography, and nothing should be banned	20	19	30	20
It's okay to be homosexual	59	20	5	5
There's no such thing as vaginal orgasm	14	8	14	33
Women should be passive while having sex	5	1	7	76
It's okay for women to initiate having sex	87	6	2	2
Abortion is every woman's right	77	8	4	5
I'm against having children because the world is such a mess	7	20	19	34
I don't believe in "going all the way" on the first date	8	14	13	43
Sexual jealousy is unhealthy	25	30	22	6
I buy magazines featuring nudity, because I like the pictures	19	21	9	24

*An additional choice of "Neither Agree Nor Disagree" was originally given, yielding numbers that were statistically uninteresting.

252

Monogamy is very important to me	27	27	12	13
Married couples should allow for "open marriages"	10	26	17	12
A woman should remain a virgin until marriage	2	2	15	68
I dig S&M	2	7	9	63
I won't have sex with anybody I don't love	12	13	28	35
Men and women are getting along better than ever	9	26	20	13
There's too much talk about sex these days	9	20	20	23
The thrill is gone	2	14	18	52
When it comes to sex, the 60's were all talk and no action	3	15	23	33
Sexual morality has reached an all-time low	6	11	22	34
Arnold Schwarzenegger is sexy	3	8	9	42
Woody Allen is sexy	8	19	13	29
Ann-Margret is sexy	18	30	10	17
Tricia Nixon Cox is sexy	3	4	10	61
I am sexy (phone no. optional)	48	30	3	1

37. During the 60's how involved were you with the following things? And how involved are you with them now?

	60's					70's				
	Used Regularly or for Prolonged Periods	Used Frequently	Used Occasionally	Used Once or Twice	Never Used	Use Regularly or for Prolonged Periods	Use Frequently	Use Occasionally	Use Once in a While	Never Use
Acid	14%	12%	19%	12%	42%	1%	3%	13%	21%	60%
Amyl nitrite	1	2	9	13	73	1	1	6	15	75
Beer	17	20	36	11	15	17	22	31	15	14
Cocaine	2	4	14	16	62	3	6	21	25	43
Cough syrup	1	4	16	21	56	0	0	9	12	76
Downers	3	6	15	18	56	2	2	12	18	65

253

	60's					70's				
	Used Regularly or for Prolonged Periods	Used Frequently	Used Occasionally	Used Once or Twice	Never Used	Use Regularly or for Prolonged Periods	Use Frequently	Use Occasionally	Use Once in a While	Never Use
Grass	43	19	18	6	13	38	16	19	13	13
Glue	1	1	2	7	87	0	1	1	1	95
Hard liquor	8	16	43	17	15	7	15	41	21	14
Hashish	17	23	26	10	21	7	9	27	24	30
Hash oil	4	6	14	16	58	3	4	14	23	54
Heroin	2	1	3	9	83	0	0	1	6	90
Mescaline	5	13	19	17	45	1	2	10	21	65
Nitrous oxide	1	1	5	11	81	1	1	4	15	77
Opium	1	3	12	24	58	0	2	5	19	71
PCP	1	1	4	13	78	0	1	1	8	87
Peyote	2	3	11	19	65	0	1	6	16	74
Quaaludes	1	2	7	10	78	2	1	7	17	71
Speed	11	9	22	17	40	3	3	13	20	58
THC	2	4	10	19	63	1	1	4	14	74
Valium	2	3	10	14	69	2	5	11	23	56
Wine	11	24	43	11	9	11	31	35	13	9

38. During the 60's how important were the following things to you personally? And how important are they now?

	60's			70's		
	Extremely Important	Somewhat Important	Not Important	Extremely Important	Somewhat Important	Not Important
Abstaining from drugs but not booze	10%	13%	74%	10%	15%	72%
Abstaining from drugs totally	10	10	78	10	16	72

254

Always having a stash	26	18	55	21	22	54
Being a dealer	7	9	83	1	4	93
Being high all the time	12	17	70	4	7	86
Being high frequently	22	25	50	13	18	65
Being high once in a while	31	29	33	24	28	41
Being with other people who like the same drug or drugs	29	29	40	12	25	60
Knowing a dealer	32	20	47	21	20	56
"Turning on" other people	20	26	53	7	14	78
"Turning on" your parents	6	9	83	3	4	91
"Turning on" the world	15	15	67	5	7	85
"Turning on" the people who give surveys (discreetly)	15	9	69	18	8	67

39. During the 60's, how involved were you in the drug scene?

Totally involved	27%
Somewhat involved	37
Wasn't interested, but used drugs if they were offered	17
Had nothing to do with it	17

40. How do you personally feel about these statements?*

	Agree Completely	Agree Somewhat	Disagree
LSD leads to enlightenment	10%	34%	33%
The more people who smoke marijuana, the better	18	29	33
I like cocaine	31	18	25
Psychedelic drugs have no place in the 70's	9	14	53

*An additional choice of "I Don't Know" was originally given, yielding statistics that in most cases correspond to the 17% that had nothing to do with the 60's drug scene (see question 39). The "Disagree" category combines the original choices of "Disagree Somewhat" and "Disagree Completely," for easier comparison.

255

	Agree Completely	Agree Somewhat	Disagree
Without drugs, there probably would have been less political activism in the 60's	12	32	32
The 60's would have been better without drugs	4	7	66
You can't understand the music of the 60's without having had the drug experience	10	33	45
I like downers like Valium and Quaaludes	8	15	65
Heroin should be legalized	19	15	55
I drink more in the 70's than I did in the 60's	32	23	37
I drank more in the 60's than I do in the 70's	15	11	65
Drugs improve sexual pleasure	12	45	25
I personally know two or three people who died from drugs	31	8	50
Marijuana should be legalized	72	15	8
Marijuana should be decriminalized	84	9	4

41. If you have used drugs, in what year did you first get stoned? Describe the circumstances.

1960—1%	1964—3%	1968—15%	1972—4%
1961—1%	1965—8%	1969—14%	
1962—2%	1966—10%	1970—5%	N.A.—14%
1963—2%	1967—20%	1971—2%	

42. How have drugs affected your lifestyle?

43a. Are the 70's different from or the same as the 60's?

Different   93%   Same   4%

256

43b. Describe what you mean.

44. If you were writing a book, your personal memoirs of the 60's, what would you title that book?

45. If you were writing a book, your personal memoirs of the 70's, what would you title that book?

46. How do you personally feel as we approach the 1980's?

Excited	11%
Optimistic	20
Encouraged	7
Serene	6
Confused	9
Worried	14
Bored	3
Depressed	3
Cynical	15
Frightened	4
Other	10

47. How do you personally feel about the following statements?

	Agree Completely	Agree Somewhat	Neither Agree Nor Disagree	Disagree Somewhat	Disagree Completely
I cannot accept a conventional way of life in society as it exists now	26%	35%	10%	20%	7%
I find the conventional way of life in today's society distasteful, but there's no other choice	3	23	10	35	27
I can fit into today's society while trying to change some of its worst features	19	50	10	12	6

	Agree Completely	Agree Somewhat	Neither Agree Nor Disagree	Disagree Somewhat	Disagree Completely
I like the way things are now and I hope they stay the same	1	5	7	35	51
If I have children, I want them to avoid a decade like the 60's	4	9	12	26	47
I cannot fit into a 9–5 routine	28	27	9	23	12
My education didn't prepare me for a job	28	25	8	17	19
Things never change	5	14	10	22	48

DEMOGRAPHICS

48a. How did you get this questionnaire? Attended session in . . .

Atlanta	7%	Boston	3%	New York	13%
Austin	5	Kansas City	8	San Francisco	7
Berkeley	3	Madison	6	Tucson	5

Requested it through the mail   37%
A friend gave it to me   6

48b. If you did not receive this questionnaire at one of the sessions in the cities listed above, in what state do you live?

48c. Age:

25	17%	29	9%	33	3%	37	1%
26	13	30	10	34	3	38 and over	2
27	13	31	8	35	3		
28	13	32	5	36	3		

48d. Sex:

Male   55%
Female   45

258

48e. Race:

White	96%
Black	1
Hispanic	1
Oriental	.3
Other	1

48f. Marital Status:

Single	43%
Cohabiting	14
Married	30
Divorced	13

48g. Education:

Some high school	1%
Graduated from high school	5
Some college	31
Graduated from college	27
Post-graduate work	35

48h. If you had college experience, what kind of college was it?

Ivy League	4%
Small private	19
Large private	10
Small public	15
State university	52

48i. Occupation:

48j. Total annual income before taxes:

Under $8,000	34%
$ 8,000–$ 9,999	14
$10,000–$14,999	27
$15,000–$19,999	12
$20,000–$24,999	6
$25,000 or more	5

48k. Family's socio-economic background:

Upper class	3%
Upper middle class	30
Middle class	43
Lower middle class	18
Lower class	5

48l. Where did you grow up?

Big city	28%	Small city	12%
Suburban	32	Outside U.S.	0
Rural	5	Moved around a lot	8
Small town	12	Other	.4

49. Is there anything else you'd like to say about the 60's and/or the 70's?

50. By the way, what sign are you?

THANK YOU VERY MUCH.
PEACE AND LOVE

Methodology

SAMPLE SIZE

There are three reasons why we believe our sample of 1005 is a firm basis for the generalizations we have made. First, there emerged from the data strong patterns (e.g., the differences between activists and nonactivists) that would not have changed substantially had the numbers been larger. Second, professional pollsters generally consider a national sample to be anywhere from 800 to 1500 people. A 1971 national Yankelovich survey of campus attitudes (*The Changing Values on Campus*, Washington Square Press) was based on a total of 1244 interviews, and Kenneth Keniston's *Young Radicals: Notes on Committed Youth* (1968) made generalizations about politically committed youth based on only 14 interviews. Third, our research consultant, Linda Waldman, says, "A thousand's fine."

THE PERCENTAGES

All of the percentages in this book have been rounded off to the nearest whole percentage. In some tables, the percentages reported add up to more—or less—than 100%. This may be because of the rounding-off, or because some respondents did not answer every question, and some gave more than one answer where appropriate. In addition, we have occasionally used only the categories of extreme like or dislike, importance or nonimportance, ignoring "neutral" or "somewhat" or "no answer." The complete results are listed in the questionnaire (Appendix A).

THE DATA

We collected a lot more data than we could possibly use. Many questions on the questionnaire yielded results that have not been discussed in this book. Some of the information falls into the "so what?" category, such as the number of people who had positive feelings about the United Nations in the Sixties (34%) and in the Seventies (23%). Some information was predictable. For example, more people registered positive about "myself" in the Seventies (81%) than in the Sixties (55%), a change which is probably due as much to leaving behind the confusion of adolescence as to leaving the Sixties behind. Some of our questions didn't work out well (response to "Pick one movie that best expressed the Sixties" gave us a tremendous list of films with no particular winners). But there is a lot more in the results that we simply hadn't the time to discuss. Perhaps you can look at the figures and draw some of your own conclusions.

Bibliography

Baskir, Lawrence M., and Strauss, William A. *Chance and Circumstance.* New York: Knopf, 1978.

Boone, Pat. *A New Song.* Carol Stream, Ill.: Creation House, 1970.

Brand, Stewart. *The Last Whole Earth Catalogue.* New York: Random House, 1971.

Brink, William, and Harris, Louis. *The Negro Revolution in America.* New York: Simon and Schuster, 1964.

Burton, Sir Richard, and Arbuthnot, F. F., trans. *The Kama Sutra of Vatsayana.* New York: Putnam's, 1966.

Charters, Ann. *Kerouac.* San Francisco: Straight Arrow, 1973.

Cleaver, Eldridge. *Post-Prison Writings and Speeches.* New York: Vintage, 1969.

———. *Soul on Ice.* New York: Dell, 1968.

Davidson, Sara. *Loose Change.* New York: Pocket Books, 1978.

Dickstein, Morris. *Gates of Eden.* New York: Basic, 1977.

Farina, Richard. *Been Down So Long It Looks Like Up to Me.* New York: Dell, 1966.

Felton, David, ed. *Mindfuckers.* San Francisco: Straight Arrow, 1972.

Forcade, Thomas King, ed. *Underground Press Anthology.* New York: Ace Books, 1972.

Franklin, Bruce. *From the Movement Toward Revolution.* New York: Van Nostrand Reinhold, 1971.

Friedan, Betty. *The Feminine Mystique.* New York: Dell, 1963.

Fuller, Buckminster. *Operating Manual for Spaceship Earth.* New York: Pocket Books, 1970.

Ginsberg, Allen. *Howl and Other Poems.* San Francisco: City Lights, 1956.

Glessing, Robert J. *The Underground Press in America.* Bloomington, Ind.: Indiana University Press, 1970.

Goldstein, Stewart, and Jacobson, Alan. *Oldies But Goodies: The Rock 'n' Roll Years.* New York: Mason/Charter, 1977.

Goodman, Paul. *Growing Up Absurd.* New York: Vintage, 1956.

Gordon, Dale *Hippie Sex.* Buffalo: Market Arcade, 1968.

Haley, Alex, and Malcolm X. *Autobiography of Malcolm X.* New York: Grove, 1965.

Heinlein, Robert. *Stranger in a Strange Land.* New York: Putnam's, 1961.

Hersey, John. *The Algiers Motel Incident.* New York: Bantam, 1968.

Hoffman, Abbie ["Free"]. *Revolution for the Hell of It.* New York: Dial, 1968.

————. *Woodstock Nation.* New York: Vintage, 1969.

Jackson, George. *Soledad Brother.* New York: Bantam, 1970.

Keniston, Kenneth. *Young Radicals: Notes on Committed Youth.* New York: Harcourt, Brace & World, 1968.

Kerouac, Jack. *On the Road.* New York: New American Library, 1957.

Kostelanetz, Richard, ed. *Seeing Through Shuck.* New York: Ballantine, 1972.

Kupferberg, Tuli, and Bashlow, Robert. *1001 Ways to Beat the Draft.* New York: Grove, 1967.

Lewis, Roger. *Outlaws of America: The Underground Press and Its Context: Notes on a Cultural Revolution.* New York: Penguin, 1972.

Lora, Ronald, ed. *America in the 60's: Cultural Authorities in Transition.* New York: Wiley, 1974.

Lukas, J. Anthony. *Don't Shoot, We Are Your Children.* New York: Delta Books, 1972.

Mailer, Norman. *Advertisements for Myself.* New York: Putnam's, 1959.

————. *Miami and the Siege of Chicago.* New York: New American Library, 1968.

Malina, Judith, and Beck, Julian. *Paradise Now.* New York: Random House, 1971.

McLuhan, Marshall. *Understanding Media.* New York: New American Library, 1964.

Mehnert, Klaus. *Twilight of the Young.* New York: Holt, 1976.

Meltzer, R. *The Aesthetics of Rock.* New York: Something Else, 1969.

Morgan, Robin, ed. *Sisterhood Is Powerful: An Anthology of Writings from the Women's Liberation Movement.* New York: Vintage, 1970.

Mungo, Raymond. *Famous Long Ago: My Life and Hard Times with Liberation News Service.* Boston: Beacon, 1970.

Neville, Richard. *Play Power: Exploring the International Underground.* New York: Random House, 1970.

Nowlis, Helen H. *Drugs on the College Campus.* New York: Anchor, 1969.

Ram Dass, Baba. *Be Here Now.* New York: Harmony, 1971.

Reich, Charles A. *The Greening of America.* New York: Bantam, 1971.

Rimmer, Robert H. *The Harrad Experiment.* New York: Bantam, 1973.

Rogers, Mick. *Freakout on Sunset Strip.* San Diego: Greenleaf Classics, 1967.

Roszak, Theodore. *The Making of a Counter-Culture.* New York: Anchor, 1969.

Roxon, Lillian. *Rock Encyclopedia.* New York: Grosset & Dunlap, 1971.

Rubin, Jerry. *Do It.* New York: Ballantine, 1970.

————. *We Are Everywhere.* New York: Harper & Row, 1971.

Sale, Kirkpatrick. *SDS.* New York: Vintage, 1974.

Sann, Paul. *Fads, Follies and Delusions of the American People.* New York: Crown, 1967.

Sia, Joseph J. *Woodstock 69.* New York: Scholastic Book Services, 1970.

264

Spiegelman, Art, and Schneider, Bob, eds. *Whole Grains: A Book of Quotations.* New York: Douglas/Links, 1973.

Spock, Benjamin. *Baby and Child Care.* New York: Pocket Books, 1977.

Tavris, Carol, and Sadd, Susan. *The Redbook Report on Female Sexuality.* New York: Dell, 1978.

Toffler, Alvin. *Future Shock.* New York: Bantam, 1971.

Vellela, Tony. *Food Co-Ops for Small Groups.* New York: Workman, 1975.

Williams, Paul. *Right to Pass.* New York: Berkeley, 1977.

Wolfe, Tom. *The Electric Kool-Aid Acid Test.* New York: Bantam, 1969.

Wuthnow, Robert. *The Consciousness Reformation.* Berkeley: University of California Press, 1976.

Yablonsky, Lewis. *The Hippie Trip.* New York: Penguin, 1973.

Yankelovich, Daniel. *Generations Apart: A Study of the Generation Gap,* Conducted for CBS News, 1969.

_____. *The New Morality: A Profile of American Youth in the 70's.* New York: McGraw-Hill, 1974.

The *Underground Press Collection,* 1966 to present, is available on Bell and Howell microfilm at public and university libraries. For more information, contact the Alternative Press Syndicate, P.O. Box 775, Madison Square Station, NYC, 10010.

Index

(Charts are indicated by SMALL CAPS throughout index)

267